Creative Careers in Crafts

Creative Careers in Crafts

SUSAN
JOY
SAGER

**ALLWORTH
PRESS**
NEW YORK

08 07 06 05 04   5 4 3 2 1

Published by Allworth Press
An imprint of Allworth Communications, Inc.
10 East 23rd Street, New York, NY 10010

Cover design by Derek Bacchus
Page composition/typography by Sharp Des!gns, Inc., Lansing, MI

ISBN: 1-58115-362-7

LIBRARY OF CONGRESS CATALOGING-IN-PUBLICATION DATA
Sager, Susan Joy.
Creative careers in crafts / Susan Joy Sager.
p. cm.
Includes bibliographical references and index.
ISBN 1-58115-362-7 (pbk.)
1. Handicraft—Vocational guidance—United States. I. Title.
TT149.S18 2004
745.5'023—dc22
2004015084

Printed in Canada

Contents

Introduction

Welcome to *Creative Careers in Crafts*! It is my hope that this book will inspire you and give you the necessary information to get started in your crafts career, make the transition from paid employment to working for yourself, and sustain you and your business for long-term survival.

It's an exciting time to be a craftsperson. Organizations, magazines, conferences, shows, fairs, and shops all exist to help you sell your work. Although selling through the Internet is a growing trend in crafts, nothing will ever replace the power of meeting you, seeing your work, and seeing your studio. Buyers want to know your story, not just buy something off the rack, or they would be shopping somewhere else.

While teaching artists and craftspeople how to sell their work over the past ten years, I have found stories about working artists and craftspeople to be extremely helpful in making the nuts and bolts of small-business management understandable to creative people. As a result, this book focuses on profiles of craftspeople who have been able to turn their passion for making things into their life's work. The craftspeople chosen give you a chance to sample different approaches, lifestyles, and value systems of craftspeople earning all or part of their income from selling their work. While I don't claim to have included every possible career in crafts, I have selected the most common. Please read the interviews in all of the sections rather than just those in your particular medium. You may find that you have something in common with a weaver, perhaps, even though you are a woodworker, and vice versa.

The book is organized by craft medium. Each section begins with general information, followed by in-depth profiles of craftspeople. For additional ideas and educational programs, see chapter 4, "Educational Opportunities, Residency Programs, and Apprenticeships for Craftspeople."

In part 7, "Transitions and Support Systems," there is a special chapter geared toward young craftspeople to help this important new generation take advantage of opportunities specially designed to nurture it. Establishing a crafts career is a challenge at any age, but with knowledge of programs and opportunities designed for craftspeople in high school, young craftspeople will have a greater chance of success. Nobody said this was going to be easy, but for many of today's craftspeople, the rewards far outweigh the efforts. The key is to give yourself a realistic amount of time and enough support to make realizing your dreams possible.

Don't put it off: There is never going to be a better time to get started. Launching a new career is an ongoing project full of chances for refinement and new ideas. Even craftspeople who have achieved high levels of success in their fields have a next step or another level of achievement they wish to reach. A career in crafts offers a fascinating opportunity to engage in lifelong learning and achievement, especially for those makers who think they can make the next piece even better.

On the flip side, you may decide that a career in crafts is not for you and keep your current job. Success is defined in many ways; the only person who really matters is you, and how you feel about your work. Some simple planning and goal setting will help you focus and measure your success along the way.

I'd like to thank Tad Crawford at Allworth Press for his interest in this project. I'd also like to thank the craftspeople who, by generously sharing their stories and photographs, helped this book exist. Talking with each one of you was inspiring for me. I hope I have been able to translate your comments, impressive résumés, and promotional materials into a profile that honors you and your work. You are an impressive bunch and your stories deserve to be told again and again.

On a personal note, I'd also like to thank my husband, Scott Moody, my mother, Clare Sager, and my son, Miles. You are my strongest supporters, and I love you.

My father died this year, and one of my first thoughts was that he would never see this book. He read *Selling Your Crafts* from cover to cover and was extremely proud of my efforts. Since he was an avid reader and daily presence at the Schenectady County Public Library in Schenectady, New York, we have endowed a chair in his memory. Dad, may the memory of your inquisitive mind, good listening skills, and ability to tell engaging stories inspire a new generation of readers who may happen to sit in your chair. We miss you and we love you.

Please contact me with questions and comments through my Web site, *www.artbiz.info*. I'd love to hear from you. This is not rocket science—if you want to have a career in crafts, you can do it! May these stories and tips inspire you to achieve greater things with your creativity. Remember, there is no time like the present to get started.

SUSAN JOY SAGER, *www.artbiz.info*

PART ONE

Craft History and the Contemporary Scene

CHAPTER 1

Then and Now

Pick up a copy of a crafts magazine and the contemporary crafts scene is right there in front of you. Full-page ads by galleries, gallery show and crafts fair reviews, profiles of working crafts-people, book reviews, and numerous opportunities to show and sell your work; all display the richness and variety of the field. The contemporary scene is an active one, jam-packed with things to do, places to show, and things to collect. Increasingly, finding your way through the myriad opportunities can be overwhelming as well as inspiring. Welcome to the crafts world of the new century!

Although there has been an explosion of interest in things made by hand in the last thirty years, there have been periods in the recent past when interest in handmade items has waned and craftspeople have struggled to make a living. Where did the crafts field come from and where is it going? Why do some people who work in crafts media call themselves "craftspeople" while others in the same field call themselves "artists?" Why are we still debating whether it is "art" or "craft"? What's in a name, anyway?

The word "craft" was first used to describe the skillful craftsmanship of Renaissance artisans, such as goldsmiths, furniture makers, and stonemasons, who created functional, one-of-a-kind objects. "Craft" has assumed many meanings over the past two centuries, and continues to evolve today. In the nineteenth century, art critics and writers used the term "craft" to distinguish unique handmade objects from what were considered poorly designed, anonymous consumer goods and mass-produced industrial objects. While "craft" came to denote functional objects and the decorative arts, the term "fine art" emerged to describe painting and sculpture, reflecting the power structure and classification system that developed in the art world. The fine arts carried greater social, aesthetic, and philosophical meaning, while crafts were linked to the material world of objects rather than to spiritual ideas, and were considered lower in the hierarchy of artistic creation.

In the late nineteenth century, theorists and practitioners sought to link craftsmanship with art by further distinguishing craftsmanship from the commercial world of design and manufacturing. The Arts and Crafts Movement was a response to the industrial revolution, advocating that well-designed buildings, furniture, and household goods would improve society. Various design reformers advocated an integrated approach to art, design, and crafts. By the twentieth century, major movements in design, such as the Bauhaus, were nourished by the creativity that emerged from this integration. No art was considered superior: They were all equal, and dedicated to the creation of the totally designed and unified environment.

In the second half of the twentieth century, the hierarchy in the arts (with the fine arts at the apex of a triangle of which crafts and design formed the base) was further called into question. Artists, designers, and crafts practitioners recognized the profound interconnections between these fields. The exploration of abstract ideas and forms drawing upon traditional crafts materials and techniques were used in creating new work. Crafts evolved into an interdisciplinary vehicle of individual artistic expression, radical experimentation, and the skilled ability to transform materials into significant forms. The art/crafts/design triangle does not reflect the true state of the arts today, which links the triangle with many other fields of creativity, including fashion, interior design, architecture, new media, performance art, and pop culture. New materials and technologies have emerged, rendering the nineteenth-century classification system obsolete. Today "crafts" stands for creative activity, process, method, and purpose, rather than a class of objects, transcending the boundaries that separate crafts, fine art, and design.

"A couple of the most dramatic changes I have seen in the last two decades are how important craftspeople's ability to market their work is now, and how important the need to command higher prices for their pieces has become," says Mary Douglas, Curator of Collections at the Southern Highland Craft Guild in Ashville, North Carolina. "In the 1970s, only a handful of craftspeople could command big prices for their work. Now it's routine for a glass artist or a potter to get over $10,000 for one piece. Commercial galleries have helped to facilitate this change and as a result, the sales figures have really grown. However, at the same time, the crafts field still lags behind other creative fields as a scholarly pursuit. The smallness of the field is reflected in the fact that there are still no craftspeople included in major history publications. Also, contemporary crafts seem to fall between the cracks in the way that art historians and decorative art historians are traditionally assigned periods to focus on in museum work. I recently attended a crafts think tank and the first priority that came out of the meeting was to create a crafts history textbook. Crafts history is not mainstreamed into contemporary art and is always seen as a subset rather than a complete topic. While there are many wonderful catalogs from shows, good chapters about crafts history scattered in various books, and several excellent books written about crafts history that concentrate on one particular media, the field needs a really good crafts history textbook. Finally, the same group of people are patrons of several major crafts institutions, such as the Renwick, the Mint Museum, and the American Craft Museum. While they are a wonderful and dedicated group of people, it makes me uneasy that such a small group may have undue influence on the field in general."

The American Craft Council (ACC) (*www.craftcouncil.org*) has enjoyed a distinguished history of innovative programming that has provided a vital base for the emergence of the contemporary crafts movement in the United States in the decades since the Second World War. The leading voice for crafts in America, celebrating the remarkable achievement of the many gifted artists working in the media of clay, fiber, glass, metal, wood, and other materials, the council supports the field with programs such as a bimonthly magazine called *American Craft*, annual retail and wholesale shows, a special library on contemporary crafts, education grants, workshops, seminars, and other services to the public. Membership is open to anyone interested in crafts.

The American Craft Museum (*www.americancraftmuseum.org*) has served as the country's premier institution dedicated to the collection and exhibition of contemporary objects created in crafts media such as clay, glass, wood, metal, and fiber. Originally part of the ACC, the museum has recently changed its name to the Museum of Arts and Design, once again creating controversy in the crafts field about the distinction between fine art and crafts. Many craftspeople have worked diligently to educate the public about the importance of crafts in our lives and are concerned that deleting the word "craft" from the name of the most prominent crafts museum in the country may only confuse the public further. According to the museum's Web site, the new name is not meant to indicate that the museum is turning its back on crafts;

rather, it reflects the increasingly interdisciplinary nature of the museum's permanent collection and exhibition programming as it explores objects created at the crossroads of crafts, art, and design. While planning to honor the rich history of crafts and craftsmanship, the Museum of Arts and Design hopes to celebrate materials and processes that are today embraced by practitioners in the fields of crafts, fine art, and design, as well as architecture, fashion, interior design, technology, performing arts, and art- and design-driven industries. To help illustrate this new direction, in 2001 the museum organized an exhibition titled "Defining Craft I: Collecting for the New Millennium." The first in a series of traveling exhibitions that will explore the changing definitions and meanings of crafts in the twenty-first century, this exhibition examined the influence and potential of new technologies such as computer-aided design and computer-aided manufacturing (CAD/CAM), one-of-a-kind objects, and craft multiples made in a series.

The California College of Arts and Crafts in Oakland, California, also recently changed its name, to California College of Arts, to reflect the full range of the college's plans and activities. "Since its founding in 1907 during the height of the Arts and Crafts Movement, the college has changed in many ways," says President Michael S. Roth. "We've added design, architecture, and writing disciplines, and experienced tremendous growth in our graduate division. The construction of the new San Francisco campus, the expansion of exhibitions and public programming with the creation of the Wattis Institute, and the founding of our community-based program, the Center for Art and Public Life, are just a few of the milestones in the evolution of the institution. Over the years, the understanding of the words 'arts' and 'crafts' has changed. Moreover, contemporary crafts are now firmly part of the most progressive work in the art, design, and architecture arenas. And the visual, performing, and literary arts are intersecting in the most productive and powerful ways. The new name is true to the evolving identity of the college and better communicates the breadth of our programs and the seriousness of our educational purpose to potential students."

In what almost seems like a reversal of the trend, the Fuller Museum of Art in Brockton, Massachusetts, decided in January 2003 to become one of the few museums in the country to focus entirely on contemporary crafts. "After reviewing the success of an exhibit of glass-blower Lino Tagliapietra in 2001, the museum realized how many world-renowned crafts artists are living, teaching, and working in southern

New England," says Dawn Wilson Low, the museum's education director. "The board of directors voted unanimously for the change. I think the stigma of crafts as being boring, stagnant, and traditional is slowly being erased. People are waking up to the notion that crafts can be exciting, lively, and thought-provoking. It is our hope as a contemporary crafts institution that we can promote craft as art." According to the former Director, Jennifer Atkinson, the reaction to the new focus has been "overwhelmingly positive from craftspeople, collectors, and the press." It is no surprise that museum attendance tends to go up when there is a crafts exhibit, because most people can relate to things made by hand, whether it is a piece of glass, furniture, or wearable art. Although many pieces made in crafts today transcend the boundaries between art and crafts, most craft items are still recognizable whether or not they are functional, and visitors feel more comfortable viewing something that is part of life.

No matter what side of the fence you are on, lively debate about these topics is a good thing. "Right now, the public conversation about crafts is very active," says Carmine Branagan, executive director of the American Crafts Council. While some people are worried that "crafts" has become a word with negative connotations, others are pleased that crafts are now being included as art.

Meanwhile, several new organizations have formed that reflect the recent growth and professional development of the crafts field, including the Annual International Exposition of Sculpture Objects and Functional Art (SOFA), the Craft Organization Development Association (CODA), and the Craft Retailers Association for Tomorrow (CRAFT).

SOFA is an event that brings together galleries (rather than individuals) to showcase the work of artists and craftspeople. Exhibits include innovative work and stylistic movements in the contemporary decorative and design arts fields that expand and inform the audience and promote quality. A series of artist presentations (exploring the aesthetic dialogue between artist, process, and material) and a resource center (made up of arts publications, museums, and nonprofit organizations that present information to attending artists, curators, collectors, and the art-interested public) are there to exchange ideas and inform the public of upcoming exhibits, conferences, recent publications, and collector group activities. For more information, check out *www.sofaexpo.com*.

The Craft Organization Development Association (CODA), best known for its landmark CODA Survey, "The Impact of Crafts on the

National Economy," published in 2001, began in 1986 as a breakout session at an ACC show. "The industry seems to need leadership in building collaborations as well as public understanding and appreciation for the crafts," says Linda Van Trump, CODA's chair and managing director. The group was founded to support the work of crafts administration professionals of state, regional, and national crafts organizations; its members also find value in networking, peer approval, affirmation, and discussion of common goals. The mission is formally defined as serving organizations with education and professional development to foster public appreciation and understanding of crafts. For more information, contact CODA at (870) 746-4396 or *www.contemporarycraft.org/coda*.

The Craft Retailers Association for Tomorrow (CRAFT), formed by approximately forty retailers who gathered in Philadelphia to establish the organization in 2002, hopes to: promote American crafts to the public, create a high level of standard business practices among crafts retailers, and provide networking opportunities for retailers, as well as programs such as health insurance for its members. Although the idea is not new (the defunct American Craft Retailers Association [ACRA] disbanded after joining the American Craft Association [ACA]), members felt a need for an advocacy group that can promote the interests of retailers and promote good business practices. A survey was distributed to four hundred retailers nationwide to determine relevant issues, and the direction of the group is based on those responses. In order to qualify, at least 50 percent of the items members sell in their galleries must be handmade American crafts. For more information, call (215) 564-3484, or visit *www.craftonline.org*.

Another interesting development in the crafts world that has helped to promote crafts was a special collection assembled in 1993 at the White House in Washington, D.C., by Michael Munroe, former curator at the Renwick Museum in Washington. Titled *The White House Collection of American Crafts*, this collection features seventy-two works by seventy-seven of America's leading crafts artists. The support, encouragement, and visibility given to contemporary American crafts in the White House by then-President Bill Clinton and First Lady Hillary Rodham Clinton served as recognition of our country's longstanding tradition of making crafts, and as a tribute to the richness and diversity of this important aspect of our heritage. The pieces, illustrating the skill, imagination, and vitality characteristic of crafts in the 1990s, were made of glass, wood, clay, fiber, and metal. The collection revealed the ability of craftspeople to manipulate materials in inventive ways, expressing their creative visions in objects of startling beauty. As the most industrialized century of our history drew to its close, this collection stood as testimony to our belief in the value of works made by hand. Despite our increasing reliance on computer technology, the intimate and physical qualities of the handmade object had never had more appeal.

Installed in various locations throughout the White House (including the Ground Floor Corridor, the Library, the Vermeil Room, the China Room, the Diplomatic Reception Room, the North Entrance, the Cross Hall, the Green Room, the Blue Room, and the Red Room), this collection of objects did not pretend to be a broad, exhaustive survey of all facets of contemporary crafts practiced today. Ordinarily, a curator organizing a collection for a museum exhibition would have the opportunity to select the pieces without regard for the architecture or decor of the museum environment. In contrast, the rationale and the parameters for selecting objects in the White House collection were narrowly defined and determined by the architecture, historical settings, and furnishings, with careful consideration given to the color, texture, and scale of the period rooms. It was important that all of the crafts media be represented: clay, wood, glass, metal, and fiber. Because there was little wall or floor space for textile hangings and furniture, certain pieces were deemed inappropriate. The most desirable settings for the objects were most often the antique pier tables, cabinets, bookcase-desks, fireplace mantels, worktables, and sofa tables that help to give the grand White House interiors their character. The selected craft pieces responded, each in their own way, to the preexisting style and ambience of these historical spaces.

The most appropriate type of object for the majority of these settings proved to be the vessel form. Among the richest areas of current craft expression, vessels and objects relating to the vessel form have been fashioned in all crafts media. A number of the vessels were chosen because they related directly to classical and traditional shapes of the past and responded eloquently to the aesthetic of their period settings.

The following sections, organized by medium, offer historical references as well as books and museums for further study and insight. Although there has not been a definitive book written on the history of crafts to date, there are many excellent exhibition catalogs available that include historical essays. For example, in 2002 the Philadelphia Museum of Art co-published a catalog with Rutgers University Press titled *Crafting a Legacy: Contemporary American Crafts in the Philadelphia Museum of Art*, by Suzanne Ramljak. Marking the twenty-fifth anniversary of the respected

Philadelphia Museum of Art Craft Show, this catalog documents the museum's contemporary crafts collection, begun in 1970, which today totals more than 315 objects. Including more than one hundred works by sixty-four artists, the catalog traces the history of crafts collecting at the museum, stressing the role the city of Philadelphia has played as a center for innovation in the field since the 1960s.

Clay

Garth Clark, owner of Garth Clark Gallery in New York and author of *American Ceramics: 1876–Present*, is considered an authority on the history of ceramics. Garth was named an Honorary Fellow of the American Craft Council in 2002, and received the Visionaries Lifetime Achievement Award from the ACC in 1999. Garth became interested in ceramics history while doing research on a book about South African potters, when he realized there was very little written about the subject. He began his own original research and has done pioneering work in the field of ceramics history ever since.

According to Garth, one of the changes in recent history has been the acceptance of new work in clay on an equal footing with other fine arts. In an essay titled "Otis and Its Influences," Garth writes, "Postwar American artist–teachers such as Peter Voulkos and Robert Arneson did not set out to found 'schools' the way Bernard Leach and others did in Europe, and did not consider imitation to be the sincerest form of pottery. They were offended if students tried to mimic their work, expecting them to seek their own visual identity. Partly this was the character of this generation of artists, but it was also cultural, part of America's obsession with individuality and innovation. What was it that the ceramics world found so exciting in American ceramics? Certainly it was the work itself, irreverent, provocative, experimental, and sometimes even glamorous. But the real achievement in the last fifty years has been to liberate the minds of ceramics artists to be more ambitious, and to use tradition as a stepladder, not as a prison. Peter Voulkos, the leader of the so-called abstract expressionist ceramics movement, was unable to get the kind of attention and respect he sought as an artist because his chosen medium, ceramics, enjoyed about as much stature as finger painting. This isolation from the art mainstream influenced Voulkos to give up ceramics in 1963 and to work exclusively in metal until the mid-1970s." To anyone new to the field today, the fact that ceramics held a low position in the art world would be a complete surprise, given the support and stature the field now enjoys.

An exhibition titled "Abstract Expressionist Ceramics" (held in 1966 at the Art Galleries of the University of California at Irvine and at the Museum of Modern Art, San Francisco) was able to define a new language of form as well as a tough and ambitious stance for ceramics. Even though the work showed a virtuoso facility with clay, it was not about technique, but about the unleashing of energy and emotion. The vessels in particular were a revelation: Michael Frimkess's ungainly and bluntly named *Pot* (1959); Ken Price's witty *Lizard Cup* (1959); Voulkos's thick, muscular *Vase* (1961), which slumped back into the earth, and a ripped and gouged *Plate* (1963); John Mason's sculptural *X Pots* (1957); Ron Nagle's luscious green and brown *Cup* (1963); and James Melchert's masterpiece, *Leg Pot 1* (1962), with its defiance of the verticality of the vessel. This group of Los Angeles artists had confidently (some of the artists say blindly) marched out of the more precious world of the decorative arts and into a new landscape that was troubling and uncharted, but promising. Of course, the work did not arrive by immaculate conception, nor was it disconnected from ceramic tradition, as some writers have suggested. Otis was very much about the continuum of extended tradition. After all, these were still pots and they carried with them all the nuances and deep associations that pots have had in the lives of man for thousands of years. But this group, working experimentally through the night in the basement workshop of the Otis Art Institute in Los Angeles, had finally crossed that line that ceramics had been pushing towards since the late nineteenth century, trying to establish an autonomous art form that was as relevant and contemporary as painting or sculpture.

Fiber

The field of fiber stretches across many media and approaches, from working in baskets, dolls, studio beads, paper, and book arts to wearable arts, quilts, and weaving. Although the historical and contemporary influences intersect, there are distinct differences, even within the same medium.

Baskets

Basket making has a long history, and there are many interesting traditions in different regions of the United States. Today, not only are some of the old traditions kept alive by groups of dedicated basket makers such as the Maine Indian Basketmakers Alliance (in Theresa Secord's profile, page 117), but contemporary baskets are finding their place in the crafts world through organizations such as the National Basketry Organization (*www.nationalbasketry.org*).

Early historic European accounts often do not distinguish between rigid baskets and the flexible bags of the Native Americans. All types of woven containers were generically referred to as "baskets," despite differences in the materials or construction techniques employed. In the Northeast, for example, storage baskets were constructed from a variety of materials, including hemp, rushes or bents, maize husks, silk (or sweet) grass, tree bark, and even horseshoe crab shells.

Basket making in the South has been part of the greater Charleston, South Carolina, communities for more than three hundred years. Brought to the area by slaves who came from West Africa, this traditional art form has been passed on from generation to generation and is one of the oldest art forms of African origin in the United States. During the days of slavery, rice cultivation, and the flourishing plantations of the Old South, these baskets were in great demand not only for agricultural purposes, but because they also brought extra income to slave owners through selling baskets to other plantation owners. During this era, large work baskets were made by men from marsh grasses, called "bulrush," to collect and store vegetables, and functional baskets for everyday living in the home were made by women from the softer, pliable grass commonly called "sweet grass." For generations, the techniques of sweet grass baskets have been passed from mother to daughter to granddaughter. In the 1930s, basket makers saw a new surge of interest from gift shop owners, museums, and handcraft collectors. The paving of roads also enabled makers to market their wares from roadside basket stands, which were directly accessible to tourists. Today, these baskets are purchased by museums and art collectors throughout the world, such as the Museum of American History at the Smithsonian Institution.

The Nantucket Lightships Basket originated in the mid-1800s in Massachusetts. Lightships, vessels that were fitted with lights and moored at sea to warn approaching ships of shallow water, were essentially manned buoys. (Men needed to be on board because the first lights were oil lamps that needed frequent refilling and repairs.) In 1856, the No. 1 Nantucket Lightship was commissioned to service, and it is believed that this is when the Nantucket Lightship Basket was born. The men stationed to monitor the ship for months at a time used their leisure time to weave baskets. Although baskets had been woven on Nantucket for as long as it had been inhabited, the Lightship Baskets were unique because of their combination of mold-woven cane sides and wood spokes emanating from a grooved wooden bottom. The first molds were made from ship masts, but later, lathe-turned molds enabled weavers to create nested sets of baskets that fit one inside the other in graduating sizes. Today these baskets are in great demand.

Dolls

The interest in doll making and collecting has never been greater. While there is a lot of variety in how dolls are made and distributed, many craftspeople are making dolls as one-of-a-kind objects as well as in series or kit form. An exhibit held in 2003 at the American Textile History Museum in Lowell, Massachusetts, called "Reflections: Fashion, Dolls, and the Art of Growing Up," explored how generations of little girls' lives have been shaped by and are reflected in their dolls. From American Girl to Barbie to Grandma's cherished porcelain-faced playmate, this exhibition was both a nostalgic trip through childhood—examining how girls' self-perceptions and the fashions they emulate have changed—and a chance to glimpse the fantasies of earlier generations of children and compare them to present-day notions of childhood, girlhood, and womanhood. This exhibit included mother-and-daughter fashions from the nineteenth century and scenes of a typical household from that time, such as Victorian women and girls engaged in play and needlework. Also featured was a wonderful collection of teatime toys and dolls exploring how girls and boys were taught behavior in the social world by bringing their dolls and other "guests" to the nursery to serve them everything from petit fours to mudpies.

Dolls also mirror our culture's attitudes and history. For example, the Philadelphia Doll Museum (*www.philadollmuseum.com*) has more than three hundred African American dolls in its collection. The museum provides a resource library of information and documentation highlighting the story of how African Americans have been perceived throughout world history, through a collection that includes African, European, and American folk art dolls, the renowned Roberta Bell Doll Collection, and internationally manufactured dolls. Established in 1988 as an educational and cultural resource institution, the museum is dedicated to preserving doll history and culture through seminars and lectures, a resource library of information for doll research (printed material, photographs, and audio recordings), exhibit exchanges, and educational workshops.

Paper

According to Faith Shannon in her book *Paper Pleasures*, a civilized world is inconceivable without paper. While the uses of paper as a medium for storing and conveying information reach far beyond the dreams of its inventors, the artistic aspect of using paper as a means of self-expression ranges from notebooks to drawings to decorative uses. Even in an increasingly computerized society, paper continues to hold a place of crucial importance.

Paper was invented in China in the second century A.D. Before paper, the Chinese drew or painted their characters on woven cloth until they discovered they could use tree barks and other fibrous materials to form thin, flexible sheets with fine surfaces. The invention of papermaking spread westward from China until it was first recorded in Europe in the late fifteenth century in the form of the famous Gutenberg Bible in Germany. European immigrants were the first to establish papermaking in North America, in Pennsylvania during the seventeenth century. As the craft of papermaking spread, the techniques became more refined, with mechanized systems replacing the use of handheld molds.

Today, while mechanized systems still create the bulk of our paper, craftspeople around the globe have revived the art of making handmade paper and are incorporating it into their work. Papermaking, decorating paper, using paper in three dimensions, and book making are current creative uses incorporating handmade paper.

The Robert C. Williams American Museum of Papermaking is an internationally renowned source on the history of paper and paper technology. Membership to the museum, which features more than two thousand books and a collection of over ten thousand watermarks, papers, tools, machines, and manuscripts, also includes membership to the Friends of Dard Hunter Inc. The original Dard Hunter Paper Museum was founded by Dard Hunter (1883–1966), who traveled extensively to document papermaking techniques and write a number of books about papermaking in various cultures. Originally housed at the Massachusetts Institute of Technology, the collection was moved to the Institute of Paper Chemistry in Wisconsin, and now rests in Atlanta, Georgia.

The Friends of Dard Hunter Inc., an international organization with 450 members, offers members three issues of the *Bull & Branch* newsletter, a listing in and copy of the FDH membership directory, advance notice of the annual meeting, and voting privileges within the organization. For more information, contact: Robert C. Williams American Museum of Papermaking, Institute of Paper Science and Technology, 500 10th Street NW, Atlanta, GA 30318, (404) 894-7840, *www.ipst.edu/amp*; Friends of Dard Hunter Inc., Box 773, Lake Oswego, OR 97034, (503) 699-8653, *www.friendsofdardhunter.org.*

Quilts

According to Ruth Marler in her book *The Art of the Quilt*, the precise beginnings of the American quilt are unknown. What is known is that three distinct types of textile work—scraps, remnants, and pieces of worn-out garment—were used to create items such as bedcovers; fabric was applied for decorative effect; and padded or quilted textiles were used for warmth. The merging of these three skills resulted in the American quilt.

The earliest surviving quilts known today are from the first quarter of the eighteenth century and were show quilts never intended to be used on a daily basis. Initially there were three types of quilts: whole-cloth (made of a large expanse of one fabric), medallion (a central motif emphasized by borders), and mosaic piecework (one shape repeated all over the quilt). Blockwork (making quilts out of squares or blocks) did not emerge until the early nineteenth century. Frequently, quilts are a combination of these styles, with a central medallion or large expanses of cloth interspersed with pieced blocks.

Technical advances in the textile industry affected how quilts were made, and changes in the methods of printing cloth resulting in the availability of cheaper fabrics (such as calico), which allowed a wider range of women to produce intricately appliquéd designs, incorporating preprinted images sewn onto the quilt rather than relying on creating imagery by piecing together different bits of cloth. Different cultures also influenced how quilts were made. For example, in the 1830s German immigrants in Pennsylvania influenced quilt design with their use of decorative art in the design of appliquéd quilts.

The development of synthetic dyes also influenced the colors of quilts as dyes evolved from natural substances (such as red from madder and blue from indigo plants) to a larger range of synthetic colors. Conversely, using the combination of blue and white remained popular, and may be traced to the official colors used by the WCTU (Women's Christian Temperance Union), which produced many blue and white quilts using aptly named patterns such as the "drunkard's path." Or it may be that blue was a lasting color and contrasted well with white. What is known is that the advantage of colorfast dyes, coupled with the availability of more reasonably priced fabric in a wide selection of patterns, ensured that more women were able to afford to make quilts.

The act of piecing and quilting has never been done solely with the goal of producing a practical, useful item. Quilting has not only afforded the maker a means of creative expression and a reason for socializing, but also the chance to express herself through themes such as political support, suffrage and temperance statements, slavery, and AIDS.

The largest show quilt ever created is the AIDS Memorial Quilt. Started in 1985, this project consists of commemorative patches sewn together that measure three by six feet. The AIDS quilt provided a traditional forum for commemoration and healing, as did nineteenth-century quilts made from clothes of the deceased. It has also proven to be the focus of a highly successful health education program and a source of fundraising for research into prevention of the disease.

Where did the recent resurgence of interest in quilts come from? In 1971, a show at the Whitney Museum in New York called "American Pieced Quilts" was considered to be the starting point for the revival of interest in quilting. The bicentennial in 1976 also stirred up interest in everything traditionally American, including quilts. According to Nancy Halpern in an article titled "Pioneers: Teaching the World to Quilt" in QNM magazine (July/August 2002), three-quarters of the quilt makers she polled in the 1980s had not learned about quilt making from their families; 78 percent claimed to be self-taught, and 87 percent had begun their learning in a class. Lacking a grandmother's knee to fall back on, the emerging community of current-day quilt makers learned from old books, observation, word of mouth, trial and error, and desire, rather than from tradition passed down through generations.

By the end of the twentieth century, quilt making continued in four distinct ways: traditional quilting in the domestic sphere, incorporating modern materials and tools (such as sewing machines and computer programs); quilting used politically for the advancement of causes like feminism and AIDS; quilt history, used to study social history to uncover the lives of ordinary people; and finally, the acceptance of quilt making as a high art form.

There are several museums around the United States dedicated to quilts, such as the New England Quilt Museum, located in Lowell, Massachusetts (*www.nequiltmuseum.org*), the only museum in the region dedicated solely to the preservation and study of American quilt making, past and present; and the Museum of the American Quilter's Society (*www.quiltmuseum.org*) in Kentucky, dedicated to educating the public about the art, history, and heritage of quilt making.

Weaving

Throughout history, people have insulated themselves against the climatic variations of their homelands by weaving cloths, rugs, and covers. Textile production has evolved over thousands of years, and while weaving is practiced in many communities around the globe, the process of weaving was developed in various regions of the world at different times.

In the United States, during the Industrial Revolution, cloth weaving became a mechanized industry with the development of steam- and water-powered looms. The invention of the fly shuttle—a mechanical device using ropes and pulleys to deliver the weft (horizontal threads) into the warp (vertical threads)—removed the need to have a weaver place the thread by hand. The fly shuttle not only increased the volume of cloth production, but it also forced technological advancement in the spinning industry by forcing it to keep up through supplying larger amounts of yarn.

The early 1800s saw the development of the Jacquard machine, a revolutionary machine with a punch card mechanism to operate the loom. Credited as the basis of modern computer science, this complicated machine was added to the top of the weaving loom, and was able to move individual warp threads up and down according to the pattern of holes punched into the cards. Cloths woven on a loom with a Jacquard machine could have more intricate patterns.

Today most of our textile needs are still supplied by commercially woven cloth made by automated machines. However, there are growing numbers of craftspeople making cloth on hand looms, in home studios, and in small weaving businesses, keeping alive the skills and traditions developed by the early weavers.

The American Textile History Museum in Lowell, Massachusetts (*www.athm.org*), known as the world's largest textile museum, brings alive the magic of spinning and weaving in nearly one hundred exhibits, ranging from the interior of an eighteenth-century Pennsylvania weaver's log cabin to a working 1870s woolen mill. Located in a restored historic mill building, the museum offers an unparalleled collection chronicling textile production in the United States from the eighteenth century to the mid-1900s, including the world's largest assortment of hand-powered tools and equipment, machinery, fabrics, and garments, in addition to a library, a state-of-the-art laboratory (for the care and preservation of textiles), and activities, including hands-on workshops, lecture series, classes, and community school outreach programs.

Glass

Until the 1960s, glassblowing had been confined to large factory settings rather than artist studios and shops. Although the last several decades have seen the field of glass explode, glassblowers still have a respect and almost a reverence for those pioneers who have gone before them.

Artists in Glass: Late Twentieth Century Masters in Glass by Dan Klein, executive director of the auction house Phillips in New York, traces the glassblowing movement through the lives and works of nearly eighty artists, exploring their influences, training, and techniques. The book also includes a glossary, a bibliography, and a list of galleries and museums where contemporary glass art can be seen.

In addition to the Pilchuck School and the Glass Art Society in the Seattle area, two wonderful museums dedicated to the field of glass are the historic Corning Museum of Glass in Corning, New York, and the Museum of Glass: International Center for Contemporary Art in Tacoma, Washington. The Corning Museum (*www.cmog.org*) offers exhibits in the Collection Galleries, views into the workshop and studio to provide opportunities to watch glassblowers at work, a research library, and a shop selling items made of glass. The Museum of Glass: International Center for Contemporary Art (*www.museumofglass.org*) opened in 2002 to honor glass artist Dale Chihuly (a Tacoma native), with 13,000 square feet of open exhibition space, a hot glass studio where artistic teams blow and cast glass, a cold glass studio for completing artworks, and a 2,200-square-foot Education Studio, which serves as an interpretive space reflecting the themes of the exhibits.

Stained Glass

Although stained glass dates back to ancient Egypt in the second century B.C., stained glass as we know it today was first used in European religious panels and cathedral windows of the twelfth century A.D. The use of stained glass expanded during the Renaissance period, with the building of grand cathedrals in Europe from the 1400s through the

1700s. During this period, although the use of stained glass outside the Church was rare, leaded clear glass windows began to be used in some non-Church construction. In Europe during the 1800s, stained glass was fitted into chateau windows in a variety of "soft" colors considered more appropriate for domestic use.

Stained glass expanded in the late 1800s and early 1900s during the Art Nouveau period, when American glassmakers began to make a translucent, "milky" glass known as "opalescent,"which significantly expanded the variety of glass available for artists' use. During this time, Louis Tiffany (1848–1933) used stained glass extensively in non-religious forms such as lamps and windows, and also promoted the "copper foil" style of stained glass construction. The copper foil technique uses tape to wrap the edge of each piece of glass, allowing each piece to be soldered to the adjoining glass pieces. A lighter method of construction than using lead, it also allowed artists to use many smaller glass pieces, permitting more detail in a stained glasswork. The extremely fine detail of Louis Tiffany's glasswork became a signature of Tiffany art glass.

The popularity of stained glass continued into the Art Deco period of the late 1920s through the early 1940s, when stylized stained glass was incorporated into the architectural design of buildings. Although stained glass work was slowed by the worldwide depression of the 1930s and World War II in the 1940s, it continued to be promoted by prominent people such as architect Frank Lloyd Wright (1869–1959) in his modern Prairie art style, and continued as a fringe art form through the early 1960s.

Stained glass gained significant popularity in the late 1960s and early 1970s as a hobby art form, but even serious artists and craftspeople also began to learn this ancient art. Environmental concerns about lead in glass panels encouraged most stained glass artists to adapt the copper foil method of construction as the standard method of stained glass assembly. In the mid-1990s, a new form of stained glass known as "stained glass mosaic" emerged, combining stained glass and mosaic techniques. Prior to this, stained glass had generally been used only in windows or lamps, and mosaics had been limited to small ceramic tile chips cemented onto floors, walls, or ceilings.

The Biographical Index of Historic American Stained Glass Makers by Robert O. Jones, which is available through the Stained Glass Association of America, broadly defines the history of stained glass in the United States, including the people and studios that practiced the trade from the colonial period up until fifty years ago. To be included in the book, the person or studio must have been actively involved in the industry in the United States or Canada. For more information, contact SGAA at *www.stainedglass.org.*

Metal

The history of metal includes jewelry, hollowware, and sculptural work created out of a range of materials such as gold, silver, iron, and steel, which have evolved over many years. Today's metalsmiths can be found working in individual studios or for industry, incorporating a wide range of materials and processes to create their work.

Jewelry

According to metalsmith Tim McCreight, in the 1960s crafts were sold through a wide array of street fairs, regional gatherings, and holiday events. In addition to exposing the buying public to a wide range of work, these activities also provided opportunities for designers to view each other's work and share their business experiences. As the industry grew in scale and professionalism, the cost of participation rose. Instead of driving to the next town and selling from a card table, jewelers needed to fly across the country, stay in hotels, and present their work in an increasingly competitive setting. This raised bar had the effect of urging commercial designers to be connected to their market and be confident that they were in synch with popular taste. Academic and gallery designers were not subject to these same pressures (they had others, of course), which led to a gap between designers who responded to the marketplace and those whose work was driven by competitive exhibitions, gallery shows, and personal expression. Currently, a sluggish economy has pushed the wedge deeper between these two groups, which has unfortunately brought confusion and in some cases a lack of generosity that was not evident thirty years ago.

Jewelry of Our Time: Art, Ornament and Obsession by Helen Drutt is one of the best books on contemporary trends in the jewelry field, praised as a "must" for those who collect or are interested in collecting contemporary jewelry as an art form in a review posted on *Amazon.com.* Because Helen knows a number of the artists personally, she is able to provide the reader with an in-depth perspective on the artists' work and inspiration. While a fair number of the artists are European, Helen also focuses on American artists.

Blacksmithing

Blacksmithing dates back to when primitive man first began making tools out of iron. While early blacksmiths were able to make simple tools such as spears, arrow tips, and cooking spits, the craft would require several centuries before mankind could realize the magnetic properties of forged metal. Early iron smelters consisted of an oven built from rocks that could withstand repeated heating. These ovens looked like beehives with a smoke vent in the top and an entry portal on the side. The hearth was filled with charcoal or coke and set afire, and the ore rocks were laid on top. When the temperature rose above two thousand degrees, the iron would flow from the ore and puddle in the fiery coals. With large tongs, these lumps of raw iron would be pulled from the oven and placed on an anvil. A man would then hammer the lumpy piece of raw iron into a flat, rectangular bar. The bar would be folded over and hammered again into its original shape. This process would continue several more times until all impurities had been driven from the ingot. The finished ingot, bearing the layers of the folding process, was called "wrought iron."

As the iron industry evolved over time, blacksmithing became an umbrella trade for other specialties. A blacksmith who made suits of armor was called an "armorer," a smith who made knives and swords a "bladesmith," locks a "locksmith," gun barrels and triggers a "gunsmith," and one who shod horses a "farrier."

In colonial America, the village blacksmith was called upon to do many different things, such as make an axe, a knife, a fireplace crane, a set of door hinges, or a handful of nails. This made his shop into the local hardware store. Without the blacksmith, the village could not survive. Over the centuries, blacksmiths experimented with iron and other metals in their search for a more durable metal, which lead to the development of the tool steels and alloyed metals we have today. Blacksmithing in America prospered until the Industrial Revolution, when by the late 1800s, railroads had linked the country and hardware was being manufactured and sold in hardware stores.

Today, a blacksmith is usually a specialty craftsperson, making both reproductions of items from the past and fine art objects. Using many of the same techniques, today's blacksmith might also use the electric drill, electric grinder, power hammer, oxyacetylene torch, and electric blower.

Wood

Making objects from wood grew out of the functional needs of building shelter, crafting furniture, carving tools to work with, and getting from one shore to another. While some woodworkers are dedicated to using only hand tools, many of today's woodworkers use a variety of hand and power tools to get the job done.

Boats

Before the development of trains and automobiles, which required roads, ships and boats were very important to daily life. Shipbuilding occurred in almost every bay, cove, and harbor. Building a vessel required a source of lumber, sail makers, ironworkers, framers, plankers, painters, caulkers, riggers, foundrymen, woodcarvers, and draymen with their teams of oxen and horses. Early boats required investors to build the vessel and fit her out for a voyage—as they still do today. Shipbuilding required a combination of crafts; it was an exciting process by which vast amounts of lumber and iron were turned into a thing of beauty and provided a livelihood to hundreds of craftspeople.

Today, although the methods of transportation have changed radically, a revival of interest in wooden boat making has emerged. Although the development of materials such as fiberglass and plastic have altered the boat world, interest in building wooden boats is a strong trend supported by hobbyists and professionals alike.

Studio Furniture

While furniture has been made for thousands of years, studio furniture is a fairly new twig on the branch of furniture history. Many furniture makers now see themselves as makers of unique objects, creating in the vein of artists rather than makers in a factory setting. Studio furniture, uniquely designed using a variety of materials, has emerged as an important trend in the contemporary furniture world.

Furniture historians have traditionally tended to organize antique furniture according to formal stylistic categories, often named after designers or rulers such as Chippendale or Louis XVI or Rococo. Style, rooted in the shop masters, client group, common printed sources, or available materials, served as the primary means of linking objects. With the revivals in the mid-nineteenth century and increased production due to mechanization, style became a less important barometer and was replaced by taste and workmanship as the important criteria.

The term "art furniture" emerged in the late 1860s as a way of distinguishing this type of furniture making from factory work. The Arts and Crafts Movement of the late nineteenth and early twentieth centuries elevated the importance of craftsmanship over decoration. Good, honest structural furniture was considered to possess great moral integrity that would facilitate the simple life pursued by many Americans. By the 1920s and '30s, modernism began as an intellectual investigation of design that quickly became a way of packaging furniture and was reduced to a style.

Today, there are multiple uses of art and styles without reference to any specific hierarchy, as in the past. The term "studio furniture" allows makers to distinguish their work from other types of furniture. The unique backgrounds of the makers; their interest in linking concept, materials, and technique; and the small shops in which they work are the common elements, rather than a technique or use of any specific material.

Studio furniture makers have not learned their skills through traditional apprenticeship programs, but have tended to master design and construction in college programs or are self-taught, learning through reading, workshops, experimentation, and comparing notes with other furniture makers. Rather than undergoing the restrictive training typical of the furniture trade, most studio furniture makers experience a longer, more self-directed, and less constrained learning period and possess a high degree of visual literacy in approaching design and construction.

One cannot intelligently discuss studio furniture without naming some of the collectors and gallery owners who have supported the movement and kept it alive. Pritam and Eames Gallery in East Hampton, New York, mounted a twentieth anniversary exhibition in 2001 that included many of the most accomplished active makers in the United States today, including Judy Kensley McKie, Jere Osgood, Kristina Madsen, Alphonse Mattia, Hank Gilpin, Wendy Maruyama, David Ebner, Rosanne Somerson, Michael Hurwitz, and James Schriber. A furniture historian could have easily conducted a stirring seminar on the recent history of the craft using only the pieces and makers in this show. Founded in 1981 by Warren Eames Johnson and Bebe Pritam Johnson, this gallery has consistently presented furniture of the highest caliber, reflecting not only the vibrancy of the field, but also the creativity and stamina of the makers. The formation of the gallery was timely, as the 1970s saw the emergence of numerous artists designing and making furniture by hand, who had relatively few venues in which to show and sell their work.

Woodturning

Although traced back to 1900, when industrial arts education entered many high schools, woodturning's growth as a popular hobby and professional art form did not reach a peak until the 1930s and '40s, when new, smaller, and safer classroom lathes were developed that were equally appropriate for home workshops, fostering a boom in amateur training. At that time, there also weren't many people like James Prestini, Rude Osolnik, or Bob Stockdale exploring the artistic potential of the turned wood bowl. Prestini and Osolnik are often credited with single-handedly reviving the field and, interestingly enough, were both introduced to the lathe in high school.

Although woodturning was taking a uniquely contemporary shape, there wasn't a national coherence to this widespread activity until 1976, when the first Wood Turning Symposium was held in Philadelphia, helping to form a national community of turners. The following years saw the field become more professional, with the emergence of significant collectors and exhibition venues. In 1985, the Arrowmont School of Arts and Crafts in Tennessee hosted a juried exhibit of turned objects with a three-day symposium that drew approximately two hundred woodturners from all over the country. The concept of a national organization of woodturners was presented, and as a result, the American Association of Woodturners (AAW) was formed.

Two woodturners are often singled out for their efforts to gain recognition as artists: David Ellsworth (see chapter 15) and Mark Lindquist. The movement from the purist form of turning to the evolution of more sculptural and experimental work that we see today bears little resemblance to historical turnings that were primarily made as parts for furniture or buildings, and instead reflects the influence of studio ceramics, with its emphasis on creating vessel forms.

For those interested in reading more about the history of woodturning, see *Wood Turning in North America Since 1930*, the catalog published in 2002 in conjunction with the exhibit of the same name. The first attempt to write the history of North American woodturning and define the field in context, this catalog is available through the Yale University Art Gallery, (203) 432-0601.

CHAPTER 2

Success Defined

What is success? Getting accepted into a crafts show or gallery? Making your living from selling your work? And after you have achieved success, how do you maintain it? The truth is that when asked whether or not they are a success, most craftspeople rarely respond with an enthusiastic "yes," even when seen as a great success by others. So what makes successful craftspeople *feel* successful?

Some craftspeople define success in monetary terms, by their ability to earn their living doing something they love. To others, a sense of community involvement and helping others is part of the definition of success, rather than just their income. Even for those who have achieved a high level of recognition and success, there is always a next step and something new to accomplish. However you choose to define success for yourself, remember that it is also a personal decision that can only be made by you. Your definition may change with each phase in your life as well, whether you are single, in a relationship, a parent, or taking care of aging parents.

Beginning in 1970, the American Craft Council has paid tribute to those whose artistry and leadership as makers, teachers, patrons, scholars, and administrators have enriched and advanced the crafts field in the United States. Now given annually, the awards include the Gold Medal (for consummate craftsmanship), Awards of Distinction (for outstanding accomplishment relating to crafts), and the Aileen Osborn Webb Award (named for the Council's founder and given to recognize generosity and leadership benefiting crafts). The Council also recognizes outstanding design and craftsmanship in the work of artists exhibiting in the American Craft Council shows through Awards of Excellence (cash prizes are given annually to outstanding show exhibitors), as well as Honorable Mention awards. Initiated in 1975, the College of Fellows is comprised of individuals who have made major contributions to the crafts field in America. The designation of ACC Fellow signifies an artist of outstanding ability who has worked in his or her respective field for at least twenty-five years. The title of Honorary Fellow is bestowed on people who have played an important role in crafts and is based on peer election. New members are named each year and are honored at the Council's annual awards presentation. Several of the craftspeople profiled in this book have either received the Gold Medal or been designated an ACC Fellow, including Arline Fisch, Gerry Williams, Dorothy Gill Barnes, Harvey Littleton, David Ellsworth, and Jere Osgood.

How can craftspeople empower themselves (as do those in sports or sales) so that they *feel* successful? Planning and goal setting can give a craftsperson a way to measure success, especially if it is done on a regular basis. However, being a success on paper and feeling like a success can be two different matters. What stands in the way of most craftspeople feeling successful?

In his book titled *The 7 Levels of Change: Different Thinking for Different Results*, Rolf Smith writes that different results do not only come out of doing something differently; they also require *thinking* differently. He identifies seven levels of change that involve moving one's thinking into action in order to drive change. Level one begins with "doing the right thing," culminating in level seven with "doing things that can't be done." In-between levels include: doing the right things right, doing things better, doing away with things, doing things that other people are doing, and doing things no one else is doing. One of the most interesting aspects of his research is his outline of the levels of fear associated with each level of change, such as seeing only the worst case, fear of letting go, and fear of self. What may be holding you back from feeling successful? He suggests that many people never take the time to think about who they are, where they have been, and who they want to become. In response, he has developed a program called "Me, Inc.," which moves readers through increasing levels of personal reflection (vision, mission, strategy, principles, values, strengths, and major goals) to help them implement change.

Self-Assessment Quiz

Here is a simple exercise I developed to help craftspeople ascertain what stage they are at in their careers and see what career choice might fit their particular lifestyle best. There are no right or wrong answers. Just circle the answer that best describes your current situation and then read what your answers signify.

1. What is your level of education and experience?
a) I have a degree in crafts or I have done an apprenticeship to learn my craft and the business. I continue to attend as many workshops as I can on both crafts and business.
b) I have a degree in another field but have taken numerous workshops to learn both my craft and how to run a business.
c) I have taken a few workshops in my craft.

DISCUSSION: While you don't have to have a formal degree in your craft to sell your work, a broad background in both the history and techniques of your craft is preferable. Expertise in running your own business can be learned on a trial-and-error basis, but many people find it worth the time and investment to take a small-business management course or to find an opportunity to work with an experienced craftsperson.

2. I want to make my living by:
a) selling my work full-time.
b) selling my work part-time and maintaining another source of income.
c) working at a non-craft job.

DISCUSSION: Whether you decide to make all or part of your living from your crafts career is a personal decision. Part-time ventures can be just as successful as full-time ones. There are also craftspeople who choose to earn their living another way and keep their crafts work separate from the demands of the marketplace.

3. I prefer my income to be:
a) it doesn't matter as long as I earn enough money annually.
b) a regular paycheck supplemented with sporadic sales of my work.
c) a regular paycheck.

DISCUSSION: Depending on your support system and comfort level, earning money on a regular basis, sporadically, or by collecting a paycheck doesn't matter as long as you have enough and feel comfortable. Once your career is established, you should have enough cash flow to be able to pay yourself on a regular basis, if that's your goal.

4. My studio includes:
   a) all the equipment I need, a large work space with an adjacent office and showroom to meet customers, and space to store my inventory and ship my work.
   b) a decent work space with the basic equipment I need.
   c) a space in a spare room or part of my garage or basement.

DISCUSSION: While many craftspeople operate their business out of their home, having a dedicated space to make work, store it, ship it, and make sales is important not only for your efficiency, but also for financial matters, such as filing your taxes. Check your local zoning laws before deciding whether or not to make sales from your home. Conversely, having a separate place to work can be better psychologically for some craftspeople who prefer to keep their business and personal lives separate.

5. My portfolio includes:
   a) digital images, color slides, black-and-white photographs, a publicity photograph of me working in my studio, and a shot of my booth, taken by a professional photographer.
   b) color slides of some of my work and a few photographs.
   c) I don't have a portfolio.

DISCUSSION: Depending on which career option you choose to pursue, you may or may not need all of these items in your portfolio, but I recommend having them ready for any opportunity that may present itself. When it does, chances are the images will be needed ASAP. You don't want to miss out on an opportunity just because you neglected to have a complete portfolio ready. With the ease and relatively small expense of having a Web site, many craftspeople design their site to function as an online portfolio as well.

6. The following phrase describes my work:
   a) a line of several different pieces created in multiples with a distinctive style, as well as a series of one-of-a-kind pieces.
   b) some pieces made in multiples and some one-of-a-kind pieces.
   c) many different styles—I like to experiment and never make the same thing twice.

DISCUSSION: The ways in which you choose to make and produce your work (i.e., produce multiple pieces or one-of-a-kind pieces) will directly affect how you market and sell your work. For example, if you choose not to make a production line, you may limit yourself to selling directly to your customers because shops may not be able to place orders with you. How you choose to produce work is not a problem as long as it is in line with your marketing methods, expectations, and outcomes.

7. **Which description sounds like a customer who would buy your work?**
   a) Someone who likes to collect unique things for his or her home as well as purchase handmade gifts.
   b) I guess the customer likes to buy unique gifts for him- or herself, but I'm not sure.
   c) I don't know who my customers are.

DISCUSSION: Identifying profiles of your customers will save you time and money in the long run, because you will know whether or not a show is appropriate and if that expensive ad in a magazine is worth the investment. Take the time to come up with a profile of your potential customers and then match it against your marketing plans.

8. **Where would your customers see your work?**
   a) at fairs, galleries, and shops; in advertisements; online; or at my annual studio sale.
   b) at a fair or studio sale a few times a year, or in a group show once in awhile.
   c) I don't show my work often.

DISCUSSION: In the beginning, you may not have shown your work very often, but you may decide to start by doing a local fair or having a studio open house over the holidays. Once they have established contacts, many craftspeople are able to cut back on doing shows and spend more time in the studio, filling orders or marketing through their own showroom.

9. **I belong to the following organizations:**
   a) local, state, and national crafts organizations.
   b) local crafts organization.
   c) I'm not a joiner of groups.

DISCUSSION: While it is not a prerequisite to belong to any business or crafts organizations in order to have a successful career in crafts, most craftspeople in business for themselves do join these groups for networking, learning about opportunities, and taking workshops. Some also offer health insurance and discounts on supplies and subscriptions. And depending on who your customers are, it sometimes makes sense to join local business organizations, such as the Chamber of Commerce.

10. What are your goals for the next five years?

a) I want to support myself with sales of my work, earning a livable wage.

b) I want to keep the security of my other job, but if the sales from my work continue to increase, I will consider pursuing my crafts business full-time.

c) I want to make pieces I enjoy without being concerned about sales.

DISCUSSION: Statistics show that people who set goals are more likely to achieve them. Having a plan not only helps you to make decisions correctly the first time; it also helps you to spend your money wisely and gives you something by which to measure and review your success.

If you chose mainly:

- (a) *answers:* You are probably already earning a living from the sales of your work. You have a good background in crafts and business, you have the studio and portfolio you need, you know who your customers are, you're promoting your work through several venues, and you know the importance of networking and lifelong learning.
- (b) *answers:* You enjoy the security of a paycheck, and yet you have a strong interest in supplementing your income with selling your work. If you should decide to make the transition to earning all of your income from selling your work, you are learning valuable skills through your part-time selling experiences. Consult an advisor if you decide you want help with planning a transition.
- (c) *answers:* You enjoy making your work, but are either not interested in selling it or unsure of how to go about running a crafts business. Consult an advisor if you decide to start earning all or part of your income from selling your work at some point in the future.

After reviewing the results of this self-assessment, you will either see that (a) you are already selling your work, (b) you are poised to start selling your work full-time, or (c) you need to take additional steps to learn more about how to sell your work or decide to make your living another way. Some of you may decide that selling your work to earn your living is not for you. Take the time to figure out what you want to do and get the help you need. You can do it!

What about craftspeople who have achieved success but still feel there is something missing in their lives? In his book *What Matters Most: The Power of Living Your Values*, Hyrum W. Smith suggests that in an age of unprecedented prosperity and opportunity, there are still many who feel that something is missing in their lives. With a strategy consisting of three steps—discovering what matters most to you, making a plan, and acting on that plan—you will not only re-embrace your values, but you will learn to make them a top priority, thus becoming the person you always wanted to be.

Who do you want to be? Who are your role models, mentors, and heroes? My hope is that from the profiles that follow, you will take away the inspiration and belief that you can do it too.

CHAPTER 3

Career Options

To launch a crafts career, not only do craftspeople have to develop their skills as good makers, but they also need to define a direction and obtain the skills necessary to succeed in the business world. For example, someone who wants to be a potter first needs to learn how to make pottery, then decide how to use his pottery skills to make a living (does he want to market his own work, or teach or work for another craftsperson?). After that, he must figure out what professional skills he needs in order to be successful, and get started.

To help you make a decision about which career may be best for you, this section profiles suggested career options available to people who are considering a career in crafts. Note that many craftspeople combine different career options to earn their living (such as selling work through crafts fairs, teaching workshops, *and* doing private commissions). For some, this is a way to get started before their careers are established; other people do it just because they enjoy it, or to keep their income diversified for a change in the economy. There is not a right or wrong way to have a career in crafts—only what works best for you, your unique situation, and your dreams.

The career options listed here offer a brief explanation to give you an idea of what may fit your current dreams, aspirations, and lifestyle. The end of this section contains a listing of business workshops geared toward creative people that are offered around the country to help you find the resources you may need.

The Self-Employed Craftsperson

Craft Fairs, Trade and Gift Shows

This career option requires someone who wants to run his or her own business, marketing his or her work through retail and/or wholesale fairs and shows. Income can be sporadic in this career choice, with cash flow either resulting immediately from retail shows or in payments over a period of time from wholesale orders.

Although some shows are starting to have tenure for repeat exhibitors, most craft fairs and shows have to be applied for on an annual basis, making it difficult to plan ahead until acceptance has been confirmed. Some craftspeople have said that one year they were awarded Best in Show, only to find out they weren't even accepted into the show the following year! Jurors change, and acceptance always depends on who else is applying.

This career choice allows you to plan your own schedule, report to yourself, and have a lot of control in what you make and when you make it, as well as what part of the country you want to live in (if you are willing to travel to do fairs and shows). For example, some craftspeople live in remote areas that allow them to have low overhead, and travel to do shows in larger metropolitan areas. After you develop contacts, you may only need to do a few fairs to run your business successfully.

Profiles to check out: Mark Bell, Peter Bloch, Pat Caska, Dan Dustin, Randy Fein, Candace Jackman, Mary Nyburg, Marylou Ozbolt Storer, Patricia Palson, Josh Simpson, Ellen Spring, Bert Weiss, and Gail Wilson.

Gallery Representation

Craftspeople who are able to market their work primarily through galleries are usually fairly established in their careers. Emerging craftspeople can usually get started in a group or juried show so that gallery owners can test the market's response to their work. If there is sufficient interest in your work, you may be given a solo show or representation by a particular gallery. However, even if a gallery decides to represent you, it may only mean a show every other year or so.

Another way emerging craftspeople can get started is by joining a cooperative gallery, where they can learn valuable skills before approaching a privately owned gallery. By being a member of the co-op, you are assured of having your work exhibited in exchange for helping run the gallery.

Although there are only a few craftspeople who are able to make the majority of their income from selling their work through galleries, most use their gallery shows to garner part-time income, as a form of publicity and additional prestige to garner sales in other markets, and as a way to exhibit new or experimental work that they might not be able to sell at a fair.

Profiles to check out: Elizabeth Busch, Katharine Cobey, Lisa Tully Dibble, Lynn Duryea, David Ellsworth, Rev. Wendy Ellsworth, Christine Federighi, Arline Fisch, Dorothy Gill Barnes, Abby Huntoon, Dante Marioni, Richard Marquis, George Mason, Mary Nyburg, Jere Osgood, Jan Owen, Josh Simpson, Rosanne Somerson, J. Fred Woell, and Eric Ziner.

Grants and Fellowships

Obtaining grants and fellowships is possible at any stage of your career, although many are designed for established craftspeople or are project-based. In an effort to help emerging craftspeople, many organizations and foundations have designed special grant and fellowship programs to help them get started.

Even if you are able to get a grant or fellowship to complete a special area of study, make a new body of work, or complete a project, grants and fellowships are usually only a temporary source of income. However, what you do with the experience is up to you. For example, buyers and collectors will be impressed by the additional credentials of your having received a grant or fellowship, the experience may take you and your work in new directions, or you may be able to obtain additional grants to carry on the work started with the first grant.

For more information, check out state art commissions, the Foundation Center's Web site at *www.foundationcenter.org*, and Web sites such as *www.artisthelpnetwork.com* for ideas and opportunities.

Profiles to check out: Amanda Barrow, Elizabeth Busch, David Ellsworth, Arline Fisch, Wendy Maruyama, Dante Marioni, and Richard Marquis.

Private and Public Commissions

Commissions can range from private ones garnered from collectors or customers to public ones available through state organizations and private organizations, such as museums or schools.

While these commissions can be invaluable to support craftspeople making site-specific work, such as for a private home or public building, the income from them is usually temporary. However, there are some craftspeople who are so successful at obtaining these commissions that they are able to work on one right after another, applying for new ones while they are completing a current project.

For more information, check out state art commission Web sites for details on the Percent for Art program (available in almost every state in the U.S.) and Web sites such as *www.artisthelpnetwork.com* for ideas and opportunities.

Profiles to check out: Elizabeth Busch, Katharine Cobey, Randy Fein, Abby Huntoon, Candace Jackman, Dante Marioni, George Mason, Jere Osgood, Jan Owen, Rosanne Somerson, and Bert Weiss.

Corporate Collections, Showrooms, and Sales Reps

Many corporations around the country have collections and someone appointed to manage them. Not only is there an opportunity to sell some of your work to a corporation, but sometimes they also offer gallery spaces to show it within the company walls.

Showrooms specializing in specific types of crafts are usually located in big cities, and can be private or found in design centers, catering to the interior design and architectural trades. While you can approach a showroom yourself, usually sales reps will make the contact and process the orders for you, because they represent many craftspeople. Another type of showroom is one that a craftsperson builds right next to his or her own studio as a way of showcasing his of her own work. The third type is an online showroom, exhibiting the work of an individual or group of craftspeople on a Web site.

Profiles to check out: Mark Bell, Marylou Ozbolt Storer, Gerry Williams, and Eric Ziner.

Catalogs

Craftspeople can either participate in an already established catalog or start their own. Catalog sales can be either part of your overall marketing plan or the bulk of it. Several craftspeople have told me that getting an order from L.L. Bean, for example, has been successful beyond their wildest dreams, but has also catapulted them into a whole new level of production.

Profile to check out: Gail Wilson.

Web Sites

More and more craftspeople are marketing their work online through their own Web sites, sites offered through membership organizations, and online galleries. At this point, most craftspeople are only making a small portion of their sales online, but say that there is growth in this type of sales and that it helps their other marketing efforts to have a presence on the Web.

Craftspeople also refer interested customers to their sites for additional information, as a way for someone interested in buying a piece to show another decision-maker the work before making a purchase, and as a follow-up tool for commissioned work.

Web site promotion might include links to other pages, direct mail, and paid advertising. Many craftspeople say that finding ways to personalize the sale is important. They utilize strategies such as quick turnaround on email responses and the use of a digital camera to show current work.

Profiles to check out: Amanda Barrow, Peter Bloch, Katharine Cobey, David Ellsworth, Rev. Wendy Ellsworth, Peter Hagerty, Candace Jackman, Jill Kenik, Dante Marioni, Josh Simpson, Deb Stoner, and Bert Weiss.

Teaching

Visiting Artist in the Schools

There are opportunities for interested craftspeople to teach their craft through public and private schools, through either the local parent/ teacher organization or the state touring artists programs. Sometimes the visit may last just a day, while other times, the teacher is there for a week or two teaching in a block format. Sometimes a craftsperson installing a piece of public art in a school is asked to do a workshop as part of the process, and teaching is another aspect of what he or she does. For most craftspeople, this career option is a supplemental rather than a full-time form of income.

Profiles to check out: Mark Bell, Randy Fein, and Jan Owen.

Private Lessons

Many craftspeople have taught private lessons in their own studio as a way to supplement their income. This career option also allows you to make your own schedule, decide what to teach, and choose which students to accept.

Profiles to check out: Katharine Cobey, David Ellsworth, Rev. Wendy Ellsworth, and Gerry Williams.

Public and Private Schools

Craftspeople who choose to teach in a school setting usually work nine months a year, teaching as many as hundreds of students for short periods of time. While this enables many craftspeople to do their own work during the summer months, this type of teaching is demanding and usually takes all of a craftsperson's energies while school is in session. However, teaching in the school system offers a steady paycheck with benefits.

Profiles to check out: Dorothy Gill Barnes and Iver Lofving.

College Professor

Craftspeople with college teaching jobs usually hold onto them, making this a very competitive profession. Hundreds of people may apply for a job, but once obtained, this career choice offers the opportunity to obtain not only dedicated students interested in pursuing crafts as their career, but also other art and crafts professors as peers. Summers off to pursue their own work, benefits such as sabbaticals, and a steady paycheck make this the career choice for many professional craftspeople.

Profiles to check out: Lisa Tully Dibble, Christine Federighi, Arline Fisch, Dorothy Gill Barnes, Abby Huntoon, Wendy Maruyama, Tim McCreight, Jere Osgood, Rosanne Somerson, Deb Stoner, and J. Fred Woell.

Continuing Education

There are numerous opportunities to teach part-time through continuing education programs, whether at the local high school or at a crafts school. While this is usually a supplemental form of income for most craftspeople, teaching in a continuing education program allows a craftsperson to share her expertise, get exposure for her own work, and have the association of working for the school as part of her credentials when selling her work. For those interested in teaching as a full-time occupation, teaching in a continuing education program helps them garner teaching experience to make their applications more competitive.

Profiles to check out: Abby Huntoon, Tim McCreight, and Jan Owen.

Workshops

Teaching workshops is a great way to supplement your income and gain exposure for your work at the same time. Many crafts schools around the country offer workshops during both the academic year and the summer.

Teaching a workshop can also be a great way for a craftsperson who usually works alone in her studio to socialize and share some of her hard-earned knowledge with others. It can also serve as a form of publicity and an additional way to show work through faculty exhibits and slide lectures.

While in many cases the income from teaching workshops is less than what a professional craftsperson could earn in her own studio, many see it as a working vacation, teaching at beautiful places such as Haystack (on the ocean) or Penland, Arrowmont, and Anderson Ranch (in the mountains). Family members are usually welcome too.

Profiles to check out: Elizabeth Busch, Katharine Cobey, David

Ellsworth, Rev. Wendy Ellsworth, Christine Federighi, Arline Fisch, Dorothy Gill Barnes, Dante Marioni, Richard Marquis, Tim McCreight, Wendy Maruyama, Jere Osgood, Peter Ross, Josh Simpson, Deb Stoner, and J. Fred Woell.

Teaching Assistant

Craftspeople interested in teaching as a career need to get experience in addition to a degree in their field, and being a teaching assistant is a great way to get started. Although this position may vary in length from assisting at a workshop to a semester-long course, it's a chance to interact with students, see what the demands of the classroom are, and gain valuable experience. Anyone getting an MFA degree should insist on obtaining teaching experience as part of the program, whether it is required or not, because there are many opportunities to teach while someone is still in school that may be harder to obtain after graduation. While this is usually open to craftspeople enrolled in an MFA program, it should be seen as an investment in learning how to be a good teacher, and it will make an application to teach later on more competitive.

Profile to check out: Lynn Duryea.

Those Employed by Another Craftsperson

In years gone by, almost every craftsperson would have worked her way up through the apprenticeship system, learning her trade by being employed by another craftsperson. Today, working for another craftsperson is still a viable career choice for many craftspeople, ranging from those just getting started to those who like to earn a paycheck without all the responsibility of running their own business. Not only does working for another craftsperson enable you to see how that person runs her business and learn from it, but it also gives you time to develop your own skills before you start your own business.

Profiles to check out: Amanda Barrow and Dante Marioni.

Industrial Designer

While crafts that are made entirely by hand in a studio setting are still the first choice of many craftspeople, there are opportunities to work in industry as a craftsperson. Whether they are designing a product or helping other people bring their ideas to fruition, today's craftspeople are an integral part of the mass market. This career choice includes doing freelance design or consulting for a company, or working as a paid employee and earning a paycheck and benefits.

Profiles to check out: Jill Kenik, Tim McCreight, and Deb Stoner.

Historic Sites and Museums

Historic sites and museums offer craftspeople an opportunity to make their crafts in the same ways that they were made in different periods of history as part of interpretive programs aimed at educating the public. While some museums have full-time paid craftspeople working at their sites, others rely on part-time or volunteer craftspeople to show visitors how things used to be made by hand. Sample sites include: Colonial Williamsburg in Virginia, Plimoth Plantation and Sturbridge Village in Massachusetts.

Profiles to check out: Paul Rollins and Peter Ross.

Restoration Work

There is a market for craftspeople to use their skills to restore other crafts, whether in a museum conservation department or as an independent business.

Profile to check out: Paul Rollins.

Crafts Administrator

Many administrators in the crafts field emerged from the ranks of studio craftspeople to educate the public and provide assistance to other craftspeople. Careers choices include working as an administrator for crafts schools, organizations, and museums; as curators for museums and galleries; or serving on boards of directors and committees.

These positions may be full-time, part-time, or volunteer, with or without benefits, but they are usually full of opportunities to make a difference.

Profiles to check out: Lynn Duryea, David Ellsworth, Arline Fisch, Theresa Secord, George Mason, Tim McCreight, Wendy Maruyama, Mary

Nyburg, Jan Owen, Peter Ross, Josh Simpson, Rosanne Somerson, Deb Stoner, Gerry Williams, and Pamela Weeks Worthen.

Crafts Publishing and Writing

With the changes in the last several decades in the crafts field, many periodicals have emerged through crafts organizations as well as privately. While many craftspeople participate in these magazines through submitting articles once in awhile, a few magazines have been instrumental in getting certain craftspeople's businesses off the ground. Publishing crafts books has also been an important addition to the field. Some craftspeople have worked hard not only to write books themselves, but to recruit other people to write them as well.

Profiles to check out: Tim McCreight, Rosanne Somerson, and Gerry Williams.

Related Jobs

Studio Resident

Places to work and live with peers in crafts have been available for the past several decades to help craftspeople bridge the distance between graduating from school and launching a successful career. While these positions can be very competitive, they offer reduced living costs, access to studio space and equipment, and a nurturing environment. See chapter 4, "Educational Opportunities, Residency Programs, and Apprenticeships for Craftspeople," for more details.

Profiles to check out: Mark Bell, Dorothy Gill Barnes, Julie Morringello, and Deb Stoner.

Studio Technician

Taking care of the physical aspects of a studio isn't just a way to learn the nuts and bolts of running a studio; it can also give access to equipment as well as much-needed support to do your work. Positions may be full- or part-time, with or without benefits. Sometimes these positions are in exchange for waived tuition to take classes as well.

Profiles to check out: Ellen Spring, Dante Marioni, Gerry Williams, and Eric Ziner.

Retail Sales

Working in a crafts supply store or retail shop can be a viable way to not only learn valuable selling or production skills, but also help you save money on supplies or gifts while earning a paycheck.

Profiles to check out: Amanda Barrow, Mark Bell, Deb Stoner, and Marylou Ozbolt-Storer.

The Non-Crafts Employee Who Maintains a Professional Studio

Finally, there are many craftspeople who are very serious about their work and maintain a professional studio, but for one reason or another, make a living another way. Some take a break from selling their work while making life changes and then return to their crafts career in a different way. Others choose to keep their work separate from earning money and make work that doesn't have to be tied into the trends of the marketplace.

Profiles to check out: Mark Bell, Lynn Duryea, Peter Hagerty, George Mason, and Deb Stoner.

Business Workshops Designed for Artists and Craftspeople

Whether you take a continuing education course, a workshop offered through a guild or association, or through a small-business center, there are many courses, advisors, and services available to help you make decisions and/or run your business better. Consider signing up for the next available business workshop, because the longer you wait, the more time you will waste before you get the help you need to get going.

Art and crafts schools are beginning to offer formal business courses to their students, as well as workshops open to the public through their continuing education programs. Not only are these geared specifically to the needs of artists and craftspeople, but they also offer an opportunity to meet other craftspeople in your own area who may be starting or running their own business too. Some workshops may be offered for college credit as well.

Business seminars may be offered at places that never offered a business seminar before, such as local art and crafts associations, galleries and crafts shops, and crafts supply stores. Call your local art school or crafts organization to see if it is aware of a course or workshop offered near you. If there is somewhere that you think should offer a class, ask them to arrange either a one-day workshop or a series of speakers on various topics. They may be surprised at the large response and the publicity it offers them.

Here are some places to take business workshops designed for artists and craftspeople, as well as some additional resources to help you figure out which career in crafts is for you, get up to speed to run your own business, and be aware of current opportunities.

The Art Business Institute (ABI)

Dedicated to providing educational resources to all facets of the arts community, ABI provides resources to maximize the perception, profitability, and professionalism within the arts marketplace through annual retreats and workshops held in conjunction with local arts organizations.

For more information: The Art Business Institute, 2229 Paseo de Los Chamisos, Santa Fe, NM 87505; (505) 424-1262; *www.artbusinessinstitute.org*

Arts Extension Service (AES)

Arts Extension Service develops the arts in communities and community through the arts, with continuing professional education for arts managers, artists, and civic leaders. AES is a national arts service organization, founded in 1973 as a program of the Division of Continuing Education, University of Massachusetts Amherst.

For more information: Arts Extension Service, 358 N. Pleasant St., Amherst, MA 01003; (413) 545-3653; *www.umass.edu/aes*

Artists Help Network

The Artist Help Network—produced by Caroll Michels, author of *How to Survive and Prosper as an Artist*—is a free online information service designed to help artists take control of their careers. The network is available to assist artists in locating information, resources, guidance, and advice on a comprehensive range of career-related topics. People working in the applied arts, arts administration, and arts-related fields will also find this site useful.

The site is organized to help you locate information that impacts your career now and in the future. It is divided into seven general categories: Career; Exhibitions, Commissions, and Sales; Money; Presentation

Tools; Legal; Creature Comforts; and Other Resources. Each general category unfolds into numerous sub-topics that offer an abundance of regional, national and international resources. Listings include publications, organizations, professionals, Web sites, audiovisual materials, and software programs.

For more information: *www.artisthelpnetwork.com.*

The Center for Design and Business

The Center for Design and Business is a joint venture between Bryant College and the Rhode Island School of Design, established in 1997 to unite the design and business communities for purposes of economic development. Services include:

- On-site incubation support to design-based entrepreneurs and innovators
- Guidance to designers and innovators in the process of bringing new product designs and innovations to market
- Training in business skills to artists and designers
- Assistance to manufacturers and business owners in utilizing design to develop more competitive products and businesses
- Connecting businesses to design resources
- Promoting the economic value of design

For more information: Center for Design and Business, 20 Washington Place, Providence, RI 02903; (401) 454-6558; *www.centerdesignbusiness.org.*

College Art Association

Founded in 1911, the College Art Association offers *CAA Careers*, a comprehensive listing of employment opportunities for artists, art historians, and other visual arts professionals. It is published bimonthly and available to CAA members only. To get a sample copy and find out about membership, contact CAA.

For more information: College Art Association, 275 Seventh Avenue, New York, NY 10001; (212) 691-1051, ext. 519; *careers@collegeart.org; www.collegeart.org.*

Kentucky Appalachian Artisan Center

Founded to support and promote local craftspeople, the center offers training in craftsmanship and marketing skills, as well as a revolving loan fund to help local artisans develop their business. A business incubator program to offer business training to artists is in the works.

For more information: Kentucky Appalachian Artisan Center; *www.kyartisancenter.com.*

Maine College of Art

This college offers a one-semester course called "Art and Business" through the Continuing Education department in the fall session. Each of the seven class meetings features a guest speaker on a specific topic, such as the art of being your own boss, marketing, getting gallery shows, portfolios, and client/project management.

For more information: MECA, 97 Spring Street, Portland, ME 04101; (207) 775-5158; *www.meca.edu.*

Oregon College of Art and Craft

Oregon College of Art and Craft offers a three-quarter-long sequence course called "Business Practices" for college credit, as well as short-term, topic-specific workshops. Practicing artists and craftspeople seeking a stronger career focus can gain skills in handling the business side of their work through presentations by business professionals and hands-on classroom practice. The sequence covers gallery representation, legal issues, marketing, grants, finances and accounting, forms of doing business, developing a portfolio, and professional presentations.

For more information: OCAC, 8245 SW Barnes Rd., Portland, OR 97225; (503) 297-5544; *www.ocac.org.*

School of the Museum of Fine Arts, Boston, Massachusetts

Since the Artist's Resource Center's (ARC) inception more than twenty years ago, thousands of artists have used its services through the subscriber-based *Artist's Resource Letter* to find jobs, internships, and information on residencies, grants, competitions, and public art commissions. Currently they offer an online service as they continue their commitment to produce only the highest quality resources for artists. The ARC specializes in: resource development, one-on-one advising, studio seminars in career planning, and an internship program. Art-Source, an online index of arts-related employment opportunities, internships, grants, residencies, exhibitions, public art commissions, and related community resources, allows practicing artists to connect to the vast, up-to-date network of career and professional development services. Helpful in-house publications include: *Résumé Writing Basics; Visual Arts Career Cameos: The Art of Presentation; Proposal Writing Basics; Career Planning Web Site Guide; Local Resources for Artists;* and *Teaching Resource List.*

The center also offers a two-semester-long credit course called "Survival and Business Skills for the Visual Artist," offered through the Continuing Education office. The course addresses the special questions that artists face in their careers: What does marketing mean? Is public art a real opportunity? How do I get grants? How do juries work? What are my legal rights? What about insurance? What about health hazards? How do I find a studio and keep it? Each session is coordinated by a professional artist and has a guest speaker who is a professional.

For more information: School of the Museum of Fine Arts, Artist's Resource Center, 230 The Fenway, Boston, MA 02115; (617) 267-6100; *www .smfa.edu.*

Worcester Center for Crafts

The Worcester Center for Crafts offers a one-semester course called "Business Practices Seminar," which covers portfolio requirements, artists statements, résumés, slide photography, taxes, business card and letterhead design, grant writing, trade shows, retail and consignment options, and gallery visits. The class has several visiting instructors.

For more information: Worcester Center for Crafts, 25 Sagamore Rd., Worcester, MA 01605; (508) 753-8183; *www.worcestercraftcenter.org.*

Small Business Centers

Small business centers can be found all over the country. Although their services are not primarily geared to the concerns of craftspeople, they can offer valuable advice and services to new businesses of any type and size.

The Small Business Association (SBA)

The SBA offers assistance for starting a business, writing business plans, and finding shareware computer programs, workshops, information files, and more. Contact them for the office nearest you.

For more information: Small Business Association (SBA); (800) 8-ASK-SBA; *www.sba.gov.*

Service Corps of Retired Executives Association (SCORE)

SCORE offers free management assistance and low-cost workshops for starting or expanding a business, given by retired executives who volunteer their time and expertise. SCORE offers pre-business workshops for people just getting started, as well as specialized seminars for those further along in the process. SCORE's volunteer leadership is divided into ten regions in order to foster the development of community-oriented chapters. For example, in 1996, SCORE offered over four thousand workshops in the United States.

For more information: Service Corps of Retired Executives Association (SCORE), (800) 634-0245; *www.score.org*.

Volunteer Lawyers for the Arts (VLA)

Volunteer lawyers offer advice and workshops on topics such as copyright law and leases in various locations around the United States to artists and craftspeople who qualify financially. Call for the VLA office nearest you.

For more information: Volunteer Lawyers for the Arts (VLA), 1 East 53rd St., 6th Fl., New York, NY 10022; (212) 319-2787; *www.vlany.org*.

To help you get started in your career as a craftsperson, consider the following:

- Buy a copy of a business book written specifically for craftspeople, such as my other book, *Selling Your Crafts*. A handy reference tool, this book includes sections on pricing, marketing, business planning, commissions, galleries and craft fairs, and the Internet.
- Take a small-business management course, especially one that includes writing a business plan as part of the curriculum. Many craftspeople lament that if they had only done this when they first started their business, it would have saved them a lot of time and money.
- Join a crafts organization. Membership has its privileges, and to be aware of marketing opportunities, having access to special workshops for members, and meeting other craftspeople to get feedback from is an important part of staying on track.
- Subscribe to a business journal such as *The Crafts Report*. Established in 1975, this is a monthly business magazine for crafts professionals. It's available in most bookstores or by subscription, or you can check them out online at *www.craftsreport.com*.

Taking workshops through continuing education programs, guilds, and associations, as well as taking advantage of the services offered through small business centers, can be important sources of business information to a craftsperson running her own business. Although craftspeople tend to want to be able to do everything themselves, getting some helpful advice from crafts and business professionals can be a real asset in figuring out what the best career choice is for you, as well as how to run your business successfully.

CHAPTER 4

Educational Opportunities, Residency Programs, and Apprenticeships for Craftspeople

Profiled in this chapter are some of the places around the country where you can take workshops, earn a degree, apply for a residency, or obtain an apprenticeship. Don't forget to check out the medium-specific schools listed in the Clay, Glass, and Wood sections for information as well.

Educational Opportunities for Craftspeople

Technical proficiency in your craft is vital to your success as a professional craftsperson, but let's not forget the importance of design, craft history, business skills, and the general knowledge gained through study of other subjects too. If you want to get an education in crafts, how do you know whether you should take a workshop or enroll in a degree program?

"There is no one correct formula for what you need to do to become a craftsperson," says Michael Munroe, former Director of the American Craft Council. "Although I was taught in a progression of courses, there are a diversity of approaches available now. I suggest people interested in becoming a craftsperson do an apprenticeship or pick someone they want to study with and take several workshops at any of the crafts programs around the country. After a quick sampling of workshops, they could quickly find out if being a craftsperson is what they want to do."

In addition to crafts schools, there are over 180 art schools, colleges, and universities around the country that offer traditional BFA and MFA programs for those interested in a degree. The College Art Association sells a directory of all the MFA programs in the United States. It is full of vital information about admissions, tuition costs, faculty, and more.

For more information: College Art Association, 275 Seventh Avenue, New York NY 10001; (212) 691-1051; *www.collegeart.org.*

Residency Programs for Craftspeople

Residency programs can help bridge the gap between graduating from school and running a business (or give someone a break from running a business to concentrate on a new body of work without worrying about meeting payroll). Why not take advantage of one of these opportunities to help you get started?

By removing craftspeople from their everyday obligations to family and work, a residency can provide uninterrupted time to work in a supportive atmosphere to try new techniques, create a body of work, and learn how to sell your work. Residencies can last from a couple weeks or months to a year, depending on needs and availability. Although many communities must charge a nominal fee to cover some of their operating costs, others require volunteer work in exchange for the opportunity. Some pay the residents a stipend. If you have to pay for the opportunity to be a resident, it may be worth it for the contacts you will make, the time you will have to develop your work and business skills, and the access to facilities.

According to Tricia Snell, former Executive Director of the Alliance of Artists Communities, there is a quiet grassroots movement growing (in response to the falling-off of public programs that support artists) to create new residencies that directly serve artists' most important needs. Collectively, artists' communities represent a century-old, national support system for artists and thinkers. A survey done in 1995 showed that there are more than seventy communities in this country that were providing 3,600 residencies to artists, craftspeople, writers, and others. The Alliance has put together a great resource book for finding out about residencies called *Artists Communities: A Directory of Residencies in the United States That Offer Time and Space for Creativity*, published by Allworth Press. This directory lists residencies available to visual and performing artists, composers, and writers, and includes:

- Complete contact information
- The art disciplines served
- Facilities
- Housing and meals
- Season and length of residency
- Number of artists-in-residence
- Deadlines and fees
- Stipends and expenses
- Duties
- Programs, history, and mission
- Well-known artists who have been in residence

For more information, contact Allworth Press at *www.allworth.com*, or the Alliance of Artists Communities, 255 South Main Street, Providence, RI 02903, (401) 351-4320, *www.artistcommunities.org*.

If you decide to pursue a residency at one of these programs, call for information and then plan a visit. Stay for a couple days to meet the current residents and see the studio facilities.

Crafts Programs

The crafts programs profiled here offer workshops, sometimes certificate and/or degree programs, and residencies. Call and request a catalog (or look on their Web sites), arrange a visit, and talk to the people currently enrolled before you make a decision about which program may be right for you. You can also ask to speak to some alumni to find out firsthand how the program helped someone else get started in his or her field.

Appalachian Center for Crafts

The Appalachian Center for Crafts is a nationally renowned facility dedicated to expanding the influence of crafts on contemporary art while preserving crafts traditions. Offering a Bachelor of Fine Arts degree and Professional Crafts Certificates in ceramics, fibers, glass, metals, and wood, the center is a division of Tennessee Technological University, located twenty-two miles away in Cookeville.

The faculty, leading professionals in their fields, strive to give the aspiring craftspeople full preparation for a career in fine crafts. Students benefit from the professionalism and experience of a faculty who continue to produce, exhibit, and sell their work, guest-teach at other institutions, actively participate in their trade organizations, and cultivate relationships with craftspeople around the world. Each faculty member maintains a studio adjacent to student work areas to encourage discussion and to teach by example.

The workshop and special events program is committed to offering the highest quality experiences in fine crafts, ranging from one-day programs for schoolchildren to week-long Elderhostels and weekend or week-long workshops for amateur and professional crafts artists.

For more information: Appalachian Center for Crafts, 1560 Craft Center Dr., Smithville, TN 37166; (615) 372-3051; *www.craftcenter.tntech.edu.*

Anderson Ranch Arts Center

Anderson Ranch is located in the resort community of Snowmass Village, Colorado, on a former turn-of-the-century sheep ranch, which was transformed into an artists' community in 1966 when a handful of artists cleared out the historic barns for studios, set up a gallery, and inaugurated an informal workshop program. Since its incorporation as a nonprofit visual arts community in 1973, Anderson Ranch has matured into a widely recognized institution. Premised on the belief that "to create is human," Anderson Ranch recognizes the need to develop personal creativity and to discover, learn, and grow throughout one's lifetime.

Each summer, Anderson Ranch offers over 130 workshops taught by today's most prominent artists and educators, who come to share their skills and experience with more than 1,200 participants. Workshops, beginning after Memorial Day and running through the end of September, range in length from two days to three weeks. There are workshops for artists of all skill levels and experience, from the first-timer to the professional studio artist. Anderson Ranch also offers field expeditions that give artists a chance to learn, create, and gather inspiration for their work through contact with other cultures, landscapes, and disciplines.

Anderson Ranch offers workshops in the following areas: Art History and Critical Studies, Ceramics, Digital Imaging, Furniture and Woodworking, Painting and Drawing, Photography, Printmaking, Sculpture, and children's courses.

Anderson Ranch also offers an artists-in-residence program to encourage the creative, intellectual, and personal growth of emerging artists. Applicants, chosen based on artistic merit, live and work at Anderson Ranch from January through March, creating a body of work.

Anderson Ranch also hosts a Visiting Artist program for established artists seeking to work on projects that foster personal growth.

For more information: Anderson Ranch Arts Center, P.O. Box 5598, Snowmass Village, CO 81615; (970) 923-3181; *www.andersonranch.org*.

Arrowmont School of Arts and Crafts

For more than fifty years, Arrowmont has dedicated its resources to nurturing the creative talents of individuals by offering art and crafts classes. In 1945, fifty students attended the first summer crafts workshops, taught by faculty from the University of Tennessee, Knoxville.

The campus, nestled on a wooded hillside in downtown Gatlinburg, Tennessee, has nine well-equipped studios and a state-of-the-art woodturning and furniture-making complex. Because the studios are located in close proximity to one another, students can easily interact with fellow students. A one-week session finds you enough time to get immersed and begin personal explorations as you thoroughly focus in your chosen medium. A two-week session offers a more in-depth, intense exploration of the subject with lots of time for experimentation, while providing maximum hands-on studio time.

An Artist-in-Residence program is designed to give pre-professional, self-directed artists time and studio space to develop a major body of work in a creative community environment of students and visiting faculty. Five artists are selected annually to participate in this eleven-month program. These artists are also involved in Arrowmont's ArtReach and Artists-in-Schools programs, which impact all eighteen schools in the local school system. Through these two programs, in the year 2000, over four thousand students were exposed to art experiences they may not have otherwise had, through their interaction with Arrowmont's residents.

Resident artists live on the Arrowmont campus in the new Pollard housing complex, enjoying private bedrooms and bathrooms; meals during workshops, conferences, and retreats; and private studios in the spacious resident artist studio complex provided for each artist. Each resident is charged a modest monthly fee for housing, studio, and utilities facilities. In addition to pursuing their own work, residents are required to work for Arrowmont eight hours per week in a variety of assignments. Several optional paid teaching opportunities are available throughout the eleven months.

For more information: Arrowmont School of Arts and Crafts, P.O. Box 567, Gatlinburg, TN 37738; (865) 436-8887; *www.arrowmont.org*.

Brookfield Craft Center

Founded in 1954, the Brookfield Craft Center has been promoting and preserving the skills and values of fine craftsmanship through innovative educational and exhibition programs for over five decades. The Center strives to engender creativity, fine design, and quality craftsmanship by offering one of the widest and most varied hands-on workshop curriculums in the nation, with more than two hundred topics each year. In 1982 Brookfield Craft Center received the state's highest award for excellence in the arts, *The Connecticut Arts Award.*

In addition to classes on the traditional subjects of ceramics, weaving, metals, woodworking, and glass, the Center offers courses in many uncommon topics, including boat building, business and marketing, and decorative arts. Workshops are taught by nationally respected visiting artists in facilities that include: seven teaching studios, an exhibition gallery, a retail shop, housing for visiting faculty, and administrative offices housed in four vintage colonial buildings on two and a half acres.

The Center also offers extensive scholarship programs, plus an innovative hour-for-hour volunteer work/study program. The Center is supported primarily by tuitions and retail sales, with supplemental funding coming from federal, state, and private sources.

For more information: Brookfield Craft Center, P.O. Box 122, Brookfield, CT 06804; (203) 775-4526; *www.brookfieldcraftcenter.org.*

John C. Campbell Folk School

The Folk School, founded in 1925, was a collaboration of two progressive educators: Olive Dame Campbell and Marguerite Butler, and the Appalachian community of Brasstown, North Carolina. Together they wanted to help people develop inner growth as creative, thoughtful individuals, in addition to developing socially as tolerant, caring members of a community. Throughout its history, the Folk School has worked towards these goals through performing arts, agriculture, and crafts rooted in the traditions of southern Appalachia and other cultures of the world.

Workshops are offered in a wide variety of topics such as: Basketry, Beads, Blacksmithing, Book Arts, Brooms, Calligraphy, Clay, Cooking, Handwork, Gardening, Glass, Metals, Mixed Media, Music, Nature Studies, Painting, Paper, Photography, Printmaking, Quilting, Storytelling, Weaving, Woodcarving, Woodturning, Woodworking, and Writing.

What makes the Folk School different from the other schools profiled in this section is the integration of art and crafts with other aspects of living, like song and dance. For example, a typical week at the Folk School begins with Morning Song at 7:45 A.M., a Danish custom of singing, folklore, and camaraderie. Evenings are filled with dancing and singing, or a chance to visit studios to see the works of other students. The week typically ends with a student exhibit and a performance of bluegrass music.

Resident and scholarship opportunities include the Student Host position—a six-month residential opportunity to learn and share at the Folk School by assisting staff and students in a variety of ways—and Work/Study positions, six- to twelve-week opportunities for living and learning at the Folk School. Work/Study participants receive one week of class for every two weeks they work in grounds, maintenance, and housekeeping and may include other tasks as well. Financial assistance scholarships may be available on a limited basis.

For more information: John C. Campbell Folk School, One Folk School Road, Brasstown, NC 28902; (704) 837-2775; *www.folkschool.org*.

Guilford Handcraft Center

The Guilford Handcraft Center was established to nurture and support excellence in the arts through education, communication, and outreach. Through its school for adults and children, its gallery, programs, shop of contemporary crafts, and special events, the Center provides opportunities for individuals to participate in the arts, to experience their cultural and historical diversity, and to appreciate the process and product of creative work. The Center further provides an environment for artists of all ages to gather, practice, teach, and advance their ideas, fostering exchange and innovation.

With an enrollment of over 3,500 individuals per year, the Center serves students of all ages in a wide range of crafts and fine art media and techniques. Supplementing the professional core faculty, visiting artists provide intensive workshops and master classes.

The Center also has a dedicated Youth Program and often collaborates with area schools, civic groups, Scout troops, and others to offer demonstrations, curriculum enhancements, and cultural exchanges.

For more information: Guilford Handcraft Center, P.O. Box 589, Guilford, CT 06437; (203) 453-5947; *www.handcraftcenter.org*.

Haystack Mountain School of Crafts

Built on forty wooded acres at the southeastern end of Deer Isle, Maine, Haystack is situated on a slope overlooking the Atlantic, offering breathtaking views of the ocean and unforgettable nature trails through woods filled with boulders, moss, and lichen.

The core season includes two- and three-week sessions in Blacksmithing, Ceramics, Fibers, Glass, Graphics, Metals, and Wood. The Haystack community is made up of approximately eighty-five participants, including staff, students, and internationally known faculty artists. Workshops are open to adults eighteen years or older, and welcome all skill levels, from beginners to advanced professionals. Studios are open twenty-four hours a day, seven days a week, with classes scheduled Monday through Friday. Students work within the format of the workshops as outlined by the instructors, and are free to work in the studios on their own. In addition to evening slide lectures by the faculty, there are presentations and performances by visiting artists and writers throughout the summer months.

Haystack also sponsors Open Door and the New England Workshops, which are designed specifically for people from Maine and New England. Modeled after the core sessions at Haystack, these two intensive fall weekend workshops are for individuals who wish to devote extended time to work in a variety of crafts media.

For more information: Haystack Mt. School of Crafts, P.O. Box 518, Deer Isle, ME 04627; (207) 348-2306; *www.haystack-mtn.org.*

Oregon College of Arts and Craft

Oregon College of Art and Craft traces its origins to 1907, when Julia Hoffman founded the Arts and Crafts Society to educate the public on the value of arts and crafts in daily life through art classes and exhibitions. Today Oregon College of Art and Craft is an accredited independent crafts college offering studio classes in Book Arts, Ceramics, Drawing, Fibers, Metal, Photography, and Wood. Students can pursue a Bachelor of Fine Arts or a three-year Certificate in Crafts, or enroll in the College's extension series of Open Program classes.

The BFA, a four-year degree in crafts, is for students who have the goal of becoming working artists, and who also value the broader education provided by a degree. It is designed to provide the skills and technical knowledge students need to follow their professional aspirations when they complete the program, such as preparing for studio practice, making a business out of studio work, getting involved in community arts activities, and going to graduate school. Students are trained and encouraged to continue producing artwork following completion of the program.

The Certificate Program, a three-year program for the student interested in studying a particular medium in depth but not interested in the academic courses required for a BFA, is an artisan program for those seeking to make a business of their craft.

The Post-baccalaureate Certificate Program is a unique one-year pre-graduate program designed for students with an undergraduate degree in art or who have studio art experience at the college level, to give them the opportunity to focus on one craft medium in depth. Students use this program in several different ways, including: as an opportunity to return to an intensive studio experience following their undergraduate degree, as a chance to learn new techniques and media, as an opportunity to create new work and update their portfolio, or as a stepping stone to graduate school.

A semester-long program for emerging artists and a summer residency for mid-career artists are also offered. The residencies are offered in each of the College's seven media areas of concentration and include housing, individual studio space, a stipend, and the opportunity to become involved in community life at the College. All residents give an introductory slide lecture and a public review of their work, while each fall an exhibition features work by the artists-in-residence.

The semester-long Junior Residency provides an opportunity for the postgraduate artist to pursue a proposed body of work over a four-month period in a stimulating arts environment, offering the time and place for young artists to concentrate on their work. The ideal resident is self-directed and relishes the challenge of time to work, but enjoys creating work in a learning environment where relationships are mutually reinforcing. The Junior Residency Program hosts two residents each fall and spring semester. Media areas of concentration are decided on a rotating basis.

The Senior Residency focuses on allowing mid-career artists a time to work during the summer. During odd-numbered years, the Senior Residency will accept applicants from all media areas of concentration for a six-week residency, and will offer residencies to three artists. During even-numbered years, seven resident artists representing each area of concentration are invited on campus for a two-week period in July. This invitational residency is a wonderful opportunity for top artists and craftspeople to gather together, share ideas and inspiration, and be a part of an intensive discourse about art.

For more information: Oregon College of Art and Craft, 8245 SW Barnes Rd., Portland, OR 97225; (503) 297-5544; *www.ocac.org.*

Penland School of Crafts

Penland is a national center for crafts education located in the Blue Ridge Mountains of western North Carolina, offering one-, two-, and eight-week workshops in Books and Paper, Clay, Drawing, Glass, Iron, Metals, Photography, Printmaking, Textiles, and Wood. The school also sponsors artists' residencies and educational outreach programs.

Founded in 1923 by Miss Lucy Morgan, a teacher at an Episcopalian school that was located in several buildings on the current campus, the school began as an organized group called the Penland Weavers, providing looms and materials to local women and helping them to market their handwoven goods. As a result of inviting guest instructors to teach weaving, requests for instruction began to come from other parts of the country, and Penland School was born in 1929. Penland has grown to encompass about four hundred acres and forty-one structures, with over 1,200 people coming each year to seek instruction in ten crafts media.

In addition to summer workshops, Penland offers a program called "Concentration," comprised of four- and eight-week classes in up to eight studios in the spring and fall. The pace is very different from the summer, both because there is a smaller student body and because students settle in for a month or two. Classes are taught by working professionals, with visiting artists coming for short periods of time, sharing their enthusiasm and expertise. The student body during Concentration is a mix of those learning a craft, who are ready for a period of focused work, and professionals who may be pursuing a new direction.

Penland core students are full-time and work for the school in exchange for room, board, and tuition. These young artists are integral members of the staff, and they serve a leadership role among work/study students. They are chosen from former work/study students based on the seriousness of their artistic intent and their ability to work with others.

The Resident Artist Program seeks to enrich the total educational experience available at Penland by providing a stimulating, supportive environment for persons at transitional points in their careers. Residents are professional-level, independent artists who live and work at the Sanford Center, adjacent to the school.

For more information: Penland School of Crafts, P.O. Box 37, Penland, NC 28765; (828) 765-2359; *www.penland.org.*

Peters Valley Craft Center

Peters Valley, founded in 1970, is located in rural northwest New Jersey, in the Delaware Water Gap National Recreation Area. Peters Valley employs nationally recognized instructors to teach intensive workshops for beginners to advanced students, offers an education center with resident and visiting artists, and is dedicated to quality education through the cultivation of the individual's artistic appreciation, exploration, and participation in the evolving tradition of craft. In July 2000, the New Jersey State Council on the Arts honored Peters Valley with both the Citation of Excellence award and a designation as a Major Arts Organization.

Peters Valley currently focuses on eight disciplines: Blacksmithing, Ceramics, Fine Metals, Photography, Special Topics, Surface Design, Weaving, and Woodworking. A full workshop schedule in all media is offered throughout the spring, summer, and fall.

An Associate Residency Program is available for up to seven months during the off-season, October to May, for emerging artists or artists in transition. This allows them to attempt new work, try out new solutions, discover through interaction with others new ways of seeing their work, or simply finish a body of work that is important to them. Others come to build a body of work for graduate school, or to explore a completely new phase in their artistic career. A nominal monthly fee is charged for housing and studio use.

For more information: Peters Valley Craft Center, 19 Kuhn Rd., Layton, NJ 07851; (973) 948-5200; *www.pvcrafts.org.*

Southwest School of Art and Craft

Since 1969, the Southwest School of Art and Craft in San Antonio, Texas, has offered a community-based art school serving established artists as well as beginning, intermediate, and advanced students of all ages. Currently over 2,400 adults and 1,600 children enroll in classes annually, while another ten thousand children are taught in special programs in schools, shelters, and community centers. Housed on two adjacent campuses, one the restored historic buildings of a former convent and the other a state-of-the-art contemporary building, the school is above all a place that kindles creativity and nurtures the creative spirit. The Ursuline Campus is located on the former site of the Ursuline Academy and

Convent, which was opened by French Ursuline nuns in 1851 as an all-girls school. In 1965, a group of San Antonians who felt that there was a need for local education in the arts began what is now the Southwest School of Art and Craft. The School offers classes taught by outstanding local, regional, and national artists, and presents exhibitions, a lecture series, guided tours, and a museum for the historic site.

Adult Studio Programs are organized into six departments: Ceramics; Fibers; Metals; Painting, Drawing, & Printmaking; Paper & Book Arts; and Photography. Classes of varying cost, length, and level are offered in three different terms per year: Fall, Winter/Spring, and Summer.

Young Artists Programs are organized into four different programs: Saturday Morning Discovery, Mobile Arts Program, Tuition-Based Classes, and the Teacher Training Initiative. Saturday Morning Discovery is a free studio art program for children and families. The Mobile Arts Program sends artist-teachers into the community to work with children in their neighborhoods or with social service agencies. Tuition-based studio art classes are offered year-round, though the Summer Art Camp is the most extensive. The Teacher Training Initiative is designed to provide training in the visual arts for classroom teachers, and to provide ideas for how to incorporate the visual arts into the regular school curriculum.

For more information: Southwest School of Art and Craft, 300 Augusta, San Antonio, TX 78205; (210) 224-1848; *www.swschool.org.*

Worcester Center for Crafts

The Worcester Center for Crafts is a leading institution for all ages dedicated to the knowledge, appreciation, and advancement of fine crafts and craftsmanship through professional education and special events. The Center's early beginnings during the late 1800s place it at the forefront of the American Arts and Crafts Movement. By 1957, the growth of the organization promoted the search for a larger teaching space. The present facility, hailed as the first American community center designed exclusively for crafts instruction, was completed in 1959.

Established in 1977, the School for Professional Crafts offers an intensive two-year program in Clay, Metals, and Wood. The accelerated, studio-based curriculum not only incorporates the technical and aesthetic elements of design and fabrication, but it also offers a range of academic, design, and business classes through the Becker College partnership.

The School for Professional Crafts currently offers two study options: the Associate Degree track and the Non-degree track. The

Associate Degree program is a unique collaboration between the Worcester Center for Crafts and Becker College. In the Center's studios, students develop an in-depth understanding of their selected media. At Becker College, students augment their study of crafts with the skills necessary to succeed as a professional. Upon completion, Becker College issues an Associate of Science Degree. All of Becker College's resources are available to matriculating Associate Degree students, including housing, financial aid, library, and computer labs. The Non-Degree curriculum addresses the needs of students who are not presently considering a degree program. Students enroll in three studio classes at the Craft Center and one course at Becker College. The program teaches students to use their craft to earn a living.

The Artists-in-Residence program at the Worcester Center for Crafts provides emerging craftspeople the opportunity to have a year to develop artistically and professionally in a creative community educational institution. Residencies are offered in clay, fiber, metal, and wood for a ten-month period, and provide studio space, the use of studio equipment, and participation in classes and workshops (in all studios) on a space-available basis. Students have access to their studios twenty-four hours per day, seven days per week. Artists-in-Residence exhibit work developed during their residency in the Craft Center's Krikorian Gallery.

Visiting artisans from all areas of the crafts professions are invited to the Craft Center each year to conduct workshops, lectures, and seminars. Workshops provide diversity and excitement and serve to supplement the education that is provided by the faculty in the Adult School and School for Professional Crafts programs, as well as the professional craftsperson.

For more information: Worcester Center for Crafts, 25 Sagamore Rd., Worcester, MA 01605; (508) 753-8183; *www.worcestercraftcenter.org*.

Apprenticeships for Craftspeople

In addition to studying your craft and participating in a residency that will help you get established, many craftspeople suggest becoming a craftsperson's apprentice to get started. Not only does being an apprentice allow you more time to develop your own work, but it also provides you with a role model of someone who is running a crafts business successfully. "I recommend craftspeople take a simple course in business and get a formal education in crafts," says Mary Nyburg, potter and owner of Blue Heron Gallery in Deer Isle, Maine. "After they graduate, they should get an apprenticeship with a working craftsperson to *really* learn the business."

What should you look for in an apprenticeship? Many arrangements exist between apprentice and crafts artist. Things to consider include:

- Is the craftsperson a good teacher?
- What are the working conditions like?
- Will the apprentice have the opportunity to do his or her own work?
- Who will pay for materials?
- Who is responsible for what?
- How long will the apprenticeship last?

Are apprentices paid for their work? Sometimes the apprentice works for free or pays the craftsperson for the opportunity to learn the business. In other cases, the craftsperson pays the apprentice, usually a minimum wage. After all, the apprentice is benefiting from the arrangement by learning the business, but the craftsperson is also benefiting by having someone contribute to the production process. Before formalizing your agreement, consult the state and federal labor laws in your area to find out what the legal requirements regarding apprenticeships are where you live. Finally, put your agreement in writing to avoid any misunderstanding, and keep a copy for your records.

How can you find an apprenticeship? "Call ahead and visit as many craftspeople as possible to just get acquainted and let them know you are looking for work," suggests Gerry Williams, director of Studio Potter and author of the book *Apprenticeship in Craft.* "If you really like one or two of them, be persistent, but not obnoxious, and keep in touch until something works out. You may soon find you have either an unstructured relationship or a formal apprenticeship." For more information, contact Studio Potter, P.O. Box 70, Goffstown, NH 03045, (603) 774-3582, *www.studiopotter.org.*

What do most apprentices get out of their apprenticeship experience? In an article titled "Apprenticeships Get Your Foot in the Door" by Daniel Grant in *The Crafts Report,* two former apprentices share what they learned:

"I learned all the processes and a little bit about design," says

Peggy Cochane, apprentice to New Orleans jewelry maker Thomas Mann from 1989 to 1993.

"I learned how to deal with galleries, how to set up a business, and a lot about marketing," says Robert Dane, a glassblower who worked for glassblower Josh Simpson from 1978 to 1982.

Whether you live in an area with a lot of craftspeople who work in your medium or in a remote area that may only offer a craftsperson working in a medium different from your own, consider working for someone on a full- or part-time basis for a period of time to learn about running a crafts business. It just might turn out to be time well invested.

CHAPTER 5

Profiles of Successful Craftspeople

Who are today's craftspeople? What can we learn from their experiences? Are there other crafts organizations that might be helpful to someone starting out? In the sections organized by craft medium—Clay, Fiber, Glass, Metal, Wood—results are presented from national surveys of craftspeople and different state governments, revealing the roles state organizations can play in supporting crafts. Each section begins with educational opportunities and organizations, followed by numerous in-depth profiles of working craftspeople. The profiles not only tell the story of how a successful craftsperson managed his or her career, they also share insights and advice to help you navigate the challenging waters of the crafts world.

The Craft Organization Development Association Survey

The CODA survey titled "The Impact of Crafts on the National Economy" has finally given the crafts field the numbers to reinforce what many have known for some time: Crafts are big business. According to the CODA survey, the fine crafts market is a $13.8 billion industry (about half the size of the $29.9 billion toy industry, roughly three times the size of the $4 billion organic food industry, and just slightly smaller than the $16 billion retail floral market). This survey did not include crafts shops and galleries, crafts schools, publications, or other venues.

In August 1998, CODA announced it was launching a nationwide study of the impact of crafts on our national economy to:

- Focus public attention on crafts as an entrepreneurial profession
- Help enhance local and national economies

- Provide data to lend credibility and legitimacy to the work of craftspeople
- Put craftspeople on equal footing with other kinds of businesses, making them more eligible for comprehensive insurance coverage, business credit, and job training

A test survey was conducted to allow CODA members to get face-to-face feedback from craftspeople around the country before rolling out the finalized questionnaire, to help spread the word, and to encourage more craftspeople to respond when the actual survey was launched. Initially the test survey was distributed at twelve crafts shows, including: Roy Helms Contemporary Craft Market, Southern Highlands Craft Guild Show, Berea, Kentucky Craft Fair, Ohio Designer Craftsmen Shows, League of NH Craftsmen Show, Pennsylvania Guild of Craftsmen Show, Florida Craftsmen Show, and the New York, San Francisco, and Chicago Gift Shows.

The Typical Craftsperson

Who is a typical craftsperson? In addition to quantifying the economic impact of crafts, the CODA survey explored the demographic makeup of the professional crafts field. A typical craftsperson is a Caucasian woman, age forty-nine, who works alone in her studio and is a member of a crafts organization, based on the following findings:

- The average age of respondents is 49
- Approximately two-thirds of the respondents are female
- The vast majority of the respondents are Caucasian (93 percent), with approximately 2 percent Native American, 1 percent African American, 1 percent Asian-American, and 1 percent Hispanic
- Nearly two-thirds of respondents report that they work alone in their studio
- Nearly 20 percent report working with a partner/family member
- Just over 16 percent are owners/partners of a studio with paid employees
- Most studios (79 percent) are located in or on a residential property
- Most craftspeople (78 percent) in this sample are members of a crafts organization
- Less than 4 percent are disabled or handicapped
- Nine percent are veterans

Economic Impact

The survey found that in general, working craftspeople contribute about half of their families' total household income. The median household income for families who derive part of their income from crafts is $50,000 (which is significantly higher than the median national household income for 1999 of $40,800, as reported by the U.S. Census Bureau). The average household income for families who derive part of their income from crafts is even higher than the median, at $65,208. The average crafts-related income of $32,624 is also higher than the median of $22,000.

In addition, approximately 22 percent reported that crafts income was their only source of household income. Household income varies by crafts medium, with the highest average income for glass, at $38,237, and the lowest for organic materials, at $21,271. Gross sales also vary greatly by crafts medium. For example, glass is the crafts medium with the highest average gross sales, at $111,051, while paper is the lowest, at $37,529.

Craftspeople Who Have Employees

Most respondents (87 percent) report that they do not employ any full-time employees, and almost 80 percent do not employ part-time employees. However, 20 percent report at least one part-time employee with some payroll expense. Craftspeople with employees employ an average of four full-time employees and two part-time employees. The average total gross payroll expenditure for crafts artists who have employees is $56,041.

It is useful to note that craftspeople with paid employees generally have:

- higher overall incomes than the crafts artists who work alone
- crafts-related income providing a greater part of household income
- an average household income of $87,992 (versus $65,208 overall)
- an average annual household income derived from crafts-related activities of $58,417 (versus $32,624 overall)
- a percentage of total household income from crafts income of 74 percent (versus 47 percent overall)
- a crafts income as the only source of household income (approximately 45 percent of this group, versus 22 percent overall)

Retail Shows versus Wholesale Markets

The average annual sales/revenue produced per typical craftsperson is $76,025. The data also provides some interesting facts, such as:

- Although there are more people selling their work at retail crafts fairs (58 percent for retail versus 27 percent for wholesale), more sales are generated through wholesale sales (53 percent, estimated at $4.2 billion to $5 billion, for wholesale versus 39 percent, estimated at $3.1 billion to $3.7 billion, for retail).
- Retail sales account for 53 percent of annual crafts sales. Crafts fairs are the largest source of retail sales at 52 percent of total sales, studio retail sales account for 27 percent, and commission sales for 15 percent.
- Selling though wholesale markets in the United States accounts for 27 percent of annual sales. Wholesaling outside the United States is very small, only .50 percent of total distribution. Wholesale distribution within the United States provides an average of $73,373 of sales revenue per year, and retail distribution provides $35,126.
- Consignment to galleries is 11 percent, or the third most common method.

Staying Close to Home

According to the survey, 60 percent of gross annual sales/revenue is generated within the maker's home state, and 39 percent outside the state. However, a large market exists for craftspeople interested in marketing their wares to tourists.

Crafts and Tourism

Tourists are defined by the Travel Industry Association as anyone who travels more than one hundred miles from home in search of leisure activities. Current estimates are that tourism will become the world's leading industry within the next ten years. Whether for business or pleasure, more money than ever is being spent on travel, and what most travelers want is to bring home a bit of the culture they've experienced on the road.

Many craftspeople who already make their living from selling their work could easily estimate the percentage of their sales that come from people on vacation, especially those craftspeople who are selling their work in an area with a lot of tourist traffic. Not only do potential customers have more time to look at and buy crafts on vacation, but the family is also together to make decisions; often a budget has been established to buy mementos from the trip or to do holiday shopping. As a result, many states are capitalizing on this trend by supporting craftspeople, shops, and galleries through advertising, travel packages, and funding for craft guidebooks.

The undisputed state pioneers in packaging crafts and tourism together are Kentucky and North Carolina. Long before other states recognized the economic benefit of linking tourism with the cultural heritage of handmade items, these states had discovered that tourists would carry home carloads of locally produced products worth hundreds of millions of dollars annually. For example, in 2001, western North Carolina alone made crafts sales of more than $122 million. Other states and regions are catching on, creating marketing and tourism promotions for artists and craftspeople as unique as the products and regions they represent.

Although state governments know what the arts and crafts do for their local economies, not all crafts activity that is geared towards the tourism industry is sponsored with state money. One enterprising couple in Arkansas, Becki and David Dahlstead, decided to organize an event called "Off the Beaten Path Studio Tour," featuring fifteen working studios. Putting their small-town connections to work, they teamed up with local lodging providers, a photographer with experience in web design, and the Chamber of Commerce to draw people from all over and even outside of their state. "Not only did people come," said Dahlstead, "but they came to buy."

A 2001 report of the National Governors Association Center for Best Practices states that the nonprofit arts industry generates $36.8 billion nationally. In the same report, crafts were singled out as an important impetus for revitalizing "underperforming" regions. Although budgets are tight, many states are doing what they can, such as offering online artist rosters with links to the artists' home pages, calendars of events, and links to specialized statewide arts organizations and guilds.

Another way some states are helping artists and craftspeople while helping themselves is by offering incentives for creative people to move to a particular area. For example, Maryland is the first state to offer communities the opportunity to become "Smart Growth Arts and

Entertainment Districts," which include tax-free housing and studio space, as well as sales and income tax breaks for writers, performers, sculptors, painters, and crafts artists who decide to live or work in the districts. In addition to supporting the arts, these programs can create a thriving cultural scene in previously declining neighborhoods.

On a different note, the Hobby Industry Association (HIA) reports that the value of the crafts and hobby industry grew to $27.7 billion in 2001—an 11 percent increase in the value of the crafts and hobby industry in the United States from 2000. Residents of 58 percent of U.S. households participated in crafts and hobbies, up from 54 percent the year prior. While these statistics are not from professional craftspeople who sell their work to make their living, this trend illustrates the fact that interest in crafts is growing.

The CODA Survey, tourism trends, and the HIA report illustrate that not only are craftspeople earning a decent living and working together with other businesses to improve the economy, but that many buyers and organizations are participating in crafts and hobbies for pure enjoyment as well.

In the sections that follow, keep the statistics you have learned in mind as you read the stories of these diverse groups of craftspeople. Who are they and how do they fit the profile in the CODA survey? Who is not represented in the surveys, and how can we help these groups build successful crafts careers too?

PART TWO

Clay

CHAPTER 6

Facts, Educational Opportunities, and Organizations for Ceramics Artists

M aking pottery to sell, obtaining public and private art commissions, teaching, writing, organizing crafts fairs, and art therapy are just a few of the accomplishments of the craftspeople profiled in this section. Many of the people in this section have worked through several stages in their crafts careers, or have combined different interests to earn a living or to live in a way that suits them best. In addition, this section provides details about running a clay business, places to study and work in clay, names of important organizations, and artist profiles.

Insight Survey Statistics on Ceramics Artists

Today's craftspeople working in clay have lots of options when it comes to having a career. To give aspiring craftspeople a clearer sense of running a business in clay, here are some statistics to help you plan. The results of the Insight Survey on Ceramics in *The Crafts Report*'s April 2003 issue featured below are based on forty-three respondents, with the average gross sales per artist being $73,441. Here are the details:

Percentage of Gross Sales from Various Sources
- 27% of their income from retail shows
- 20% from wholesale shows
- 32% from selling directly to galleries
- 11% from their own studio or gallery

- 1% from Internet sales
- 1% unknown

Amount Spent on Materials
- 12% spent less than $1000
- 65% spend between $1000 and $10,000
- 9% spent between $11,000 and $20,000
- 7% spent between $21,000 and $50,000
- 7% spent over $50,000

Number of People Working in Studio
- 47% work alone
- 35% have 1 to 2 people
- 7% have 3 to 5 people
- 12% have 6 to 10 people

Time Selling Crafts
- 0% less than 1 year
- 19% 1 to 5 years
- 21% 6 to 10 years
- 2% 11 to 15 years
- 58% more than 15 years

In addition, 63 percent owned a Web site, 35 percent sold their work through an online gallery or crafts site other than their own, and 33 percent said their crafts business was the only source of income in their household.

Educational Opportunities for Ceramics Artists

There are numerous places to learn how to make things with clay. In addition to workshop and degree programs, there are two special places where clay is the focus: the Watershed Center for the Ceramic Arts in Maine and the Archie Bray Foundation for the Ceramic Arts in Montana.

Watershed Center for the Ceramics Arts
Housed in a former brickyard, Watershed offers people working in clay ample studio space, communal living with fabulous meals, a quiet land-

scape for reflection, and a common purpose. The mission of Watershed is to provide serious artists with time and space to create in clay, focusing on a small and intimate communal approach open to experimentation, exploration, collaboration, and growth.

Current programs available include:

- *Summer Residencies:* Work, eat, and live in the intimate community setting of house, studio, woods, and fields in mid-coast Maine.
- *Artists Invite Artists:* Summer sessions are held to allow one or two professional artists to arrange a residency with their peers.
- *Workshop for People with HIV:* This workshop gives people with HIV the opportunity to experience themselves as creative beings living and working in a creative environment. The workshop staff includes a therapist, ceramics artist, and an artist/therapist who help people explore images of personal and collective healing through clay, drawing, painting, and mask making. No prior experience with clay or other art materials is necessary for attendance.
- *Summer Slide Lecture and Open Studio Series:* Resident artists show slides and speak briefly about their work, followed by open studios where the public can talk one-on-one with the artists and view current works in progress.
- *Winter Residency:* A nine-month session during which four artists work, live, and teach community classes in clay.
- *Mudmobile:* A traveling ceramics resource center in a van that brings clay arts education to children and adults in diverse sites throughout Maine, including community and cultural centers, social service shelters, senior programs, and public and private schools. The van is used to transport clay, tools, glazes, reference materials, and anything else needed to hold a clay workshop at the host site. Work is brought back to Watershed for firing. The Mudmobile is staffed by artists with advanced degrees and years of practice in the ceramics arts as well as experience teaching adults and children.
- *Clay Arts Workshops:* Instruction in pottery and sculpture for any age group as well as resources and information about brick making and pottery's role in Maine's history, geology, and archeology in the area.
- *Exhibitions:* Art galleries, academic settings, and community venues around the country sponsor exhibits featuring ceramic work by past Watershed resident artists.

- *Professional Development Workshops:* Integrated curriculum workshops sponsored for teachers, school administrators, parents, and community members.
- *Special Events:* Special events, such as Salad Days (held every summer to offer visitors a firsthand look at the residence program in progress and a chance to take home a piece of pottery made from Watershed earthenware clay), as well as benefit dinners and lectures help keep Watershed artists in contact with the public throughout the year.

Here are comments from summer residents about their Watershed experience:

"My time at Watershed allowed me to focus on trying out new ideas for a production line I plan to launch which will include decorative home accessories, vases, platters, lamps, small shelves, and mirrors," says Scott Zimmer. "The other artists, staff, and of course the food were incredible and made my time at Watershed truly memorable!"

"My two weeks were some of the most informative and interesting that I have had in the ceramic world since graduate school," says Melissa Maxfield. "It was a wonderful chance to immerse myself in making clay objects and experiencing people with the same passion for clay. I am sure these relationships will continue to exist in my life. Experiencing the process of clay firsthand, from digging it out of the ground to building with it, has enriched my life, and my art making process has been encouraged to change and flourish in whatever direction it needs to take. I was able to listen to my intuition and just simply work without any distractions. I have been able to reconnect with what makes me tick and make art in my own personal way. I have since been able to take this experience back to the classroom and share my ideas with my students and colleagues."

For more information, contact: Watershed Center for the Ceramic Arts, 19 Brick Hill Road, Newcastle, ME 04553; (207) 882-6075; h2oshed@ midcoast.com; www.watershedcenterceramicarts.org.

Archie Bray Foundation for the Ceramic Arts

Founded in 1951 by brick maker Archie Bray, the Bray is dedicated to the enrichment of the ceramics arts, offering residencies and specialized workshops to ceramics artists from around the world in a nurturing environment that supports ongoing experimentation. In the words of its founder, Archie Bray, the mission is to simply "make available for all who are sincerely interested in any of the ceramics arts, a fine place to work."

Located on the twenty-six-acre site of the former Western Clay Manufacturing Company, the Bray facilities and programs include:

- *Year-Round Resident Studios:* Provided with studio space and excellent facilities, resident artists pursue their personal artistic goals and stimulate an exchange of ideas by bringing together artists of diverse backgrounds, cultures, and approaches to clay. Throughout the year, nine resident artists work in the studio, with ten additional artists joining them in the summer. Costs to residents are kept low for studio space, firing, and materials; affordable housing can be found in Helena. The artists are selected on the basis of their commitment to their work and the work itself (functional, sculptural, or experimental), and the length of residency can vary from three months to two years.
- *Taunt and Lillian Fellowships:* Awarded on an annual basis, two $5,000 fellowships are available by application for resident artists. Beneficiaries are expected to embrace the Bray experience of community and exchange, and will have the opportunity to focus their attention to produce and exhibit a significant body of work during their residency. Jason Walker, a recent Taunt Fellow, said of his experience, "This has been the perfect place to cultivate my transition from teaching to setting out on my own as a studio potter. Getting the Taunt Fellowship means that I don't have to get a job while I am here and I have more time to experiment, more time in the studio, and that's what a fellowship is designed to do."
- *Community Classes:* Adult community classes are offered to the public throughout the year for beginning and advanced students; each class is ten weeks long (summer sessions eight weeks long). "Ceramics for Kids" classes are offered throughout the year in five-week sessions with special workshops in the summer. Taught by resident artists, these classes offer a unique and diverse opportunity for learning in the Helena community and provide income and teaching experience for residents.
- *Workshops, Lectures, and Community Events:* Throughout the year the Bray presents resident and visiting artist lectures, workshops, and

community events for the general public. Annual open-house events give an opportunity to visit and enjoy what the Bray has to offer. Self-guided walking tours are available anytime during daylight hours, with special group tours arranged through the office.

- *Gallery and Ceramics Collection:* The Gallery is open year-round for exhibition and sale of work by resident artists. Featuring solo exhibits for departing artists (with additional exhibits presented in a 3,500-square-foot gallery space called Warehouse Gallery), the permanent collection, containing more than 700 pieces, can be viewed at the gallery and includes work by world-renowned artists such as Bernard Leach, Shoji Hamada, Peter Voulkas, Rudy Autio, Ken Ferguson, and David Shaner.
- *Clay Business:* The Bray operates a retail ceramic supply business with an extensive inventory of pre-mixed and dry clays. A complete line of studio equipment, glaze materials, and ceramic literature are also available. Profits generated help support operations at the pottery.

For more information, contact: Archie Bray Foundation for the Ceramics Arts, 2915 Country Club Avenue, Helena, MT 59602; (406) 443-3502; *archiebray@archiebray.org; www.archiebray.org.*

Organizations for Ceramics Artists

There are several organizations dedicated to those who work in clay profiled here. Don't forget to check out local clay guilds in your area as well.

American Art Pottery Association (AAPA)

The American Art Pottery Association's mission is to: promote an interest, understanding, appreciation, and recognition of American Art Pottery; unify and strengthen the voice of collectors and dealers of American Art Pottery; and foster a members' Code of Ethics for buying, selling, exhibiting, and publishing about American Art Pottery. Membership benefits include:

- Six issues of the bimonthly *Journal of the American Art Pottery Association*
- Having your Web site linked to AAPA

- Attending the annual National Convention, Show, Sale, and Auction
- Submitting your "mystery pots" to the AAPA Mystery Page for identification
- Posting your "wants" on the AAPA Member Want List
- The camaraderie of networking with and learning from other collectors and dealers of art pottery
- A copy of the Directory of Membership, Code of Ethics, and Bylaws.
- The right to display the AAPA Member sign, signifying your membership
- Appreciation

For more information: American Art Pottery Association, 17736 HWY 442, Independence, LA 70443; *www.amartpot.org.*

American Ceramic Society's Potters Council

The American Ceramic Society, which is dedicated to the advancement of ceramics and is the publisher of *Ceramics Monthly* magazine, has a nonprofit subsidiary called the Potters Council that is dedicated to meeting the needs of studio potters and ceramics artists by providing forums for knowledge exchange and professional enhancement. Goals include:

- Supporting studio pottery as a professional and recreational activity by providing valuable programs and services
- Providing forums for discussion of issues, and a means to address them
- Tapping into the American Ceramic Society's wealth of technical knowledge in ceramics
- Organizing groups on local, regional, national, and international levels to work closely with and support existing arts organizations
- Providing business and career opportunities
- Supporting the American Ceramic Society's efforts to promote ceramic awareness

For more information: American Ceramic Society, Attn.: Potters Council, 735 Ceramic Pl., Westerville, OH 43081-8720; (614) 794-5890; *www.potterscouncil.org.*

National Council on Education for the Ceramic Arts (NCECA)

NCECA is a professional organization primarily focused on the ceramics arts that aims to:

- Stimulate, promote and improve education in the ceramics arts
- Gather and disseminate information and ideas that are vital and stimulating to the teachers, studio artists, and people throughout the creative arts community
- Provide a meeting place for professionals in the ceramics arts to communicate with each other in a variety of ways

Members include: teachers; artists in functional and/or sculptural works in clay; students; museum professionals; writers, critics, and editors of ceramics arts publications; museum and gallery directors and curators; collectors/patrons of clay art; and others interested in the ceramics arts.

Programs include:

- NCECA Exhibitions Program: two high-quality exhibitions that encompass the full spectrum of ceramics art
- The NCECA Clay National: national juried exhibition
- The NCECA Invitational: an exhibition
- The NCECA Regional Student Juried Exhibition: an exhibit opportunity for students to showcase their work

Publications include:

- *NCECA Journal*: A record of conference presentations
- *NCECA News*: Published quarterly
- The *NCECA* membership directory

For more information: NCECA, 77 Erie Village Square, #280, Erie, CO 80516-6996; (866) CO-NCECA (266-2322); (303) 828-2811; *www.nceca.org.*

Studio Potter

When Studio Potter began in 1972, the founders wanted to start a magazine that specifically addressed the needs of studio potters rather than schools or galleries. The first issue included articles on apprenticeship, photo-resist, and homemade pugmills, as well as an excerpt from Paulus

Berensohn's then-unpublished manuscript titled *Finding One's Way with Clay*. Over thirty years later, although Studio Potter has changed the editorial focus from technology to aesthetic philosophy, some things have remained the same: an essential belief in functional pottery, a reverence for new talent and old masters, the encouragement of first-person writing, education as self-discovery, service to the field, and an overriding commitment to humanitarian values.

Studio Potter is:

- A nonprofit organization dedicated to the service of the international community of ceramics artists and craftspeople.
- An advertising-free professional journal for potters and others.
- A network designed to promote interaction and exchange among potters everywhere through:
  - Publishing books and a semiannual newsletter
  - Network News
  - Maintaining a circulating video library
  - Sponsoring workshops
  - Running a bed and breakfast program
  - Maintaining an archive

For more information: Studio Potter, P.O. Box 70, Goffstown, NH 03045; (603) 774-3582; *www.studiopotter.org*.

These places to work and study, as well as the organizations, will go a long way in helping you stay on track as your career develops. If you can, consider attending a workshop or a program, or doing a residency at either Watershed or the Bray. Pick out at least one organization to join so that every month when you receive your newsletter or magazine, you can read about what is happening in your field around the country, in addition to the opportunities to promote your work that you may not have known about otherwise. If memberships are out of your reach right now, ask a family member or friend to give one to you as a gift.

The next chapter is devoted to profiles of craftspeople working in clay. Read them and enjoy. If you have any questions for any of the people profiled and they have a Web site, feel free to learn more about them and even contact them with your questions and comments.

CHAPTER 7

Ceramics Artists' Profiles

Potters

Gerry Williams, Potter
www.studiopotter.org

Gerald Durette

In 1949, at the age of 23, Gerry Williams moved to New Hampshire to become a potter. Never having worked with clay in his life, he had been inspired by a book about a man who earned his living as a potter. From these humble beginnings, not only did he train himself to become an internationally known master potter, but he has also dedicated enormous amounts of time and energy to educating and inspiring future craftspeople, as well as promoting and furthering the development of pottery making on a global scale through Studio Potter.

Early on in his career, Gerry worked for the League of NH Craftsman as a stock boy and driver for $15 a week while taking his first classes in pottery at the League's Concord headquarters. "It was an exciting time for me to be associated with the League," says Gerry, "and I soaked it up like a sponge. Living in and being part of that dynamic crafts community, many of whom were nationally known artists, was heady stuff, and I loved it."

In 1951, Gerry became an apprentice of John Butler of Philadelphia, who had recently opened a new production pottery studio in Wolfeboro, New Hampshire. The apprenticeship experience had a lasting impact on Gerry and in 1978, he directed the first national conference on apprenticeship in Purchase, New York, followed by a lecture on the value of apprenticeship at the World Craft Conference in Kyoto, Japan. Then, in 1983, he served as a delegate to the first International

Conference on Apprenticeship held in Sydney, Australia. Having trained numerous apprentices himself, Gerry published a book titled *Apprenticeship in Craft* to help others learn about training apprentices.

In 1952, Gerry opened his own studio in Concord with a 12" × 12" electric kiln and kick wheel in an unheated room which he rented for $7 a week. "I worked fourteen- to sixteen-hour days back then, throwing hundreds of cups, saucers, cereal bowls, dinner plates, and mugs," says Gerry. "I worked mostly in low-temperature earthenware. Every piece shows more than a passing debt to some other potter, but you have to start somewhere."

The 1950s was a time of intense learning and experimentation for Gerry. "I bought every book I could on historical pottery making," he says, "and I visited other potters as much as I dared without endangering my friendships with them." His work evolved from low- to high-temperature stoneware, and he mastered a technique of using copper red glazes. (He still fires several kilns a year using these glazes for a group of admirers.) He built a home and studio in Dunbarton, New Hampshire, where he still lives and works today.

During the political turmoil of the 1960s and 1970s, Gerry's work changed from being primarily utilitarian to including architectural murals, wall plaques, decorative urns, and sculptures reflecting social, political, and racial themes, followed by "political folk art" work, including photographic images accompanied by written statements. He attributes his strong sense of social consciousness to his childhood years spent in India, where his missionary father worked at the height of Gandhi's nationalist movement for independence. "There is a lot of India's spirit in my work," says Gerry, "but it is less about politics than it is about a way of life. The rural ambiance, the importance of manual labor, the practical and symbolic role of craft making in India added dignity to a person's life, and they have had a lasting impact on my life."

In 1972, Gerry started the renowned Phoenix Workshops, providing intensive master classes. Through his work with the New Hampshire Potters Guild, he helped form the Daniel Clark Foundation (named after an obscure colonial potter in New Hampshire whose fame came principally from a diary he left upon his death) to educate and provide support for the pottery community on a national scale. (The organization was later renamed the Studio Potter Foundation.) Gerry published *Studio Potter* magazine with coeditor Peter Sabin, which serves almost 4,500 subscribers today. Volume One, Number One began with words that still define the publication: "*Studio Potter* is a magazine for the community of potters everywhere. It is written by potters and directed towards fellow potters who earn their living making pots." The Foundation also publishes a network newsletter for almost twelve thousand subscribers who belong to forty-seven pottery groups around the world. Gerry's current work includes developing a "Global Ceramics Culture" through the Studio Potter Foundation, various government institutions and universities with initiatives including: archival preservation, art education for secondary schools, conferences on art, and historical and cultural information on pottery making from every country in the world.

Now in his seventies, Gerry still considers himself primarily a potter, even after years of work and service with the Studio Potter Foundation, his many publications, teaching workshops, and earning an international reputation as a visionary craftsman. "I'm satisfied—happy is not the right word—with my career," says Gerry. "I have felt that through the magazine we have contributed to a meaningful dialogue. It's been both a high and low road, but overall, a wonderful experience. I have friends all over. I never had any regrets and found that what I was doing was exactly right for me. The work that grew out of that decision to be a potter was based on my background, culture, the times, and a need to perform. I never completed college, but have earned two honorary degrees. My wife, Julie, has been a partner in all this by aiding and abetting me in my activities. I still maintain a studio and showroom and love making work that people can use and enjoy as a result of my deep commitment to and interest in social, classical, and traditional reasons. I am glad to be working in clay, interpreting my sense of aesthetics with my social commitment. I have tried to be proactive and help the community in any way that I could." Gerry also finds inspiration in a big vegetable garden, reads voraciously ("I buy too many books"), loves classical music (like Mozart), and travels. Gerry credits mentors such as Paulus Berensohn from Penland and M.C. Richards. "I have tried to be progressive in my attitude in exploring the work," says Gerry, "with needs to communicate political, emotional, and personal issues to the viewer. Through history and tradition, I have reached deep inside of me to get to a place where the material comes from, whether it was a poem from childhood or anger at what was going on around me."

When asked what he would say to potters who are just getting started in their careers, Gerry suggests that success requires a commitment to developing and learning to make meaningful work while trying to understand your needs of expression. "Don't worry about following trends or styles," says Gerry. "Just try to make sense of your own way of looking at things by paying attention to your inner wellsprings of inspiration and giving form to the where, why, and how. Then make it meaningful in both form and style."

Mary Nyburg, Potter

Darwin Davidson

With a crafts career spanning over forty years, it's hard to believe now that Mary Nyburg didn't discover clay until she was almost forty years old. "I grew up in a small town in Maine during the depression and came back to Maine every summer," says Mary. "One year, I went to the Skowhegan fair to see the races. In the exhibition hall, I happened to see someone demonstrating at a potter's wheel. I had never seen one before and was absolutely fascinated. I never made it to the race. I went back to my home in Baltimore, Maryland, and started taking pottery classes at the museum. In 1961, my teacher suggested I take a clay workshop at Haystack. When I went home, I quit my job and made a studio in my garage."

Continuing to take clay workshops at Haystack until 1966, Mary shared her knowledge by teaching workshops at places like the Maryland Institute of Art, Peters Valley Craft Center, and Haystack. "Workshops are especially good for women," says Mary. "It doesn't matter how much time you have; you can just give it your best and skip the mid-life crisis."

Before discovering clay, Mary had already had a significant career in retail, in advertising, as a research assistant at John Hopkins Hospital, and as Regional Field Director for CARE, traveling on assignment as far as South America. Over the years, Mary has also contributed time and energy to other worthy causes such as Planned Parenthood, and to the local hospitals as a board member and volunteer. In the crafts field, Mary went on to become a well-known potter, teacher, and gallery owner, and contributed significant time and energy to several crafts organizations including the Maryland Craft Council, the Crafts Emergency Relief Fund (CERF), Haystack Mt. School of Crafts, and the American Craft Council (ACC).

Over the next several decades, Mary made her living selling a range of work (such as mugs and covered jars) at fairs by taking orders, going home, and filling them. "When I started selling my pots at fairs, we put bedspreads on the grass to spread out our wares, or tailgated in the backs of our vehicles," remembers Mary. "Later on I was involved in the first crafts fair sponsored by the Northeast division of the ACC in Stowe, Vermont, the grandfather of all ACC fairs. We had sixty-seven exhibitors and grossed $18,000 total, an amount we celebrated at that time."

Mary continued to visit Haystack every summer. "I stuck my nose in every year, at least for lunch," says Mary. After the death of her husband, she moved to Deer Isle and started the Blue Heron Gallery, still a successful venture today. "I had always wanted to come back to Maine to live. I bought my house and thought about starting a gallery," says Mary. "I asked friends to send pots and starting showing the work of the Haystack faculty. The gallery went ahead of itself for years." A seasonal gallery, up until two years ago, Mary still made pots in the winter to put in the gallery in the summer, when the business took so much time and energy that there was no time for studio work.

"I feel that I have been successful in my career," says Mary. "I don't know that I get a star, but I had a good time with it. Being surrounded by a circle of like-minded people has been wonderful. I believed in my work with the ACC, and my involvement with Haystack over the years has been a labor of love."

Mary suggests that aspiring craftspeople be patient, create work they like rather than worry about the market, and give devoted time to their work. "When you work, give it your best," says Mary. "It doesn't get much better than that."

Mark Bell, Potter

Mark Bell starting making pots in high school and focused on ceramics throughout his studies. He graduated with a BFA degree from the University of Wisconsin in 1982 and an MFA degree from Arizona State University in 1986, including a one-year residency at Millersville College and several sessions at Haystack. After graduate school, Mark made his living from a combination of being a visiting artist in schools, selling his pots, and painting houses. Ten years ago, he was able to stop painting houses. These days, Mark is 100 percent self-supporting through sales of his work. He has benefits, his house is mortgage free, and he is enjoying a new studio.

Mark suggests that aspiring craftspeople get a job in retail to interact with customers and learn how to sell. Once they get in the rhythm of selling, they can take it from there. "My father was a salesman, and I saw how he was able to be with people, follow up on leads, and make his clients feel special by giving them gifts at the holidays," remembers Mark. "When I was younger, I had a paper route and sold cookies from a cart, which enabled me to learn how to interact with customers and sell in a way that wasn't as personal as selling my own work. Now my job is 50 percent making and 50 percent selling, and I have to be good at both to prosper." Mark also suggests devising a system to keep track of all of your sales, and coding it carefully to use for targeted mailings to keep customers informed.

Mark has exhibited his work nationally, is represented by several galleries, has participated in several of the country's top crafts fairs, and sells from his own showroom. "I have had good success with craftsperson-owned galleries and have been with one for eleven years," says Mark. "Although I do very little gallery stuff now, I am now looking for name recognition from galleries who will place national ads rather than solely sales of my work. I have also found hosting events at my studio to be very successful. I invite people to come to my studio when I am opening my kiln after a firing, and give a small cup to everyone who attends. At the last opening, I had forty people here at 7:00 A.M. and they went nuts! Influenced by what they see other people buying, I sold an entire kiln-load of pots (approximately 150) in a day." Mark also suggests that rather than trying to hold on to work and sell it themselves, craftspeople should give galleries and shops great work because they will sell it.

An active member of the board of directors at Watershed, he has both given and received from the experience. "I have made some great connections through my involvement with Watershed," says Mark. "Some of the other board members have become collectors of my work, one even setting up a sale of my work the past four years in New York City."

"All my life I wanted to be a successful artist and I am now," says Mark. "I have ten pieces in the collection at the Everson Museum, as well as pieces at the Currier Gallery of Art. When I started, I had low expectations and thought I would probably fail. Sometimes I still pinch myself when someone buys a pot, and think, Why are they doing that? People love my work and love the idea that they have discovered me.

Many of them return again and again to see my progress. Selling my work has been like throwing pebbles in a pond, first making little circles, then intertwining, and going out from there."

"I suggest that aspiring craftspeople develop their work first and keep expenses low," says Mark. "Consider having a retail space where people can come, even in your house, to look at work anytime. Choose an area tourists frequent to increase traffic flow and get repeat visitors. Stay in one place so people can find you easily. Let the work sell itself by giving it a place to be seen, whether it's at a local fair or the Smithsonian. Don't overlook the importance of hosting events at your studio, no matter how small, so people can see other people enjoying and buying your work."

Public Artists

Randy Fein, Clay Sculptor, Installation Artist, Instructor

"When I was a child, my parents and teachers were always supportive of my artistic abilities. I thought I would be either an inventor or an artist when I grew up," says Randy Fein. "I always had a definite interest in the arts. My love affair with clay didn't start until I was a sophomore in college. Now, after over twenty-five years of making a living with clay, I've finally realized I'm also an entrepreneur. I earn my living from a combination of selling my clay sculpture, producing public commissions, coordinating an annual crafts show, and teaching workshops."

Randy's interest in art started early on. "As a kid, I started drawing in pen and ink, and always had art supplies," says Randy. "When I was nine years old, I did a still life on the dining room table. We lived in the projects in Manhattan, and there was a settlement house where I could take free art, music, and dance classes as an inner-city kid with artists and musicians in after-school workshops. I always had a great imagination, and made toys out of Play-Doh and papier-mâché. I even played museum by setting up a mini-museum with pictures and figures."

Randy earned a BFA degree with a BS in Art Education from SUNY New Paltz in 1975. A lucky break came before graduating, when she submitted slides of her work to the prestigious ACC Crafts at Rhinebeck fair and was accepted. "Students weren't supposed to apply, but I wanted to make a living from my artwork after graduation and this show seemed like a great opportunity," remembers Randy. " I knew nothing about having a business card or a booth or selling wholesale. Marketing skills were not taught then in art school. Luckily, my peers helped me." She sold clay pots, plates, and whimsical creatures at the fair, and her porcelain building façades were picked up by a gallery on Madison Avenue in New York. "My prices were low and I was almost giving my work away because I was so happy to sell them," says Randy. "My work evolved into a line of brownstone cookie jars and canisters, and these sold very well. Immediately after graduation I was working out of a shared house, making my pieces in my bedroom/studio and taking the pieces to a local studio to be fired in a kiln. I never saw what I was doing as a business and would back off when I saw a potential market because I wanted to remain a hands-on creator. However, looking back, if my pieces had been marketed differently, I would have made more money. However, I felt that I would have become more of a manufacturer than an artist and I wasn't willing to do that."

In 1977 Randy moved to Maine and continued to do crafts fairs to make a living. "I was making my own way, got my studio together, and figured out which shows to do," says Randy. "I knew that to be successful I needed to keep my overhead low, so I set up my studio in my home. Currently my schedule follows a pattern of gearing up for wholesale shows and teaching school workshops in the spring, with crafts shows in the summer."

Randy is well known for her teaching and mural workshops with children in the schools, and has completed fifty mural projects with students to date. "Last year I worked with almost six hundred kids in three different communities in about seven weeks' time, where we created three permanent clay murals in each town," says Randy. "I enjoy the contrast of the solitude of working in my studio with the upbeat energy of working with students and teachers during a mural workshop." Although Randy is on the Touring Artists Roster through the Maine Arts Commission, usually the teaching assignments are obtained through word of mouth. "I have developed a talent for working in the schools as a visiting artist," says Randy. "The kids I teach in the schools say they want to be an artist just like me when they grow up. I keep thinking the teaching work will dry up because I don't advertise, but fortunately my schedule keeps filling up. Although it suits me, my lifestyle would not be for everyone." Randy has also taught at the college level at Babson College in Wellesley, Massachusetts, where she set up the school's ceramics program with a business module.

Randy has done a large number of mixed media commissions as the result of winning public art competitions. "I received a commission to do a piece for Vermont State College titled 'Millennium Transformations,'" says Randy. "There were 165 applications, then 60, then 9, and finally, 2 finalists. I make a good portion of my income from doing these commissions. They require coordination between many people and can sometimes take two years to complete. I find creating art for public places extremely rewarding and particularly enjoy doing community-inspired installations. I believe that art is for everyone and creative expression is within reach of each of us. As an artist, I want to bridge that gap and make art and expression a normal daily occurrence in the lives of everyday people."

Recently Randy helped coordinate a local tour of artists' studios, and had over 150 people come to her open house. "They bought all kinds of stuff and I talked to several people about tile commissions," says Randy. This was the first time she had participated in an artist studio tour, and she thinks it has great potential. "I finally see the value of a mailing list too, and I'm working on one after all these years," says Randy.

"I consider myself a clay expert, and when I am working on a piece, I have a feeling of satisfaction and can use the materials with a confidence that only comes from experience," says Randy. "As a visual artist, I have recognition in my community as the result of both focusing my artistic abilities and being in one place for a long time.

Randy advises emerging artists to get involved in their local community. "Believe in your creative powers and don't doubt your artistic talent, because if you do, it will cause you to falter and weaken with rejections," says Randy. "Learn how to manage your money and understand cash flow. Don't do the numbers every day, but be sure to have a nest egg of money socked away for the in-between periods, or you may starve and be tempted to get a 9-to-5 job."

Abby Huntoon, Ceramics Artist

"When I visualized my life in clay," says Abby Huntoon, "I thought I would be a mom with a studio in the basement. I never thought I would be looked at as a real artist or teach at the college level. I'm happy and have already accomplished more than I ever thought possible." Abby's accomplishments include earning an MFA degree in Clay from the Program in Artisanry at Boston University, being a co-owner of a cooperative studio called Sawyer Street Studios, completing a significant number of public art projects and commission pieces, showing her work extensively, teaching at Maine College of Art in Portland, Maine, and being awarded an NEA grant in 1988.

"In seventh grade I took a clay class and hated it," remembers Abby. "It wasn't until the summer before my senior year in college that I got hooked on clay. I was assisting a teacher with teaching crafts to kids in Rockport, Massachusetts, during the day, and I decided to take a pottery class at night. I discovered I loved the versatility of clay. I was attending a liberal arts college that did not offer a clay program, so when I returned to school that fall, I enrolled in a clay course at a nearby art school, where I took one year of ceramics. I was always interested in art, but up until that point I had not settled on a medium. I had considered going to art school in high school, but I was intimidated by art schools and had ended up attending a liberal arts school instead."

After graduation, Abby moved to Boston and spent as much time as possible at a studio called Mudflat, continuing to take classes there and using the studio. She then joined a cooperative studio called Clay Dragon. To make a living, Abby was doing odd jobs, but she continued to develop her work and began to market her dinnerware sets through the gallery at Clay Dragon. Then she signed up for a clay workshop at Haystack. "I took a workshop with Rick Hirsch and liked him as a teacher and a person," says Abby. "After the workshop, I went to talk to him at the Program in Artisanry at Boston University, where he was teaching. He convinced me that graduate school would be a good move for me. I had gotten to a place in my work where I needed to learn how to judge my work and how to know whether or not it was a successful piece. He told me I would not necessarily learn all the answers, but I would learn the important questions to ask myself about my work. I enrolled, my work changed, I changed, and he was right."

After receiving her MFA, Abby moved to Portland, Maine, and shared a studio with several clay people she had met during the workshop at Haystack. After several years, when the rent on the studio was about to be increased, Abby joined with several other clay artists to form a new cooperative, Sawyer Street Studios, purchasing and renovating a former pizza parlor into studio space. "Working in a group studio situation is wonderful," says Abby. "I have gotten many opportunities from being here. For example, if a gallery owner comes to the studio to see someone else's work, he also has an opportunity to see mine, and everyone shares information about upcoming shows. I also obtained a corporate art rep from Boston and sold several pieces as a result of being here. But most importantly, I have received a lot of emotional support." Abby still maintains her studio there today.

Abby has also done a fair amount of teaching clay, both at Maine College of Art in the summer program and as an adjunct professor with the ceramic majors, and at Sawyer Street Studios. "I have taught community classes for twelve years here at Sawyer Street," says Abby. "The students are varied and range from beginner to quite accomplished."

"I think aspiring craftspeople should keep their work as a focus in their lives and must have a true passion for it," says Abby. "Many people want to, but they let obstacles get in the way of actually doing it. Love it, do it, and be open to what comes. Accept your work and don't be critical—just see where it leads. Most importantly, set up a community to support you emotionally and as a potential way of making connections to market your work."

Sculptors

Lisa Tully Dibble, Sculptor

"If teaching part-time at three different colleges, raising a child, and trying to knock out an occasional sculpture in my basement studio is of interest to your readers, then include me in your book," wrote Lisa Tully Dibble in response to my interview request. With a BFA degree from Kansas City Art Institute and an MFA degree from the Program in Artisanry at Boston University, Lisa's list of accomplishments include: exhibiting her work nationally, teaching ceramics at the college level, being a visiting artist, and taking part in planning the NCECA conference recently held in Kansas City. Not bad for someone who describes her life as a juggling act.

"My professional life changed when I had a baby," admits Lisa. "I had to stop working for awhile and learn to accept where I am and not be concerned with 'should have.' Just continuing to make my work is a challenge now, especially coupled with teaching three courses. However, when I pull out my sculptures and look back at my work, I do feel I have accomplished something. Although I had different plans for my career after graduate school, most of the time I feel successful."

Lisa currently makes large-scale clay sculptures that are typically larger than life, using bright colors, layers of texture, and several different materials in addition to clay. All treat overtly feminine roles such as housewife, mother, and fertility goddess with a more ironic than feminist thrust. "There is an autobiographical nature in my work," says Lisa. "By placing various objects in and on my self-portraits, I create imagery alluding to the roles, myths, and emotional states of each piece. I think of my art as dramatizing conflicts rather than taking a specific point of view." Very labor-intensive, these pieces are more suitable for group and solo gallery shows than for sales at crafts fairs. "So far I have not been successful in selling a lot of my pieces," says Lisa, "although several have been purchased and are in the collections of museums like the Fuller Art Museum and the Zone Art Center in Massachusetts and the Daum Museum of Contemporary Art in Missouri. But I keep making the pieces and figuring out a way to make it work. I have thought about making the work smaller, but I see the work at the scale that it is currently."

Lisa finds that being married to an artist is an asset. "Ted can be critical and honest about my work," says Lisa. "He knows and cares about the work and understands the time and the thought process it requires. I have found that although my work tends to come from making other work and writing in my journal, it certainly helps to be married to an artist who is supportive."

Lisa recently discovered how helpful it is to belong to a crafts organization and network. "I didn't attend the NCECA conference for years, and now I have gone twice and found it very inspiring," says Lisa. "I took pages of notes and saw both of my professors from graduate school. By not attending, I have missed a lot. I enjoyed helping to organize it and found it was well worth the time and expense involved."

"You have got to love what you do," says Lisa. "Find ways to keep interested, set tangible goals, but also let yourself dream. Find ways to do something towards your goals always. If you aren't doing it, it's not feeding you."

George Mason, Sculptor, Acupuncturist

After earning degrees from the Cranbrook Academy of Art and Alfred University's College of Ceramics, creating over thirty public art commissions, winning three National Endowment for the Arts grants, numerous solo and group exhibitions, participating in a vast array of teaching experiences, and cofounding the Watershed Center for Ceramics Arts, George Mason went back to school of become an acupuncturist. "Ceramics is my home," explains George. "Becoming an acupuncturist is not jumping ship. They don't have the same requirements. Now I don't have to look to my work with clay to make money, and that takes the pressure off. Earning part of my living as an acupuncturist has opened up the inquiry and what excites me about trying new things in my studio again. I'm so excited to be back in the studio again."

After college, George taught ceramics at several schools in the United States, such as Cranbrook Academy of Art, Ohio State University, and the College of Ceramics at Alfred University, followed by schools in Israel and Indonesia. Returning to the United States, he bought an old Methodist church in Maine and made it into his home and studio. "When I first got out of school," remembers George, "I did a teaching stint. Then I concentrated on the Percent for Art program commissions. After doing commissions for ten years, I decided to go back to school to study acupuncture. Now I do both." The shift towards becoming an acupuncturist happened gradually. "I started having acupuncture myself," says George, "and found it to be poetic and visual and about the cycle and energy of the seasons. I started to incorporate the colors and emotions of it into my work. Then I realized I was going to have to study it."

George is more interested in the inquiry involved in making than he is in producing a product to sell. "Selling my work has always been an issue for me," says George. "Although I loved working with the committees and towns and finding out what they wanted to create the public art pieces, I needed to back off from doing them. Recently I found that holding an open house to benefit Watershed was a delightful way of selling my work and helping Watershed at the same time. The open house felt more like an offering rather than selling. People came to visit my family and looked at my work and it just felt right. I don't want people to feel cornered, I don't want to feel misunderstood or overlooked. With the open-house format I was able to set the parameters and share the work. It was fun for me and for my family. It really felt right and I want to explore this more." With the open house format, George is able to redefine how customers see his work, allowing them to just enjoy it first rather than be concerned with wondering how much it costs.

"At this point in my career, I feel as if I am taking back the direction," says George, "and following my nose. The payback will be finding out what it feels like and enjoying the process. I have learned many lessons in my career and don't need to keep doing things to reassure myself that I am still in the loop. I'll try a lot of things once and trust what my gut is saying for a true read. I'm so excited to be back in the studio and so is my family. It's wonderful to think about art in relation to my family life in a way that includes my family and doesn't put me in opposition to my family. I don't want to feel sequestered in the studio and miss something that is happening with my family right outside my studio door. When I needed to make my living from solely selling my work, I found I had to rewrite the script around parenting to not feel in conflict. Now with my acupuncture office in town, when I am in the studio it is just my creative time."

George suggests that aspiring craftspeople carve out a support system for themselves. "I have had a number of studio assistants over the years," says George. "They are often just out of school and about halfway through the first year when they start wondering why they are doing art. Without the support system of school, they often fall on their face and then have to locate their voice and figure out if this is what they really want to do. A support system creates context and reason and meaning for making art, whatever form it takes. It gives them someone else to bounce ideas off of as well as company. In the long run, if you want to stay in the ring, it is important to nurture yourself as a creative being. It's an ongoing process. I value how I have been brought to my knees in the studio. I have let go of my shoulds and fantasies and instead looked for my voice and a connection. For me it's about the inquiry process itself, which is an open-ended thing . . . and it's not over yet!"

Teachers

Lynn Duryea, Ceramics Artist

In the early 1970s, Lynn Duryea had a bachelor's degree in history from Bucknell University, a half-finished master's degree in art
history at New York University, an assistant's
job at the Metropolitan Museum of Art, *and* a
headache at the end of every workday. Looking
for something to ease the stress, she signed up
for a pottery class. "I remember just where I was sitting in the room
that night, watching someone throw a pot," says Lynn. "I couldn't get
over it. I was mesmerized right from the beginning."

Lynn's career to date includes not only a successful production pottery business (including clients like the famous Tiffany's in New York),
but also lots of service work for others. Lynn is a Founding Trustee of the
Watershed Center for Ceramics Arts in Maine as well as past Program
Coordinator and current Artist Facilitator for the Watershed Workshop
for People with HIV/AIDS. Lynn is also one of four owners of a collaborative gallery called Sawyer Street Studios in South Portland, Maine,
which functions as a studio, showroom, and gallery space. In addition,
Lynn has exhibited her work nationally and taught numerous courses
and workshops. Recently, in her fifties, Lynn decided to go back to
school and completed a Master of Fine Arts degree at the University of
Florida. A new phase of her career is currently unfolding, with college
teaching as the primary focus.

After her initial pottery class, Lynn continued to take more classes
and then signed up for a clay workshop at Haystack Mountain School of
Crafts, never anticipating that this experience would inspire her to
make a major move from New York to Deer Isle, Maine. In the years that
followed, Lynn would return to Haystack again and again, first as a student, then as a studio monitor, teacher, and member of the Deer Isle
community. In 2001, Lynn had work in the Center for Maine Contemporary Art exhibition titled "Haystack: Pivotal Transformations." She
summed up her connection with Haystack like this: "My experience at
Haystack in 1972 and 1973 helped make the decision to give up a career
as an art historian and to leave my job at the Metropolitan Museum.
Until recently I had no formal training in art. In many ways, Haystack

provided me with an education. Sessions at Haystack removed me from my studio so I could think differently, try new techniques, work in other media, be exposed and challenged by excellent teachers and other artists. The slide presentations by artists from all over the globe, lectures, and casual conversations with mentors and peers wove a richness into my creative life."

After her move to Deer Isle in 1974, Lynn worked with two potters, supplemented sales of her work with part-time jobs, and kept her overhead low. For two winters she worked in a sardine factory and did substitute teaching and a lot of other things, until her work started selling consistently. In 1976, Lynn co-founded a cooperative gallery on the island called Eastern Bay Gallery. "The reason cooperatives work so well in Maine is that the volume of business is not large enough for one person to earn a living running the store," says Lynn. "It makes more sense to have a cooperative gallery where a lot of people share in the running of it. The audience here is quite sophisticated because of Haystack and summer residents, so it's been good in terms of actual sales and exposure."

Wholesaling her work began with the first order from Tiffany's in 1981. "The volume of that order overwhelmed me, as did the short delivery time. I was catapulted into a totally new level of production," remembers Lynn. To keep up with the demand for her quilt-patterned tableware line of pottery, Lynn hired employees and worked with business advisors, making her living selling at numerous retail and wholesale shows around the country.

After living year-round on Deer Isle for over a decade, Lynn started spending winters there and eventually moved to Portland, Maine, year-round, teaching at Portland School of Art (now Maine College of Art) and becoming involved in the Sawyer Street Studios. She continues to maintain a house and studio on Deer Isle, which still serves as an important refuge today.

In 1986, Lynn, Chris Gustin, George Mason, and Peg Griggs conceived of a ceramic residency retreat, and the Watershed Center for the Ceramic Arts was born in an old brick factory on the coast of Maine. Hundreds of clay artists have worked there since its inception, and Lynn has been actively involved since the beginning. In 1991, Watershed launched the Workshop for People Living with HIV/AIDS, with Lynn serving as both the Program Coordinator and Artist Facilitator for the workshop. As the coordinator, she developed the workshop and did all of the administrative work, including fundraising. Since 1998 she has retained the role of facilitator. "I've found these students, as a group, to be incredibly direct, full of life, and wanting to get as much as they can out of the time they have left," says Lynn. "In the early days, AIDS was considered a terminal illness, and generally within two years of each session, most of the participants would die. At the time, people with AIDS were so feared and avoided that, as one participant said, it was a great relief to come to Watershed and be treated as a creative person instead of a sick person."

By 1994, it was time to make another change. "I got restless and felt that my time was spent as a manager doing lots of travel rather than in the studio," says Lynn. "I knew something else was coming, and that made it possible for me to eventually stop doing the production work. I wanted to get someplace else with my work and I thought that if I stay the same, work with the same people, have the same conversations, exist in the same places, my work will never change. I knew that more was possible." All along the way, while selling the production work, Lynn had been creating sculptural work that included mixed media collages, one-of-a-kind plates, wall planters, and tall vessel shapes. She phased out of her commitments and worked for a few years as a sales representative for a publishing company before starting graduate school at the University of Florida in 1999. She received a master's degree in Fine Arts in 2002 after working as a teaching assistant in the Ceramics department, gaining valuable teaching experience at the college level, to prepare herself to become a professor.

Lynn has just accepted a position at Appalachian State University in Boone, North Carolina. "I could find other ways to make money, but I love teaching and feel it is a sacred endeavor," says Lynn. "Teaching provides an important opportunity for connections between people. I love to teach all kinds of people, and my teaching experiences have ranged from marginalized people such as those in correctional facilities to nursing homes to people with HIV/AIDS to students at the studio, Haystack, or the university. I need time alone in the studio, but it is not enough. I want to be a professor to transmit information as well as to guide others in their creative process."

"I suggest that aspiring clay artists work part-time at first with another source of income, as sales from your work will take time and shows can be unpredictable," says Lynn. "Be honest with yourself: How much uncertainty can you live with, and what are your physical, emotional, and financial needs? Running your own business is an enormous amount of work and takes a commitment over a long period of time. Also, think about what you want the work to give you on an emotional level. As time went on, I found the bottom line squeezed the life right out of me and I had to make a change. A group studio with a private space is a good combination."

"I love being an artist," says Lynn. "The creative problem-solving, a rich interior life, the conversations I have with myself and the whole world. The field is so wide and so many variations are possible. Although my work has been rewarding, other things that inspire me include gardening (it doesn't get critiqued or bought), swimming, reading, travel, and my friends. Life provides so many variations and inspirations."

Christine Federighi, Professor of Ceramics, Ceramics Sculptor

"I took art classes in high school and my mother always had us doing art projects," remembers Christine Federighi, "but I thought I was going to be a veterinarian. With encouragement from my art teachers, I naïvely ended up going to art school to study painting. I only took ceramics because my roommate was taking the course." Over thirty years later, Christine is a tenured Professor of Ceramics at the University of Miami with an extensive exhibition record, impressive list of workshops and lectures, successful sales of her work, representation by several prominent galleries, and work in over two dozen collections. She has been the recipient of the Florida Fine Arts Council Individual Artists Grant several times, as well as receiving a National Endowment for the Arts Individual Artists Grant.

Christine earned a BFA degree from the Cleveland Institute of Art in 1972, followed by an MFA degree from Alfred University College of Ceramics in 1974. She spent one summer during college studying glassblowing at Pilchuck Glass School as well. Her thesis work was a combination of blown glass, sculpture, and functional ware. Then at the age of twenty-five, Christine was hired to teach ceramics at the University of Miami. In the beginning, she not only taught the students, but she built kilns and cleaned the studio as well. She worked hard, and over the years, she has created an outstanding ceramics program with highly praised student exhibitions. She and the students also created the

Potter's Guild, holding annual sales to generate funds for visiting artists and new equipment. "I originally planned to teach for five years," remembers Christine. "I always wanted to have my own studio and didn't want to be in Florida. Things happened and here I am. I definitely like to do both my own work and teaching. Students' feedback surprises me and keeps me alive. I have been lucky with my job and my schedule has allowed me enough time to do my artwork."

The field of ceramics has changed greatly over the years. "I have never been good at networking," admits Christine. "The people I went to school with weren't as career-oriented as the students are today. Although I was able to put together a nice portfolio, I had the romantic notion that I would just work in my studio. In the mid-1980s everything got sophisticated. At the last NCECA conference I attended, everyone had Palm Pilots! When I started teaching, I did my work and sat on committees and got tenure just by using common sense. Now they even have workshops on how to get tenured."

Christine's work has changed over the years too. In the beginning, she was making functional pottery and selling her work through fairs and galleries. "I did a lot of local shows back then," says Christine. "After I moved to Miami, my work shifted from bread-and-butter functional ware to more sculptural creations. I started to do what I wanted and felt happy and inspired. In 1979, I had a show of my new work and all the pieces sold." Christine began to hit her stride when she abandoned utility and started thinking about the poetics of the pot. "There are all these figurative descriptions of the pot, such as the lip, belly, shoulder, and foot. It's sort of a magical thing," says Christine. "Then there's the interior and exterior of a vessel, reflecting infinity and soul or site and culture, and the idea of containment, of spirit or narrative. All of those can be visually poetic and enigmatic subjects." Current galleries include: Ann Nathan Gallery in Chicago, Sandy Carson Gallery in Denver, Jaffe Baker Gallery in Boca Raton, R. Duane Reed Gallery in St. Louis, and Lisa Kurts Gallery in Memphis.

For Christine, her work is a diary. "The changes my work has gone through all relate to my life," says Christine. "In many ways, sculpture is a journey. First there is the physical transformation of the materials. Then there is my own. My interest in American Indian art and tribal art fostered the development of decoration that wraps the form. It also helped me to see the use of symbol as narrative. I developed personal symbols such as the early dogs, and later built structures, spiral forms, house images, stairs, plant forms, water references, and landscapes. These images developed because of personal experiences, but can also represent more in the larger realm of universal symbol. For example, mystics considered the house a feminine symbol and equate it with the repository of wisdom. Stairs are the link between the various levels of the psyche. The spiral talks of the evolution of the universe. Each piece has energy and meaning alone and yet together, something totally different."

Christine feels that her teachers and gallery owners gave her the extra support she needed to become successful. "One of my undergraduate professors, Joe Zeller, was a mentor. He helped me focus and gave me not only guidance but a structure on which to build," says Christine. "Although he was strict and tough, he saw that I was a hard-working student. He also helped me get the proper slides and get ready to make sales." Another early supporter was a local gallery director in Miami named Robert Sindelit. "He had faith in me and encouraged me to do a big commission in 1977," says Christine. "He not only ran his own gallery, but he was also the first Director of Art in Public Places in Miami. He believed in artists and helped them."

"Yes, I feel successful," says Christine. "There are some things I would change. For example, I think my work should sell for more than it does! Aspiring craftspeople need to love what they do because they will do it their whole life. I've found that if you work hard and love what you do, you will find a way."

Iver Lofving, Artist, High School Teacher

A ceramics artist, printmaker, and painter, Iver Lofving is also a high school art and Spanish teacher. "I've been teaching high school ceramics for fifteen years," says Iver. "The school year is usually very hectic, but during the summer, I get a lot of work done in my studio. We spend the summer in Swan's Island, Maine, where I try to keep a schedule of at least five hours a day working in my studio.  With the security of the paycheck from teaching, I can take the time to do my work in the summer instead of looking for work. However, during the winter, it's harder to find the time to work in the studio."

Iver received a Bachelor of Fine Arts degree from Alfred University in Alfred, New York, and a master's degree in Education from the

University of Maine. After going to New York City to see if he could make it as an artist, Iver decided to join the Peace Corps. "I was assigned to Guatemala and Costa Rica for two and a half years to help people build small water tanks to provide a clean water supply," remembers Iver. "In the United States, we live in a different world, but not one that is necessarily better. I found that being in a different culture really gave me perspective on how the world works."

Although Iver was inspired by Guatemala and did paint a few watercolors, it seemed like a luxury to make art. When he returned to the United States, he started teaching Spanish and art in a private school in Vermont. Then he moved to Maine and began his master's degree program and became a Peace Corps representative. "I always took art classes, even when I was getting my master's at the University of Maine," says Iver. "I also coordinated a show featuring art from Guatemala, as well as photographs and textiles, which were displayed in the Student Union and very well received."

After becoming certified to teach Spanish and art in the public schools, Iver got a job at Skowhegan High School in Skowhegan, Maine, where he is still teaching today. "I encourage aspiring craftspeople to take advantage of whatever is available in your community. For example, we have done a number of art shows over the years in a local bank with the art students from the high school, and they have been a big success. The students had to do everything, we had an opening, and the TV crews even came to film it for the evening news. I like teaching and feel it is a socially redeeming profession. And I hope that I am having an impact on some of the students by helping them get into something worthwhile."

"I go to workshops whenever I can to keep inspired," says Iver. "I did a summer residency at the Watershed Center for Ceramic Arts, which was wonderful. I also go to weekend workshops for art teachers at Haystack whenever I can. It's a chance for the teachers to make art and is a very magical time for us."

"I suggest interested people get their studio set up and leave it set up so that they can work in it whenever they have some time," says Iver. "You can set it up over a period of time, but just having it will enable you to do more work, even if you only have a small amount of time. By the time you are ready to do your work on a more full-time basis, the studio will probably already be paid for. I have a tiny setup at my home to use during the school year, which I can heat quickly. Then I have a better setup at Swan's Island that I am able to work in on a daily basis during the summer. Currently I am working on a line of silk-screened T-shirts to sell, which I call "IverStudio." I have a tourist-trap booth set up out in front of our house with a locked metal box, so people can do self-serve, buying their shirt and leaving the money in the box. It's one step above a lemonade stand, but it works pretty well for me. I also have my work in different shops around the area. Put something out there to sell. Just do it!"

PART THREE

Fiber

CHAPTER 8

Facts and Organizations for Fiber Artists

This section includes craftspeople working in baskets, beads, book arts and calligraphy, dolls, quilts, wearable art, and weaving, all under the Fiber umbrella. While many make their living selling their work, others garner grants and fellowships, teach, or run fiber organizations. Many of the people in this section have worked through several stages in their crafts careers, or have combined different interests to earn a living or to live in a way that suits them best. In addition, this section provides some details about running a fiber business, with the results of a survey, important organizations, and artist profiles.

Although there are not many schools devoted just to the study of fiber, there are many excellent programs available at crafts schools and colleges all over the country. See "Educational Opportunities for Craftspeople" in chapter 4 for more information.

Insight Survey Statistics on Fiber Artists

Today's craftspeople working in fiber have lots of options when it comes to having a career. To give aspiring craftspeople a clearer sense of running a business in fiber, I have included some statistics to help you plan. The results of the Insight Survey on Fiber from *The Crafts Report*'s October 2002 issue featured below are based on thirty-nine respondents, with the average gross sales per artist coming out to $78,640. Here are the details:

Percent of Gross Sales from Various Sources
- 56% retail shows
- 23% wholesale shows
- 9% sell directly to galleries
- 4% consign to galleries
- 1% Internet
- 7% other

Amount Spent on Materials
- 5% less than $1000
- 46% $1000 to $10,000
- 21% $10,001 to $20,000
- 13% $20,001 to $50,000
- 15% $50,000+

Number of People Working in Studio
- 62% work alone
- 23% 1 to 2 people
- 13% 3 to 5 people
- 3% 6 to 10 people

Time Selling Crafts
- 0% less than 1 year
- 15% 1 to 5 years
- 26% 6 to 10 years
- 18% 11 to 15 years
- 41% more than 15 years

Forty-one percent owned a Web site, 10 percent sold their work through an online gallery or crafts site other than their own, and 33 percent said their crafts business was the only source of income in their household.

"Most fiber artists can't afford to live on only the income generated by the sales of their work," says Sandra Bowles, editor of *Shuttle, Spindle and Dyepot* magazine. "Even those who have achieved a level of success, have worked for years, have been persistent, and have had the support of their family, a spouse, or partner. All artists face this, but fiber artists have an added challenge since almost every aspect of fiber is extremely labor-intensive. I suggest an artist join a fiber organization to take advantage of the international network of artists, educators, and members. Read *The Crafts Report*, join a local art association, research trends, and talk with gallery and shop owners and other artists to determine if there is a market for your work. Develop a business plan, apply to local crafts shows, and as your success increases, apply to national shows. At the top of my list is having good slides or high-resolution digital photographs taken of your work. If the real estate mantra is location, location, location, make yours presentation, presentation, presentation!"

Organizations for Fiber Artists

Although many of the major fiber organizations are profiled in this section, there are also many active local and regional guilds. If you are not aware of them, contact one of these larger organizations for referrals or stop by a supplier near you to inquire.

The Center for Bead Research

The Center for Bead Research offers memberships as well as an extensive Web site that includes information on the history of beads, bead use in different cultures, and current research topics. For craftspeople looking for a local organization to join, it also lists bead guilds all over the country. A basic guidebook called *Beads Around the World* by Peter Francis Jr. is available for collectors, covering the most easily available and collectible beads. It introduces you to basic materials, beadmaking techniques, bead trade, and their ultimate uses.

For more information: The Center for Bead Research, 4 Essex Street, Lake Placid, NY 12946-1236; *www.thebeadsite.com*.

Bead Museum, Washington, D.C.

Founded by the Bead Society of Greater Washington, this museum is dedicated to furthering the understanding of beads and ornaments with a mission to encourage the scholarly study of beads and foster public appreciation of beads as objects of beauty, adornment, status symbols, and protective amulets in ancient, ethnic, and contemporary cultures.

The Society pursues its mission by:

- Disseminating knowledge through publications, conferences, and educational programs
- Sharing resources through an extensive research library

- Developing the Bead Museum as an international center for the collection, interpretation, and exhibition of beads and related ornaments

The focus is on what beads tell about people: the men and women who have worn them, made them, traded them, and treasured them; their aesthetic impulses and artistic abilities; their technological skills and trading patterns; their hopes and fears and social roles. The goal of the Museum is to enlighten the individual and enrich the community, for understanding different cultural heritages fosters understanding among people.

For more information: Bead Museum, Washington, D.C., The Jennifer Building, 400 Seventh St. NW, Ground Floor, Washington, D.C. 20004; (202) 624-4500; *www.beadmuseumdc.org.*

Fabric Workshop and Museum

The Fabric Workshop and Museum is the only nonprofit arts organization in the United States devoted to creating new work in fabric and other materials in collaboration with emerging and nationally and internationally recognized artists. Founded in 1977, the Fabric Workshop and Museum has developed from an ambitious experiment into a renowned institution with a widely recognized Artist-in-Residence program, an extensive permanent collection of new work created by artists at the Workshop, in-house and touring exhibitions, and comprehensive educational programming including lectures, tours, in-school presentations, and student apprenticeships.

For more information: Fabric Workshop and Museum, 1315 Cherry St., Philadelphia, PA 19107; (215) 568-1111; *www.fabricworkshopmuseum.org.*

National Basketry Organization

Promoting the art, skill, heritage and education of traditional and contemporary basketry, the National Basketry Organization is dedicated to basketry and everyone who appreciates this unique art form. Currently a volunteer run organization, membership includes a newsletter, biennial national conference, and special exhibitions with plans for a magazine in the future.

For more information: National Basketry Organization, 11730 Mt. Park Rd., Roswell, GA 30075; (770) 641-9208; *www.nationalbasketry.org.*

Hand Papermaking Inc.

Hand Papermaking Inc. is dedicated to the advancement of traditional and contemporary ideas in the art of hand papermaking through publications and other educational formats. Founded in 1986 with the first issue of *Hand Papermaking*, the organization's primary goal is to provide information to a diverse international audience of paper artists, mills, dealers, historians, conservators, and other aficionados of handmade paper.

Hand Papermaking offers:

- A summer and winter issue of the magazine *Hand Papermaking* with articles written by experts. Each magazine includes at least one unique sample of handmade paper.
- A quarterly newsletter with timely information and listings for national and international exhibitions, lectures, workshops, competitions, and tours. Short articles on Web sites, technical questions, contemporary research, and recent books supplement the listings.
- Limited-edition portfolios.
- A slide registry of two hundred artists, available in slide kits with audio tapes or as a video.
- An annual auction.

For more information: Hand Papermaking Inc., P.O. Box 77027, Washington, D.C. 20013-7027; (301) 220-2393; *www.handpapermaking.org*.

Handweavers Guild of America (HGA)

An organization dedicated to encouraging excellence, inspiring creativity, and preserving fiber traditions through education, HGA encompasses weavers, spinners, dyers, beadweavers, felters, basket makers, and other fiber artists who share a passion for fiber. The Guild was founded by a handful of weavers in 1969; within six months, they had a thousand members. In 2003, the American Craft Council gave the HGA its Award of Distinction.

Although you do not have the know how to weave, spin, or dye in order to become an HGA member, for those who are interested, there are programs available for novices and professionals to learn and further their skills, such as:

- The Learning Exchange (correspondence study groups where handweavers or handspinners swap swatches or skeins for critique from an experienced craftsperson)
- Teaching and Learning through Correspondence (a one-on-one study program tailored to meet students' needs)
- the Certificate of Excellence Program (a rigorous program for handweavers, handspinners, dyers, or basket makers, certifying proficiency in their chosen field)
- the Textile, Video, and Slide Library Rental program, as well as books available through the Laughlin Collection

Another benefit of membership is *Shuttle, Spindle and Dyepot*, a quarterly magazine offering articles on design, history, wearable art, shows, books, techniques, product and equipment reviews, and reports from museums, guilds, and members all over the world. Sample copies are available upon request.

In addition, a biennial conference called Convergence offers keynote speakers, workshops, seminars, exhibits, special events, and a vendors' hall of fiber and fiber-related equipment.

For more information contact: Handweavers Guild of America, 1255 Buford Highway, Suite 211, Suwanee, GA 30024; (678) 730-0010; *www.weavespindye.org*

Knitting Guild Association

The Knitting Guild Association offers:

- *Cast On* magazine, packed with innovative designs, technical articles, profiles of leading experts in the knitting industry, and news about and for knitters from around the world. Check out the "Guild News" section, filled with listings and information about knitting groups in almost every state, patterns, and new product and book reviews.
- Correspondence courses that include topics such as professional finishing, how to get started with machine knitting, and hand knitting basics, as well as master knitting programs.

For more information: Knitting Guild Association; *www.tkga.com*.

Studio Art Quilt Associates

Founded in 1989, Studio Art Quilts Associates seeks to:

- Establish a place for art quilts among contemporary fine art
- Document the historical significance of the art quilt movement
- Educate the public
- Serve as a forum for professional development of quilt artists, and
- Act as an information resource for curators, dealers, consultants, teachers, students, and collectors

Members receive a quarterly journal, on-site use of archive material, and notice of exhibitions, meetings, and symposia. They are eligible for juried exhibitions and can have their artwork represented in rotating portfolios and an artists' slide registry.

For more information: Studio Art Quilt Association, P.O. Box 2231, Little Rock, AK 72203-2231; (501) 490-4043; *www.saqa.org.*

Surface Design Association

Surface design is the color, patterning, structuring, and transformation of fabric, fiber, and other materials, and can include textile painting, printing, dyeing, quilting, weaving, stitching, embroidery, beading, knitting, and utilizing computer-assisted textiles. Since 1977, the Surface Design Association has promoted contemporary textiles from the perspectives of education, studio practices, technical development, marketing, and critical thinking.

Members include: independent artists, designers for industry, educators, scientists, manufacturing technicians, entrepreneurs, curators, gallery directors, and students.

Membership benefits include:

- *Surface Design Journal*
- *SDA Newsletter*
- National and regional conferences
- Networking opportunities
- Slide registry
- Publicity and a free classified ad

For more information: Surface Design Association, P.O. Box 360, Sebastopol, CA 95473-0360; (707) 829-3110; *www.surfacedesign.org.*

These organizations will help keep you informed, inspired, and on track as your career develops. If you can, pick out at least one organization to join. Every month when you receive your newsletter or magazine, you can read about what is happening in your field around the country, as well as find out about opportunities to promote your work that you may not have known about otherwise. If memberships are out of your reach right now, ask a family member or friend to give one to you as a gift.

The next chapter is devoted to profiles of craftspeople working in fiber. Read them and enjoy. If you have any questions for any of the people profiled and they have a Web site, feel free to learn more about them and even contact them with your questions and comments.

CHAPTER 9

Fiber Artists' Profiles

Basket Makers

Dorothy Gill Barnes, Studio Artist

Tom Grotta

With an eclectic background in sewing, pattern drafting, weaving, ceramics, and painting, Dorothy Gill Barnes's "baskets" didn't start to emerge until midlife. "I didn't start until I was forty-three years old," remembers Dorothy. "In the beginning, I had no success or recognition or way of knowing I was on the right track." Thirty years later, having been named a Fellow of the American Crafts Council and awarded the Ohio Governor's Award in the Arts, Dorothy has achieved a level of professional recognition that only a small number of craftspeople enjoy.

"My intent is to construct a vessel or related object using materials respectfully harvested from nature," says Dorothy. "The unique properties I find in bark, branches, roots, seaweed, and stones suggest a work process to me. I want this problem-solving to be evident in the finished piece. Some of these structures are basket-like." In recent years, her work with Habitat for Humanity has added the use of power tools to her repertoire, enabling her pieces to become larger and more complex.

As a child, Dorothy remembers playing with dolls, carving in snowdrifts, and making her own clothes. After attending Coe College in Iowa and the Minneapolis School of Art, Dorothy earned a bachelor's degree in Art Education from the University of Iowa, then taught for a year before returning to school for her master's degree in Art Education. After accepting another teaching position, she decided to make a change. "After graduate school, I taught home economics for a year and didn't like it," says Dorothy. "Then I went to Cranbrook Academy of Art for a summer. The experience at Cranbrook, studying with internationally known people, was quite an experience for me, and gave me the courage to leave my job and concentrate on my work."

During the next phase, Dorothy got married and taught part-time while she had babies—three boys and then a girl. She continued to take classes in ceramics and weaving, and loved it. "I looked after the kids and did some substitute teaching at the high school and preschool level," says Dorothy. "I did a little of this and that." Her career got a boost when she won an award at a show in 1978, the year her daughter was eight. "I had done some local shows and decided to enter a miniature textiles show in England," remembers Dorothy. "I was juried in and traveled there to see the exhibit. I felt recognized by this show and received a lot of encouragement. My own direction came through and things came together for me. I loved being outdoors, using the tools, sewing, and the structure of cloth. Mine was not a traditional way of doing things, but it felt right to me."

Along with more opportunities, Dorothy had her share of rejections. "Opportunities came my way and I had a few things published in *Fiberarts*," says Dorothy. "Jack Lenor Larson wanted some of my work to show at Elaine Benson Gallery in New York. But I had my share of rejections too. I applied to the National Endowment for the Arts and was rejected because I worked in several styles instead of a unified style. I felt that if I worked only one way it would take the fun out of it, so I never applied to the NEA again."

Although Dorothy has been widely recognized for her work and there have been lucrative years, her primary support has come from her musician husband. "Except for one major show and receiving awards," admits Dorothy, "my income has always come from other sources. I was an instructor at Capitol University for twelve years, until I retired in 1990. One of the benefits of doing my studio work (and something that has been more important to me than money) has been the opportunity to travel and do residencies, not only in the United States but also in places like New Zealand, United Kingdom, Australia, and Denmark."

World peace is an important part of Dorothy's life, and she has done her part to make a contribution here as well. "I am a member of a group called Weave a Real Piece, which encourages craftspeople in underdeveloped countries," says Dorothy. "I also have done work with Habitat for Humanity." Like any true volunteer, Dorothy says she gets more than she gives.

"I'm more into woodworking now," says Dorothy. "I'm playing in the studio again and it feels so good to just be doing something for myself, enjoying harvested material in my hands. At seventy-five, I don't like the idea of quitting at my age. I suggest aspiring craftspeople do the things they love to do, no matter what they are. You can still accomplish something, even if you start later in life. You don't have to quit when you get older. And remember, some things are not meant to be kept."

Theresa Secord, Basket Maker; Executive Director, Maine Indian Basketmakers Alliance

Trained as a geologist, Theresa Secord took a job in 1984 to manage a geological and mineral assessment program encompassing 200,000 acres of the Penobscot and Passamaquoddy trust lands in Maine. Little did she know that less than ten years later, she would become the founding director of the Maine Indian Basket-makers Alliance (MIBA), assisting tribal basket makers in the preservation and marketing of traditional ash and sweet grass baskets. "I worked for the tribe in 1984 as a geologist," says Theresa. "I decided to study the language with one of the elders, Madeline Tomer Shay, who was a basket maker and one of the last elders to have a natural command of the Penobscot language. She shared her love of making baskets with me. My great-grandmother, Philomene Nelson, had been a basket maker and I was given her tools. After five years of study, in her mid-seventies, Madeline agreed to take me on as an apprentice. Later on when she died, I was determined to keep traditional basketry alive. The traditional arts program coordinator from the Maine Arts Commission asked me to get involved, and the Maine Indian Basketmakers Alliance was formed." Recently, Theresa was awarded an international prize from the Women's World Summit Foundation for her work at MIBA in increasing creativity in rural communities and empowering rural women.

In addition to the Traditional Arts Apprenticeship Program sponsored by the Maine Arts Commission, the National Endowment for the Arts in Washington, D.C., has also helped to recognize the importance of the work by traditional basket makers. "Clara Keezer and Mary

Mitchell Gabriel have both been recognized by the NEA," says Theresa. "This has helped to validate tribal traditions."

Although Theresa grew up in southern Maine, her mother had been raised on Indian Island, and she maintained close links with the tribe throughout her childhood. After receiving her MS degree in Economic Geology from the University of Wisconsin, she returned to Maine to work on the assessment program at the reservation. "I value my education in science, but I realized that there are other things for me," says Theresa. "Even though I grew up off-reservation, our culture was always important to our family. So coming to work for the Alliance wasn't that much of a stretch."

The MIBA has enabled basket makers to work together not only to market their work, but also to increase their membership and help keep traditional skills and methods alive. "In the beginning, I was nearly the youngest and one of only a dozen people making baskets," remembers Theresa. "In 1992, we had 55 members. Since then, 18 have died, leaving 37 members, whose average age is 63 years old. By 2002, we had 115 members and the average age was 43 years old. Through MIBA, including the help and guidance from our Board of Directors—who are also Wabnaki basket makers—we have more than doubled our membership as a result of teaching, hosting gatherings, and training apprentices."

Another important benefit that the MIBA has been able to offer the community has been the opening of the Wabanaki Arts Center Gallery in Old Town, Maine. "We found that in order to save the traditions, we had to provide a year-round place to sell baskets," says Theresa. "Currently the Center carries the work of forty basket makers as well as another twenty artisans who make carvings, jewelry, and educational exhibits. Having a formal place to sell their work has enabled basket makers to increase their prices too." The Wabanaki Arts Center is part of a complex called Marsh Island Carry that was constructed with a cultural heritage theme to serve as a hub for the City of Old Town's downtown and riverfront development scheme.

MIBA also is the publisher of *A Wabanaki Guide to Maine*, a tourist guidebook made possible by grants, which has enabled MIBA to contribute to the heritage tourism industry in northern Maine. "We had the product and we had the history," says Theresa. "We knew we could draw people here and add to the heritage tourism theme. The guidebook has enabled us to do that."

Although Theresa primarily makes her living as the Executive Director of the MIBA rather than as a full-time basket maker, she enjoys having a job that gives her a way to practice her culture as a Penobscot.

"The Alliance is excited to have opened the gallery in Old Town," says Theresa. "It is located a stone's throw away from where all these baskets were originally sold. We have more than a hundred postcard images of Indian Island going back to the 1800 with basketmakers, including members of my family. Through the MIBA, we have been able to showcase our culture and communicate to the state and nation that we are still here. But the most important thing for me has been seeing younger basket makers come along and choose basket making as an alternative lifestyle. The MIBA is able to help them not only learn basket making skills, but also find outlets to sell their work. Basket making is important for the economic development of tribal people, who have a lot to offer. I suggest that craftspeople considering forming an organization work together as a group to accomplish their goals, have a place where people can come to buy your products, and team up with other organizations to receive assistance and funding. It must be remembered that it took us ten years to reach the point we are at today, and nine years before we could open up the gallery. Before that, we were teaching and building up the number of basket makers and it was just a dream. You need to take a long-term approach."

Bead Artists

Rev. Wendy Ellsworth, Studio Bead Artist

Rev. Wendy Ellsworth is on a journey, albeit a slow journey—one bead at a time. "I am captivated by the rhythm of stringing beads and the patience it requires to sit and bead for hours and hours," says Wendy. "It slows down the frenetic pace of my hurried life and helps me find perspective. It's also a way of assessing my inner self. Very few people in this day and age allow themselves the time to do that. We're always in a hurry." With beaded pieces that can take anywhere from 100 to 150 hours each to create, Wendy is certainly not in a hurry.

In 1970, Wendy moved to a log cabin in Aspen, Colorado, and began making leather bags decorated with beadwork. "Going back to the land looked pretty good to me," remembers Wendy. "After dealing with the insanity of campus life in the 1960s with the Vietnam War, I was on a spiritual journey. I wanted to figure out what was going on and what we are here to do, and stick my head in the clouds. My work progressed, and I sold it in stores in Aspen and did commission work. Then in 1981, I met David, and we decided to move East to settle in Quakertown, Pennsylvania, where we have been ever since."

Wendy and David (a woodturner profiled in the Wood section) both maintain studios where they do their own work and teach workshops. Being married to another craftsperson has been a positive force in Wendy's creative life. "David has been so encouraging to me throughout my career," says Wendy. "A big part of my success has resulted from being married to another artist. If I had to solely support myself through sales of my work, I would approach it differently. Instead of being primarily concerned about dollars and cents, I have had the creative license to make what I want to make."

With over thirty years of experience doing bead work, pieces in the collection of the American Craft Museum (now the American Museum of Art and Design), representation with galleries such as the del Mano Gallery in Los Angeles, and an impressive list of exhibitions and teaching gigs, Wendy currently makes about 50 percent of her living from selling her work and 50 percent from teaching. "I used to make more income from selling my work at shows and fairs," says Wendy, "but I found I didn't like doing the fairs. My work is incredibly labor-intensive and the venue wasn't always a good fit. Teaching is very important to me. I want to pass on knowledge to help broaden the field, not only to pass along techniques and a historical perspective to future makers, but to educate collectors as well."

One reason for concern has been the fact that recognition of beadwork as a serious creative profession has been slow in coming. "Many shows still do not have a bead category," says Wendy. "As a result, I can be included under the heading of any number of other media. For example, recently I have shown my work in the following categories at shows: contemporary baskets, fiber art, handweavers, jewelry, and glass! At present, the field is about ten years behind woodturning and contemporary baskets in terms of professional recognition." Wendy credits other artists like Joyce Scott with making the field of beading more professional. "I call Joyce the 'Queen Mother' of bead art," says Wendy. "I was at SOFA NY a couple years ago and a gallery director asked me if my work was Joyce Scott's. I said that although the work was mine, all of us in the field owe a huge debt of gratitude to Joyce for the work she has done, and I honor her for that."

After twenty years of making the leather bags decorated with beadwork, Wendy started making beaded sculptures and vessels. Wendy made her first beaded vessel in the shape of a simple cylindrical vase with a tiny ruffle stitched around the opening. "One day, as I was packing my work to send to a gallery, I started stacking the vessels one inside the other to save space," remembers Wendy. "A basket maker friend of mine picked up one of the stacks and exclaimed, 'Look at this—you've really got something here!' I looked into the box to see what she was talking about and saw all these ruffled lace edges bunched together. This was the inspirational breakthrough that led me to create the 'Sea Form' series I am working on now."

Wendy is happy with her lifestyle and range of interests. "There is a balance in my life right now," says Wendy. "I have a granddaughter, I was recently ordained an Interfaith Minister, I maintain both a flower and vegetable garden, and I look forward to our annual pilgrimage to the mountains of Colorado. I like the meditative aspect of playing with beads, with bits of color and light. For me, beadwork is spiritually based; it allows me to access my creative center. My current body of work is done freeform; thus, I am creating my own roadmaps as I bead along, not necessarily knowing the destination, but enjoying the journey. I will work on the 'Sea Form' series for a long time."

"I suggest aspiring craftspeople take classes from nationally recognized teachers and learn hands-on," says Wendy. "Buy magazines, books, and videos devoted to beads. Attend national events such as the Bead and Button Show and check out exhibitions such as the Bead Society Museum in Washington, D.C."

Book Artists

Amanda Barrow, Artist

Guenter Wehrmann

Although she is the recipient of an impressive list of grants from places such as the New England Foundation for the Arts, the Massachusetts Cultural Council, the St. Botolph Club Foundation, and a Fulbright Research Grant, when asked what she does, Amanda Barrow might easily reply, "I make stuff." "I always made stuff," remembers Amanda. "I have always been interested in having the correct visual alignment of the things in my house. For example, when I was a kid, my mother took two photographs of me. In the first, I was moving a flower to line up with the wallpaper. This was followed by another one of me standing there beaming with a look saying 'I did it!' It just looked better to me in the new spot and I felt compelled to get it right." With an impressive list of exhibitions and works in numerous collections such as the Museum of Modern Art in New York, Yale University in Connecticut, the Art Institute of Chicago, Rhode Island School of Design, and Massachusetts College of Art, Amanda certainly does make "stuff."

Amanda started out making jewelry in high school and was amazed when her teacher wanted to buy it. Not even thinking of an art career, she received her BA degree in 1982 from Colorado State University in Humanities (after switching majors from Geology). However, the switch to art didn't officially start until Amanda attended Summervail Workshops during the summer and met a lot of artists who left a lasting impression on her. "Nilda Getty and Richard DeVore were important influences in college," says Amanda, "and later, Richard Milhoan, the workshop's organizer, and Peter Dean, a painter, from the Summervail Workshops in Colorado."

After a move to Boston, another important shift in Amanda's thinking occurred in 1985 when she made a conscious decision to put her own work first. "I decided that if I was ever going to get anywhere with my art career, I had to stop working full-time and do only part-time work to pay my bills," says Amanda. "I left a full-time office job at the Program in Artisanry at Boston University and began making a concerted effort to do my own work." From that point forward, Amanda did part-time studio jobs to pay her rent while maintaining a studio. "I was a studio assistant to the printmaker/painter Michael Mazur. I did a little bit of everything, ranging from stretching canvas to taking inventory, buying materials, shipping, and all kinds of odd jobs. Although I wanted to just do my own art, I still had to work to pay my bills."

After moving to New York and working for a gallery there, Amanda received a Fulbright Research Grant to study in India. "The first time I went to India was in 1986," says Amanda. "I was raised in a religious setting and was always interested in different religions. I had a friend who had gone to India to study music, and I wanted to hike and walk in Nepal. I went for three weeks and was seduced by India. I made up my mind that if I went back, it would be to stay longer and get paid to do it. While I was working at a gallery in New York, one of the artists there got a Fulbright, and I thought I could get one too. I had a writer friend help me draft my application, I got it, and I lived there for a year." Several important series of work resulted from her experiences in India.

Amanda returned to Boston and worked for Michael Mazur as a studio assistant again. A few years later, she married a musician, bought a house, rented a new studio, and continued to work part-time work as a salesperson at the Society of Arts and Crafts. "My first studio was at 59 Amory Street in Jamaica Plain in 1986," says Amanda. " After living in India and New York City, I moved my studio back to 59 Amory Street in 1996 and stayed until recently. The building was bought a couple years ago, and I think it will eventually be sold as condos. The new owners raised the rent 25 percent and started not renewing leases, letting spaces go empty. Currently we are moving to New York so my husband can attend CUNY for an advanced degree. As a result of the experience of the studio being sold, I am now buying a condo to have more professional control over my space. Although the move will be good for my career, I had grown to love my community at the studio and feel bittersweet about the move. My studio situation was not always perfect, but when I'm ready to leave something, I tend to see it in a different way. I have a theory about how getting established and making a dent in a place and getting name recognition takes seven years. It will be good for my career to be in New York."

"I suggest interested craftspeople develop a tribe for support, whether it is family or friends or other artists," says Amanda. "There are some people I only see once a year, when they attend my open studio, who I consider supporters. Ask for what you need, whether it's more money or to make a trade of work or services. I always figure, What is the worst thing they can say but no? Keep doing your work. Even when you don't feel like it, just like doing exercise, you need to go to the place and paint a little bit. Find yourself in that space and the time will go by. If you don't go, your motivation will expire. Remember to play and don't be too serious. Listen to music, create a chunk of time, and make a few things. Then share it, get feedback, and take it from there. Invite people to your studio to get a critique, have something to eat, and ask what they think of the new work. Consider joining an artist studio building to keep from getting isolated. It is good to have a community and to go to a building where other people are working. You will have to seek it out, but it's worth it."

Jan Owen, Artist

"I always knew I would be an artist," says Jan Owen. "I majored in art in college and loved printmaking. In 1969, after graduation, I worked as a graphic designer. I loved moving the blocks of text. When I gave birth to twin girls, my life completely changed. I decided to teach myself calligraphy because it was something I could pick up and put down, do at my own pace, and work on right at my kitchen table. It met my needs as a mother perfectly. I would get up early and practice my ABC's. When the kids were three years old, they went to nursery school. I found doing the calligraphy to be not only be a way to survive the demands of having twins, but I also enjoyed doing a skill that required practice, like music."

Over thirty years later, Jan is an accomplished artist with an extensive list of exhibitions to her credit, numerous teaching experiences, awards, and work in the collections of places like the National Museum of Women in the Arts in Washington, D.C., the Houghton Library at Harvard University, and the Portland Museum of Art, Portland, Maine. She was also a string bassist with the Bangor Symphony Orchestra in Bangor, Maine, for twenty years.

"Everything I did or was involved in was good experience for what I do now, " says Jan. "For example, when the kids were in school, I volunteered at the school and did projects making books with the students, which helped me later on when I decided to do school residencies. My association with the Maine Crafts Association was very helpful and extraordinarily good. Not only was I a founding joiner, but I also enjoyed getting the newsletter, hearing about a lot of opportunities, and taking workshops. I was also a board member and I got to see how other artists did things. My involvement with MCA helped to raise my awareness of the possibilities."

After only one year of study, Jan started to teach through a local art space. "I started to teach at places like the local Y and the University of Maine," says Jan. "I didn't want to teach out of my home, as many other artists do. For me, I liked the validation of teaching at a place and having references." For over ten years, Jan has also been a visiting artist in public schools. "Sometimes I am hired for just one day, while other times I may have five days with a class of third-graders," says Jan. "I love going into the schools. I teach book arts and calligraphy and tie it in with computers. Many of the kids have no sense of history about where fonts come from, for example, and so I tell them the history of letter forms, write their name out in that style, and let them keep it. I think it is important for kids to see people do something and watch something be made."

When Jan's kids were in eighth grade, she had an illness that took several months to recover from, allowing her time to assess her direction. "I had an 'aha!' moment when I was sick," says Jan. "I had time to think and decided that my artwork was important to me. After that experience, I claimed mornings as mine, from about 7:00 A.M. to noon, and only did my commission work in the afternoon. Even if I just sat and looked at something, it was okay. It was my time, and I had realized what was important."

Another aspect of her career that has been helpful has been meeting with other artists on a regular basis. "I used to get together with four or five other artists in the Bangor area who did calligraphy," remembers Jan. "It basically functioned as a support group and really helped me keep going. I was also a member of another art group that met monthly at each other's homes, but it got too big and too social. In the long run, the smaller group worked better for me."

Although Jan does not earn a regular paycheck, she contributes to the family income. "My income is sporadic," says Jan. "My husband works and we have health insurance through him. But my income is important. Currently I make one-third to one-half from teaching and the rest through commissions and one-of-a-kind pieces. In the beginning, I would do things like calligraphy on wedding envelopes, which I called fun, dumb work. Now I sell more books and would like to do more gallery shows in the future. I suggest interested craftspeople develop a support system and learn to be patient with themselves, because it can be a long learning curve."

Doll Makers

Gail Wilson, Doll Maker

"I had an actual dream that I should make kits," says Gail Wilson. "Before my dream, whenever someone said 'kits,' I pictured sequins on

a Styrofoam ball. My response to requests to
make kits by museums and companies was to
feel insulted. Then, after I had the dream, I
began to market a simple kit to make a tiny
felt bear (which later grew into my Basic Bear
Series of bears, their clothes, their furniture,
and accessories). The kits dramatically
changed my business, which was a small one-
person operation carried out mostly on a trea-
dle sewing machine in a one-room house.
Suddenly the kits caught on, and the old
sewing table became a memory." Like many craftspeople, Gail was look-
ing for a product that would enable her to earn enough money and still
be made with a high level of craftsmanship and integrity. Her version
of "kits" was the answer. However, the kits are only part of what Gail
produces. She made her career and name with dolls that she makes and
sells as finished dolls.

A graduate of Skidmore College in Saratoga Springs, New York, she
chose that school specifically for its Studio Art department while still
being a good academic school. After graduation, she combined her love
for early American antiques and museum dolls with a strong business
sense, influenced by a grandmother who was a businessperson. "I didn't
call myself a doll maker until a couple years ago," admits Gail. "I
wanted to be a craftsperson, working in maybe jewelry or pottery, but I
ended up making dolls. I realized that not only was I a doll maker, but
that other people saw me as a doll maker." With numerous wholesale
accounts, sales through direct mail and her Web site, teaching all over
the world, and commissions, Gail has parlayed her love of dolls and
antiques into a very successful business.

Although Gail has always earned 100 percent of her living from
making her dolls, in the beginning, she lived a hand-to-mouth exis-
tence, until the kit idea caught on. "I started out at crafts fairs, doing
the ACC shows, Smithsonian, Philadelphia, and the annual League of
NH Craftsmen show at Mt. Sunapee. Meanwhile, the response to my kits
opened my eyes to a new direction," remembers Gail. "Then, because
many fairs and shows do not allow kits, I started doing major trade
shows, such as the New York Gift Show in the Crafts Section. I
approached the quilt market and got accounts established there. My
business has gone from mostly retail to wholesale and back again. However, wholesale has always been good for me in the museum market.

Museums often ask me to replicate dolls from their collections. I have found this challenging because working with a board committee is very different from working on my own." In addition to marketing the kits and producing replicas of dolls for museums, Gail still makes and sells her own dolls.

A commission from Disney came during the filming of "Tuck Everlasting," a story about the members of a colonial family who drink from a spring that causes them to live forever. But the Tuck family realizes that living forever is not as wonderful as it sounds. Everything grows old, even the mother's cherished doll. To show the passage of time, Disney commissioned three dolls: the first to appear slightly worn, the second to look as if it were a hundred years old, and the third to be used in a house fire from which the mother attempts to rescue the doll. "I felt like I was the real winner in this challenge," says Gail. "I have a new doll to market, I am able to say that I did a doll for Disney, and I learned many new techniques that I can now incorporate into other dolls and the classes I teach."

Although Gail started out working by herself, she now employs three part-time employees to keep production of her line of dolls, kits, and accessories moving. "I have three employees who work until 2:30 P.M.," says Gail. "I came up with this schedule because I need part of my day to myself to have some privacy. One employee also works at home, and another has worked for me for twenty years! I like the fact that I have been able to offer employment to women who otherwise might be without jobs. I couldn't do the amount and scope of work by myself. However, I insist that every single item go through my hands."

Teaching workshops in designing dolls has been an important part of the business to Gail. "Teaching is like an investment in yourself," says Gail. "Teaching is not that lucrative by itself, but it is part of a package of reaching out to others and gaining new customers and long-term students."

Her Web site has also been an important part of her business. "The Internet has been a successful medium for me," says Gail. "Doll makers are networkers, and there is a lot of traffic to my site. Collecting dolls is a growing thing right now."

These days Gail only does one retail crafts show, the League of NH Craftsmen show at Mt. Sunapee, as a way to stay in touch with the buying public (besides her Web site). She has also worked as a volunteer to help make the show what it is today, serving on the Fair Committee as well as assisting with the jury process.

"Yes, I feel successful," says Gail. "Not that I have done everything right. I still have days when I wish I could get more done. However, I wouldn't trade my life for anything. I was even given a very tempting offer a few years ago to sell my business for a good price and still be retained to run it for a lucrative salary, but I couldn't give up my freedom. There are days when I kick myself because I still don't have a retirement fund, but I know I will probably do what I do for a long time. It's a lifestyle. In the meantime, I also enjoy gardening, kayaking, our sailboat, and skiing. I live in a good town and enjoy being active in community events."

"I suggest interested craftspeople keep a mailing list and work the list and keep it current," says Gail. "Always send postcards to your list before a show and consider offering a special to people who come to the show with your postcard, like a discount, a prize, or even a reimbursement for admission costs."

Pat Castka, Doll Maker

"I have very devoted customers and I can see the looks on their faces and the tears in their eyes when they look at one of my dolls," says Pat Castka. "I even get little notes from people who have purchased one of my dolls. One woman wrote to say she had bought a little boy doll I had made and when she got it home, she realized that it looked like her father's picture from when he was a boy. When she looked at the tag, it even had the same first name as her father! She saw this coincidence as a message from her deceased father. That's what really does it for me, that's what really gives me to desire to keep going: the satisfaction that my customers have with my dolls." Pat, who makes handcrafted collectible animals, dolls, and other "dear companions" from vintage and aged fabrics, has been professionally creating for over twenty years. A juried member of the Pennsylvania Guild of Craftsmen, her work has appeared in magazines such as *Early American Life*, *Country Living*, *Country Home*, *Dollcrafter*, the *New York Times* and *Newsweek*. And she claims she hasn't been discovered yet.

Pat's love for making things started when she was a small child, watching her grandmother and aunts make things. "My father's family was very creative," remembers Pat. "My father could do anything and wouldn't rest until he did it well. My aunts were ace seamstresses and would make shirts, sports coats, and wedding and christening dresses. It fascinated me that you could make things, especially because my mother didn't do it. I remember sitting on a blanket and spending hours making doll clothes. All my friends made their own clothes too. I went on to make my own wedding dress and even my bathing suit!"

Although Pat tried all kinds of creative endeavors (including needlework, cross-stitch, rug hooking, and rug braiding), it wasn't until the Bicentennial that she came up with an idea to make a product to sell rather than for herself or as a gift. "I had always loved antiques and cloth dolls," says Pat. "While raising my family, I couldn't afford to buy things, so I tried to make them instead. I decided to make animals out of old quilts and asked people I knew for old quilts to cut up. One woman invited me over into her basement, where she did restoration work, and it was full of vintage fabrics. She supplied me with the fabrics, and the animals sold like hotcakes for about three years. When the interest in them died down, I started to make dolls. This same woman had a cloth doll collection that inspired me and enabled me to see how they were made. The dolls took right off and my business was born."

In the beginning, with children still at home and her husband working full-time, Pat only did local shows. A few years ago, her husband retired; Pat now travels all over the country marketing her work through both retail and wholesale shows. "I have found that magazine articles and other craftspeople telling me where to apply have helped me to find the best shows for my work," says Pat. "I have gotten into better and better shows, and recently did my first wholesale show. Although making my work has always been purely an emotional thing for me since I always let myself be inspired by the materials, I now have to fill orders. The orders are good on the one hand, but can be a thorn in my side because they limit what I can do to get ready for a retail show. I can sell whatever I make, but I can't always make enough. Each doll takes a lot of time." Pat has named her line of dolls "Old Friends"— handcrafted, one-of-a-kind dolls that are made without molds, utilizing vintage fabrics and trims that are appropriate to the era or size of the doll. Inspired by wonderful dolls she has researched in collections, museums, and books, they have a timeless charm and appeal.

Although Pat works long hours between shows by herself (usually from 7:00 A.M. to 11:00 P.M.), she is not looking for fame or even necessarily money. What Pat wants is for people to respect and love what she makes. "I only make things I would want to buy," says Pat. "I want the dolls to touch me. It is getting harder to achieve this level in my work. Although I am busier and know I could probably do anything else and be better off financially, my business does contribute to our family income. However, I have to admit that it is nuts to live this way!"

Doing the work part-time does not seem feasible to Pat. "I have wondered if I could just work part-time," says Pat. "But I have decided that I can't. So much needs to be invested to do this as a career. It takes a tremendous amount of time and requires total commitment in order to reach any level of achievement. Whether you work alone or have ten people working for you, you still have to generate the ideas and do it, keep doing it, and not give up on it. Developing a niche and style so that your work is recognized is important. I never really thought I had one, and was always critical of my own work. Sometimes it seems that as soon as I come up with something new, there is someone ready to copy it. Although I have tried to make things that are not easily copied, I also need to get my things to market quickly."

The market for selling dolls in high-end fairs is a competitive one. "It's one thing to be creative," says Pat, "but you also have to be savvy enough to make sure your name is out there. Everything I do somehow relates to self-promotion. Every move I make is noticed by someone, sometimes even more than the work itself. The market is getting more and more sophisticated and it is difficult to compete. There is not the time there used to be to learn as you go; you need to get to the top fast. If you are not an expert at running your business, you will get trampled. I haven't been discovered yet, so I'll have a long career, because the minute someone is in a magazine, she is either already yesterday's news or needs to come up with something new to top what she just did!"

"I suggest that interested craftspeople commit the time necessary to be successful," says Pat. "Develop a niche and recognizable style and try to design your work so that it can't be copied easily."

Quilt Makers

Elizabeth Busch, Artist

Although Elizabeth Busch graduated from the Rhode Island School of Design in 1964 with a degree in Painting, it wasn't until 1987 that she left her job in an architectural firm and started earning her living as a

studio artist full-time. "Every day I was working in architecture I was trying to figure out
how to not work in architecture," says Elizabeth. "However, all the years that I did that
type of work, I was learning something in
spite of myself. I wouldn't be doing the
commission work I do now without the background I learned on the job." Two opportunities presented themselves in 1987: a big quilt
commission in Austin, Texas, and acceptance
into a show called "10" at the Portland

Nancy Crasco

Museum of Art. "I couldn't physically have taken advantage of these
two opportunities if I was working full-time," remembers Elizabeth. "I
figured I could always get another job if I had to, but opportunities like
these might not present themselves again." She left her job and has
been self-supporting ever since.

Elizabeth makes her living from a combination of public art commissions, teaching, and art quilts. Her commission work is installed in
public buildings such as the Corbett Business Building at the University
of Maine and a library in West Linn, Oregon. She has also participated
in a national juried quilt show called Quilt National, where she won
Best of Show in 1989 and was later a juror. In 2003, she was awarded the
Quilts Japan Prize at Quilt National, and as such will travel to Japan as
an emissary for Art Quilts in 2004. Elizabeth is successful at obtaining
public art commissions while being a sought-after teacher and a talented artist.

For those thinking about leaving paid employment to work for
themselves, Elizabeth says that when the time is right to make a
change, you will know it. "When the opportunity came, I knew it. It
couldn't have happened earlier," says Elizabeth. "You may not know the
reason you are doing what you are doing, and it can be hard, but it's
clear to me now that there is a script written for my life, and I accept
that and I don't ask why. I try to stay in today as much as possible and
have no idea what lies ahead."

Elizabeth has found a balance in what she does between the commission work, teaching, and her art quilts. "I love it all," says Elizabeth.
"I don't want to give up any of it. My own work and teaching have
grown as I have, and it's very exciting. My quilts are starting to look like
the sculpture and vice versa. I didn't even realize that it was happening
until someone visiting my studio pointed it out to me." Every piece is

different, posing new challenges, new spaces, and new audiences. "For example, I just did an installation in a library in West Linn, Oregon, and I hadn't seen the space until I arrived to install the finished work," says Elizabeth. "I had made a model and designed and made the pieces, nobody had seen my work, and it knocked their socks off! I don't usually stay for the opening, and I am so concerned with the logistics of installation that I usually don't get any feedback while I'm there. My son was with me for this installation, and having him see the space before and after the installation gave him new insight into what I do every day and I take for granted. Getting the responses was wonderful."

A member of several organizations, such as the American Craft Council, the Surface Design Association, and Studio Art Quilt Association, Elizabeth joined for the connection to the outside world in terms of shows and exhibits, the announcements and opportunities, and the magazine and newsletter subscriptions.

When asked what she does for inspiration, Elizabeth said told me she spent the morning in her perennial garden and the afternoon at the ocean. "I've also gotten together with two other artists from Deer Isle, Maine, for support and critiques," says Elizabeth. "I am at a point now where I am ready to move back to Deer Isle and be a part of an active artists' community again. I want to be in a smaller house with a bigger studio, near the ocean and Haystack, and not have to drive an hour and a half each way to attend a lecture."

Elizabeth usually has several commissions lined up, and while making one is applying for others. She tries to keep her teaching commitments to five or six a year in order to have time to do some of her art quilts.

"I suggest that interested craftspeople get together with other artists to support and to critique each other's work," says Elizabeth. "Join organizations to help you keep connected with the art world, even if it just means getting a subscription to a magazine or newsletter."

Pamela Weeks Worthen, Executive Director, ABC Quilts

"There are no coincidences," says Pamela Weeks Worthen. "This was meant to be my job. I'm also studying to become a quilt appraiser through the American Quilter's Society. What other gigs could I get that would enable me to get paid to look at other people's quilts?" The Executive Director of ABC Quilts (which stands for "At-risk Babies Crib"

Quilts), Pam spends her days running the organization, and her free time making quilts, studying about quilts and their history, or buying quilts and restoring them. "I call myself the 'quilt rescue league,'" says Pam. "I will buy any old rag for $25!"

Her love for quilts grew out of having a grandmother who was a craftsperson, an aunt who made quilts, and her own involvement in 4-H as a kid. "I learned to sew in 4-H," remembers Pam. "I had a fabric stash and used my scraps to make quilts of my own designs based on tradition. But as an adult, it was during the Bicentennial that I really got involved in the craft of quilting. Although I started out making art quilts, currently I am more interested in historic quilts and restoration. I used to have a really strict attitude that quilts should be kept stored away, but now I think they should be used or displayed. All objects are trying to go back to their original form, dust, so you should enjoy them while you can."

Throughout her career, Pam has worked in a number of fields: selling real estate, coordinating events, and serving as the Acting Director at the League of NH Craftsmen. "I always worked," says Pam, "and I didn't do a lot of my own quilting when I was working, but I always had a project going. One of the great things about quilting is that it is portable—you can set up a sewing machine anywhere. I believe I am better qualified than most people for my present position, not only because of my background in quilt making, but also because of my experience in fundraising, public relations, and coordinating events. Having my greatest love, quilts, relate to my day job is great."

ABC Quilts began in 1988 after a woman named Ellen Ahlgren read an article by Elisabeth Kubler-Ross about the tragedy of HIV-infected babies, many of whom were orphaned or abandoned, destined to live their short lives in hospitals. Remembering how her grandchildren had loved the quilts she made for them, she wondered if quilters across the country would join her to provide a "blankie" for each of these babies. ABC Quilts, an all-volunteer grassroots project, was born.

Early on, a network of volunteer coordinators and distributors was established in every state. The project network was further strengthened with the establishment of zone coordinators in each of the four time zones. "So much is donated," says Pam. "The materials and labor, of course, but even our office space and utilities are free. The organization has a small budget and only two part-time paid employees: a director and an assistant."

Early publicity in *Quilters Newsletter Magazine*, an international publication, and an association with the National Association of Children's Hospitals and Related Institutions (NACHRI) helped jump-start the project. Quilts began pouring in from all over the world, and the institutions were lining up to receive them. Each quilt is valued at $30, a modest sum that includes two and a half yards of material and approximately two and a half hours of labor. The organization makes approximately four thousand quilts a year, or approximately $1 million worth of quilts. To date, that small, volunteer-run organization has delivered close to 500,000 quilts to babies born with AIDS or affected by the drug and alcohol abuse of their mothers while pregnant. Distribution has included the United States, Puerto Rico, Chile, Romania, and the former USSR, to hospitals, foster homes, daycare centers, and homes of children who are out-patients. ABC Quilts were also recently given to family members from the World Trade Center disaster as well as to the children of lost firefighters and policemen in the days after the attack.

One of the most visible ways that ABC Quilts makes quilts is at summer "quilt-a-thons" at craft and quilt festivals around the country. A state juried member of the League of NH Craftsmen, Pam saw the need for a hands-on activity at the annual fair. Setting up a tent, borrowing sewing machines, and obtaining donated materials has enabled ABC Quilts to harness volunteer time to create as many as four hundred quilts in little over a week at their annual quilt-a-thon. "We aren't babysitting when we have a quilt-a-thon at a fair like the League's," says Pam. "We provide sewing machines and eight-and-a-half-inch squares with instructions to work in a format of five rows of five squares. The result is a soft, cuddly, and serviceable baby quilt. I also have the opportunity to network with teachers as they come through and may talk with as many as one to three hundred in a week. Our mission statement talks about increasing awareness. We can't measure prevention, but we can measure awareness, and teachers are an important group to us."

In addition to making and distributing the quilts, ABC Quilts has addressed the interest in HIV/AIDS prevention by teaming up with teachers, Scout groups, 4-H Clubs, and Sunday school students who have experienced the joy of giving, along with learning about the disease and its prevention. Recently a program has been developed called "Tips for Teachers," which contains three chapters of lesson plans for elementary, middle, and high school teachers, as well as other chapters on making the ABC Quilts project part of a school or youth program. It is packaged with a book called *Kids Making Quilts for Kids* and two videos. Contact *info@abcquilts.org* for ordering information.

Pam is looking forward to making more of her own quilts again. "I would like to enter quilt competitions sponsored by the American Quilter's Society again," says Pam. "What started out as an interest in quilt appraisal is leading me to research quilt history and material culture. I have several signed quilts that I have tracked down the genealogy on and have learned about their unusual construction techniques. I want to know how something is made and find a historical reference. I am looking forward to attending the American Quilt Study Group's annual conference."

"I suggest interested craftspeople be true to their star," says Pam. "Don't worry about the money; you can get by. Stay committed and do what you can to live within reasonable means."

Wearables Artists

Ellen Spring, Fiber Artist

"The first time I brushed a stroke of dye across a shimmering field of white silk, I knew I was in the right place," says Ellen Spring. "During all the years I studied art, I never encountered surface design or fiber, yet somehow I was prepared to fall head over heels for silk painting when I came across it. I never wanted to be anything but an artist. I don't stop and make decisions. I'm not organized. I follow my heart. I have ended up where I think I should be." Ellen has followed her heart to a successful career that has included some of the country's top wholesale and retail shows and work shown in all three Vermont State Craft Galleries, numerous crafts galleries, and boutiques across the country, as well as at SOFA Chicago.

"At the Lake Placid School of Art, I studied printmaking," remembers Ellen. "After graduation, I took a summer job there as a teaching assistant in the Parsons program and worked with a silk painter. I began making hand-painted clothing, first for a local clothing company in Burlington, Vermont, painting their designs, and then for myself. Scarves were my bread-and-butter work in the beginning. My designs were reminiscent of drawings I remembered doing when I was a kid."

These days Ellen does two big shows a year, has accounts at galleries and boutiques that carry her work, exhibits at Frog Hollow outlets in Vermont, and does special orders. "I think it is about quality, not quantity, when it comes to selling my work through shops and galleries," says Ellen. "I like the people who run them and they like me. It's important to not only establish but also maintain those long-term connections."

Ellen has learned about running a business the hard way. "In the beginning, I had no idea how to make a living as an artist, and my bookkeeping system was a shoebox where I kept my receipts. When it was time to do my taxes, I would go through the box. I'm intelligent, but I am not a numbers person. So now I retain a bookkeeper who comes in once a month, and I use a computer program to keep track of my income and expenses. I've even graduated to using an accordion file instead of a box!"

Memberships in crafts organizations have served Ellen well in establishing her business. "I was a member of the ACC for fifteen years and found their services useful," says Ellen. "I am currently a member of the Vermont Craft Council and Vermont State Craft Center. I market my work through their Web sites and shops."

Ellen's definition of success has changed over the years. "I've come full-circle," says Ellen. "Before kids, I was at the peak of my success on paper. I did all the big shows, had people selling for me and working for me, and made lots of money. Then, after the birth of my second child, I hit a wall. There wasn't enough of me to spread around. I wasn't doing a good job as either a mother or an entrepreneur. Our society supports doing more and more, and I got on a roll. I wasn't following my heart when I was the most successful. One time I left my kids for a week to do the Baltimore show, and it was so painful that I decided I wasn't going to do that again. I'm glad I did it so I could understand what it was like, but I like what I am doing now better. I'm back to working by myself again, and I'm happier.

"Yes, I feel successful," says Ellen. "I have a much healthier success now than when I did all those shows. I would have said I was successful then too, but with reservations. My life is more balanced now as an artist and a mother. I recently turned forty and realized I'm mortal. If I'm lucky, I'm halfway. I plan to continue to market my work through retail shows, build up a larger wholesale base, and do sculptures. This feels right. I suggest that aspiring craftspeople start by doing what they love. Also, hire a bookkeeper, and most importantly, let your heart be your guide."

Marylou Ozbolt-Storer, Fiber Artist

Well known for her merino wool coats and jackets with their delightfully bold, color-infused appliqués, braids, buttons, and embellishments like stars, Marylou Ozbolt-Storer frequently receives fan mail. "Women send me letters all the time saying, 'You can't believe how happy this coat makes me feel,'" says Marylou. "One woman even said it changed her life. That's an awfully big statement, but I know what she means about beautiful garments making you feel special. I feel so blessed to have found something I love to do that also makes people happy." A self-taught weaver and sewer who studied pattern making, Marylou has not only successfully marketed her work through the best crafts, trade, and fashion shows in the country, but she has also received the NICHE Award for Wearable Art twice and been featured in magazines like *Ornament* and *Fiberarts*.

Growing up, Marylou was inspired by a family member who was an upholsterer and maker of drapes. She also gained invaluable skills working in her family's florist shop. "Not only was working with my family helpful in terms of business skills and developing a color sense," says Marylou, "but it also gave me an opportunity to interact with customers. I still find my customers not only fascinating, but also full of great tips. I think it is crazy not to acknowledge what customers want. As a result, we have just designed a new line of interior, lightweight office clothing in response to requests from customers who already own my coats but wanted to be able to wear my pieces inside."

In the mid-1970s, while studying pattern making and apparel and fabric design at the Northeast London School of Design, Marylou returned home to join her sister in opening a florist's shop. She arranged flowers by day and continued her weaving and apparel design after hours. A year later she decided to take her apparel to an industry trade mart in San Francisco. "I thought I knew what a line was, but I realize now I had no idea," says Marylou. "I didn't have a clue. My line was all over the place. I wove all the fabrics, made all the designs and patterns, and did all the sewing." Orders came in as a result of the show, and Marylou was officially in business.

Ten years later, she decided to quit weaving and devote herself to pattern making and the design of visual embellishments for which she is known today. "I haven't woven for fifteen years," says Marylou. "I use all commercial fabrics. I have watched wovens go from a heyday period, take a nosedive, and then come back again. I admire weavers who have hung in there through that cycle. For me, I was feeling I didn't have it in me to continue to do all the weaving. The first show I did with the purchased material was really scary. I hung my work on separate racks and watched as everyone went immediately to my new work. I learned that it is important at times to take a leap of faith. Whatever it is that is causing you to take a risk may become a strength in your work and will be accepted. Customers are always ready for new work."

Marylou sees her relationship with show promoters as mutually beneficial. "I always do a mailing before every show," says Marylou. "I think it is absolutely necessary. I feel an obligation to help the promoters keep people coming in to see that show, and to let my current customers know what to expect." Marylou currently does about ten shows a year, traveling about a week for each of them. One change in the show process that Marylou has noticed is in using computers to submit show applications. "Last year, the Smithsonian had us apply through the computer," says Marylou. "Many of us in the field are not as comfortable with computer-generated art as the new designers are. I'm concerned about what's going to happen as we try to learn how to compete with this new medium."

Success for Marylou has come in various forms, including recognition from her peers. "I just came back from a western show in Denver," says Marylou. "I found that there was mutual admiration between the people who are in manufacturing and someone like me, who only do high-end work by hand. They sell numbers, and I am happy to sell a few pieces. However, when they reviewed my work according to the industry standards that they live by, they seemed incredulous when they told me my work was perfect. I haven't compromised and it really meant something to me that my work was appreciated by them." Marylou is also an Advisory Member for the Fashion Design department at Seattle Central Community College as well as having served as a juror for craft shows such as ACC.

However, having other people in the industry eye her work with approval hasn't always been a good experience. "These are my original ideas and I don't knock off other people's work," says Marylou. "I recently had the experience of one of my buyers tipping me off that someone else had copied my ideas. Although she was kind enough to let me know, she also said she was going to buy her pieces from the company that was copying me because the look was the same, the pieces were cheaper, and she would make a greater profit. I located the exhibitors who were copying me two booths down from me at a show, got an attorney, and realized my goal to have them cease copying my work. It is very inexpensive to get work copyrighted, and it can even be done as a group of pieces for the year."

Marylou works out of a farmhouse on the same property as her home. "For the first fifteen years, I ran my business out of the house," says Marylou. "I slowly took on employees, and for many years, my bedroom was the only private room of the house. Then we built a new home. Now, our employees include an appliqué cutter, presser, patternmaker, sewer, and office person. I work alongside them, elbow-to-elbow. One floor is where we stock and design, another is an office, cut and pattern room."

A self-described workaholic, Marylou has learned not only how to delegate, but how to design a schedule to give herself much-needed breaks. "The employees work a Monday-through-Thursday schedule," says Marylou. "I work alone on Fridays in the office or doing design work. I'm also a really passionate gardener, mostly flowers, on our five-acre property. We just built a Victorian potting shed and have a bonsai, Japanese-type garden as well. On weekends, you can either find me out on our boat or in the garden."

"For craftspeople interested in starting their own business, I suggest they copyright all of their designs," says Marylou. "Don't be afraid to take a leap of faith when you have a good idea. If you just do what you are passionate about, the rest will fall into place."

Weavers

Patricia Palson, Handweaver
www.artfulgift.com

Eric Palson

"I love weaving," says Patricia Palson. "It's a passion or maybe even an addiction. I just know that I have to do it. When I think about myself on a deserted island, I think I'd be okay if I had a loom. I work from seven in the morning till nine or ten at night, with various breaks like walking with friends, meals, or going to the post office. But the fact of the matter is that I love my work. How many people can say that?" With numerous successes to her credit—such as being the winner of the Handweavers Guild of America Award, a two-time grant recipient from the Massachusetts Arts Lottery, and a three-time recipient of the Best of Show Award at the League of NH Craftsmen's annual crafts fair—Pat's love of her work certainly is evident to others.

Originally Pat studied to be an interior designer, and had a successful career that spanned fifteen years before she made the switch to weaving. "In college, I majored in interior design and took weaving as an elective," says Pat. "I loved it. I bought a table loom after graduation and made everyone Christmas scarves. Then I got a floor loom that made it faster, easier, and more enjoyable to weave. I started thinking about quitting my job. Three years later, when I was a project manager for an interior design firm, with lots of people on my team and making good money, I decided to quit. My friends thought I was out of my mind. I started out slowly, having children along the way. Five years later, I turned a profit and my business was launched."

In the beginning, balancing the responsibilities of being a mother of three children, Pat could only work for short periods of time. "My life only allowed me to weave for around five or ten minutes at a time," remembers Pat. "During nap time I might be able to work for twenty minutes! But weaving helped me to retain my sanity, and I made a lot of baby blankets." It was during this time that the integrity of her work led the Schacht Spindle Company to choose her to endorse their looms in weaving magazines.

These days Pat works by herself at home, with the help of one sewer who can do work from a sketch and a prototype. Her work has evolved from scarves to contemporary handwoven clothing based on historic textiles and incorporating silk, merino wool, chenille, and rayon. "Originally, I was interested in eighteenth- and nineteenth-century coverlets woven in overshot patterns," says Pat. "I was able to research the patterns by painstakingly counting the threads by hand on coverlets tucked away in museum collections, with the aid of two Massachusetts Arts Council grants. After I made coverlets for a few years, I added shawls to my repertoire, thinking my customers might enjoy wearable art. They loved them. Then my work evolved into the one-of-a-kind coats and jackets I market today."

Pat travels to five or six shows a year, supplying additional items to existing customers. "I do mostly retail fairs to sell my work," says Pat.

"I started out doing consignment in shops, then graduated to retail shows, and now do a combination of retail and wholesale shows. I love selling my work. The fairs provide a chance to see new things as well as to see my own garments come alive as people try them on in my booth. The League fair is phenomenal. The same people come every year, primed to buy while they are on vacation. Maybe they saw something last year and are ready to get it this year. It's also a great chance for me to be with other craftspeople and do some design work during the slow periods. I leave not only with sales, but also with a notebook full of ideas for next year." Since 1993, Pat has participated in shows such as: ACC/Baltimore and West Springfield, Crafts at the Castle, Paradise City Festival, Danforth Museum, Guilford, and of course, the League of NH Craftsmen's Fair at Mt. Sunapee. "I suggest that aspiring craftspeople simply get a great set of slides," says Pat.

To stay inspired, Pat does a lot of reading and is involved in a weavers' support group. "I subscribe to magazines like *Handwoven, The Crafts Report, Ornament,* and various fashion magazines," says Pat. "I network through organizations and formed a support group that meets two times a month. We meet at each other's homes and review samples in a non-competitive way. It's a double reward for me."

Pat plans to keep on doing what she is doing for the rest of her life. "I still love it so," says Pat. "Retirement is not even on my radar. I hope to do more travel as time goes by, and more research. I love the independence of my life, making my own schedule and being my own boss. It's a dream life."

Yarn Artists

Peter Hagerty, Peace Fleece
www.peacefleece.com

"If I hadn't had kids, I wouldn't have started Peace Fleece," says Peter Hagerty. "Kids change everything, and I don't want anything to happen to them. I served in Vietnam and when Reagan was threatening war with Russia, I had to do something to help diffuse the threat of nuclear war. So, in 1985, I went to Russia to buy wool and see if we could establish a relationship there, because I thought if we could call and talk to someone over there about the state of affairs, it would help. I visited a man who exported wool, who looked over my request and told me it was too small an order to be worth his while, because of all the paperwork involved. I had the feeling that if we weren't able to make a deal that day, the relationship between the two countries was doomed. I said to him that I had a ten-year-old daughter and that I believed if we didn't do something to make a difference, the likelihood of her growing up and having a family would be greatly diminished. It turned out that he had a daughter too, and my plea touched him. He agreed to process my order."

The challenge of importing the first shipment of wool did not stop there. "In the spring of 1986, when the shipment arrived, the longshoremen refused to unload it because it was from a communist country," says Peter. "We held a press conference, and the wool was unloaded. It was normal wool, but it was the first time it had been imported. Our story was picked up on the AP wire, and all of a sudden we were in *People* magazine, on the *Today Show*, and being talked about by newscaster Walter Cronkite. As a result, we were the poster children of the late 1980s. The basic line was, If this couple from Maine can make a deal with Russia, why can't the government?"

Peace Fleece is not a typical yarn company. By working with people who tend livestock every day, Peter and his wife, Marty Tracy, hope to find a common ground between people in different cultures that leads to mutual understanding and economic independence for all people.

In 1973, Peter moved to Maine to work as a logger and met Marty, a potter. "In the beginning, we had the farm and we had our kids," says Peter. "It was hard to make a living just by producing wool ourselves, and we were looking for a niche. Our wool was scratchy and coarse. We went to merino wool because it is very fine and soft and comes from semi-arid places around the world. We blended the wools from different places to produce a wool that is soft, looked pretty, and held up over time." Peace Fleece has worked with shepherds from Russia, Kygyzia, Israel, and the West Bank, as well as Montana, Ohio, Texas, and Maine, to produce and market knitting yarns as well as knitting and felting accessories.

Currently, Peace Fleece has about 400 stores and 8,000 customers in the United States, and their products are reaching a diverse market. "It is so important today to use our hands, feel proud of what we do, pass on these skills and traditions, and gain a sense of spirituality through making something," says Peter. "It is not the same as a store experience. I know two thousand of our customers by name, and they can be really helpful. A couple of them actually helped us out of a jam when they were in Russia, and loved it. Our typical customers fall into three categories: college students who are in a knitting group of maybe ten women, grandmothers who knit for everyone in their family, and finally, what I call high-intensity CEO-type women who bring their knitting to board meetings, and find that knitting brings a greater sense of order to their lives."

Operated out of a barn on a sheep farm in Maine, Peace Fleece employs two additional people to help run the business. "Things slow down for us during the summer months," says Peter. "This is actually a good thing, because not only do we have time to do farming, but I don't think we could operate at the same intensity all year long as we do between September and April. We also have unbelievable support from the other companies that we work with, such as Harrisville Designs in New Hampshire, who do our spinning. Without the help of other people, we wouldn't be able to do it."

A few years ago, Peace Fleece made the decision to go from a paper catalog to a Web site. "About 90 percent of our orders come through the Internet now," says Peter. "Although we lost some people with the change, the mailing, printing, and labor to produce the paper catalog were very expensive. A lot of catalogs were not getting delivered. The Web site offers enormous flexibility and our base of customers has grown very quickly. However, having said all that, we are putting out a paper catalog again this fall."

Current events affect Peace Fleece in both positive and negative ways. "Our sales tend to follow current events," says Peter. "We had enough product to fill orders until the Russian revolution in 1991. Things dropped off, and so did sales. That was fine, because it was happening for a good reason. Then we started another project in the Middle East, getting shepherds from Palestine and Israel to work together. Both villages worked together until 1997, when the shepherds from Palestine refused to work with the shepherds from Israel. At this point, we are just working with Russia again, and it's a full plate."

Peace Fleece has also teamed up with other organizations to make a difference by using knitting as a way to welcome refugee families to the United States. "There were between seven and ten thousand Kosovar refugees who made their way to Fort Dix in New Jersey. We were asked by the International Rescue Committee to help develop a very unique component of the resettlement process," says Peter. "We donated knitting yarn and knitting needles to help people begin the healing process. We also called for volunteers from the greater New York and New Jersey area to go to Fort Dix and work with the refugees. Projects focused on making clothing and simple furnishings like prayer rugs or wall hangings. We had seen knitting and healing go side by side during the Rainbow Socks Project in Bosnia and Croatia, and we hoped it would be repeated at Fort Dix. A thousand pounds of yarn were donated by Bartlett Yarns, Peace Fleece, Jagger Bros., Harrisville, and Green Mountain.

"We are struggling every day to make sense of things," says Peter. "Working with the Russians is not different from working with our own family. What we do is not extraordinary. Although I do feel successful, every time I go overseas and return, I feel like I know less. As I get older, I realize there is no answer. I didn't figure out what I wanted to do until I was forty-two years old. These days, instead of asking people what they do, I ask them what they are passionate about, what they would love to be doing. We all need to have the courage to examine what we are doing, to not listen to the voices that tell us what we ought to be doing, and then to do something else to make a difference."

Katharine Cobey, Knitting Artist
www.katharinecobey.com

Katharine Cobey already had an established literary career—a BA degree in Language and Literature from Bennington College, a published book of poetry called *The Alice Poems*, and numerous pieces in anthologies and magazines in England and the United States—when health concerns brought knitting back to the forefront of her life. "I learned to knit at age eleven from a neighbor who had no daughters," remembers Katharine. "I tried to knit from patterns in *Vogue* during college, but it wasn't intellectually acceptable then. After I had children, I took up knitting again, but in those days I saw myself as a poet, not an artist. Then I hurt my back and I couldn't walk well. I had to do something besides reading and writing, so I started to knit again. Knitting was my therapy." Twenty-five years later, with numerous exhibitions and juried shows to her credit; articles in *Surface Design* and *Spin Off*; and a profile in *Fiberarts*; and workshops, talks, and demonstrations around the country, Katharine is one of the top artists in the country who use knitting as their medium. Katharine is also a board member of Maine Fiberarts, an organization devoted to promoting the enjoyment and quality of Maine fiber work through education, display, celebrations, and networking.

A change in direction came on a trip to Pennsylvania, when Katharine found some handspun wool. "I found some beautiful, bright red handspun wool and asked who made it," says Katharine. "I called and met Peg Fike, who lived on a farm in West Virginia. She had taught herself to spin from a book. I bought her yarn and began making things with it. Then she taught me to spin. Before Peg taught me to spin, I was sure that it was too hard, that it was necessary to look exactly like a fairy godmother to qualify, and that spinning would take too much time away from knitting. I was forty-six. Now that I am in my sixties, I know that my students learn the basics of spinning in three lessons, I still look like myself, and spinning my own yarns has liberated my knitting. So much is luck. Finding Peg's yarn and then meeting Peg was certainly lucky for me."

Katharine applied and was accepted into a prestigious artist studio building in Alexandria, Virginia. "I got into the Torpedo Factory and found out there was a fiber group," says Katharine. "In that group, I discovered that my stuff was not pretty enough. I found myself walking around the factory, wondering what I was doing there and how I fit in, when I chanced upon a sculptor's studio. I remember thinking, *He is making shapes and so am I. It's okay.* I decided to work in a way that mattered to me. Don't get me wrong; I find nothing the matter with lovingly made clothing. Hand knitters have all this creativity, but nobody wants to pay for it. Great traditional knitting has stayed behind other fiber arts."

Katharine started experimenting to figure things out for herself. "I started working with the handspun yarn and decided I would just do it," says Katharine. "Part of me loves taking risks and being out on a limb. I may fall or fly, maybe flap my wings like mad, but mostly I fly. Occasionally I plummet. Sometimes I make clothing, sometimes art, and sometimes art that is clothing, playing back and forth over the line. I find it absolutely fascinating to be on the razor's edge between craft and art." Katharine makes custom clothing, sweaters, shawls, vests, and coats. Each piece is hand-knit and no two are the same. "I believe that clothing should comfort the wearer and delight the eye," says Katharine. "It should also be simple and graceful, and enhance movement. Quality materials and loving workmanship reflect my commitment to the meaning and importance of daily life."

In addition to selling her knit clothing, Katharine makes her living from teaching knitting and spinning workshops. "My field is a small pond, and I'm pretty well known for what I do," says Katharine. "There are two levels to my work. Although I can sell my coats for thousands of dollars, I can only sell a dozen or so a year, and would not be able to make enough money to eat if I had to support myself with just that. Yet I am at the top of my field. When people ask me if they can do this as a profession, I say 'yes,' but you have to figure out a way to eat. Maybe some people could do it with the aid of a knitting machine. A catalog company approached me and I did the math and found that even with hiring people, it would be impossible to make a profit. I buy back my time to work in the studio by teaching and lecturing." Katharine not only runs workshops out of her studio in Maine, but she also travels around the country to places like Penland School of Crafts and Haystack Mountain School of Crafts. She teaches knitting design, focusing on construction techniques. "I do not need to teach creativity, but I hope to encourage it," says Katharine. "I am determined to make knitting understandable to free students from following pages of knitting instructions. I work with knitters on how they can make their own plans, and then I teach them techniques with an eye to how they fit their plans. I want knitters to take what they knit into their own hands."

Katharine also makes sculptural work. "It took me six years to knit and do the carving for a large-scale boat sculpture," says Katharine. "I am so glad I did it. It is important for me to be able to look at that piece of work and say I did it. Even if I can't make money purely on my art, I have made the boat. I decided to make what I want to make and not worry about selling it."

PART FOUR

Glass

CHAPTER 10

Facts, Educational Opportunities, and Organizations for Glass Artists

The field of glass is rapidly growing, with new museums opening and lots of interest from the buying public. The glass artists profiled in this section produce their work for galleries, retail, and wholesale customers, as well as private commissions. Many of them have worked through several stages in their crafts careers, or have combined different interests to make a living or to live in a way that suits them best. This section also provides information about studio glass programs and organizations, and details about running a glass business to help you make informed decisions.

The studio glass field as we know it today is relatively new, with interest stemming from the early 1960s, when Harvey Littleton conducted his infamous workshop at the Toledo Museum of Art after researching small glass shops in Europe. Although each craftsperson has chosen a different path to make a living, several of the profiles read like a *Who's Who* in studio glass history, such as those of Harvey Littleton, Josh Simpson, and Richard Marquis.

Insight Survey Statistics on Glass Artists

Today's craftspeople have lots of options when it comes to working in studio glass. Here are the results of the Insight Survey on Glass Artists from the June 2003 issue of *The Crafts Report*, based on twenty-four respondents, with average gross sales per artist of $107,585.

Percent of Gross Sales from Various Sources

- 16% retail shows
- 15% wholesale shows
- 10% sell directly to galleries
- 37% own gallery/studio
- 5% consign to galleries
- 6% Internet
- 11% other

Amount Spent on Materials

- 0% less than $1000
- 52% $1,000 to $10,000
- 17% $11,000 to $20,000
- 17% $21,000 to $50,000
- 13% $50,000+

Number of People Working in Studio

- 34% work alone
- 38% 1 to 2 people
- 13% 3 to 5 people
- 8% 6 to 10 people
- 4% 11 or more

Time Selling Crafts

- 4% less than 1 year
- 50% 1 to 5 years
- 8% 6 to 10 years
- 13% 11 to 15 years
- 25% more than 15 years

Sixty-three percent owned a Web site, 50 percent sell their work through an online gallery or crafts site other than their own, and 58 percent say their crafts business is the only source of income in their household.

Educational Opportunities for Glass Artists

Pilchuck Glass School

Founded in 1971 by glass artist Dale Chihuly, with the support of patrons Anne and John Hauberg, Pilchuck Glass School has become the largest, most comprehensive educational center in the world for artists working in glass. Pilchuck is dedicated to advancing artistic expression in glass and furthering the awareness and understanding of glass as a visual arts medium.

Located on a fifty-four-acre wooded campus north of Seattle, Washington, the remoteness of the setting allows artists to focus on their work without distractions in facilities that include: two hot glass shops, a studio building and kiln shop, a coldworking studio, a flat shop for torch work, a wood and metal shop, and a glass plate printmaking studio. Supplementing the studio experience are a gallery that showcases work created by resident artists and a library that holds an outstanding collection of books, periodicals, catalogs, files, and videotapes for research and study. Residential facilities vary in type and allow the participants to live and work together in community.

Every year, from May through August, Pilchuck offers twenty-five intensive residential sessions. Five classes run concurrently through each of the two-and-a-half-week-long sessions, with classes limited to ten students. Areas of study include: glassblowing, casting, fusing, neon, stained glass, painted glass, flameworking, mixed media sculpture, and engraving. Courses emphasize experimentation and teamwork while fostering individual initiative and expression. Slide shows, discussions, and demonstrations occur daily and provide opportunities for dialogue and exchange across disciplines.

The educational experience is not about producing a body of work, attaining production training, or amassing technical information; it is about developing a personal voice. Artists share their thoughts and feelings, discoveries and experiences, successes and failures in ways that challenge participants. While the end result may include a notebook of sketches, a mind full of ideas, and a handful of experimental artifacts, many times these may be the seeds of a learning experience to come later on.

Classes range from beginners to advanced students. Although admission can be competitive, applicants for courses are selected through a lottery to ensure fairness. Pilchuck is not open to the public on a daily basis, but does host an annual Open House and Members' Day to respond to public interest. The Annual Auction features hundreds of works by leading glass artists and newcomers, with sales benefiting the school.

In addition to attending a course during a summer session, there are several types of residency programs available, including:

- *The Artist-in-Residence program:* Two professional-level visiting artists who work in media other than glass live and work at the school during each of five summer sessions
- *The Emerging Artist-in-Residence program:* For artists in the early stages of their careers who need financial support to work on special projects or develop their work
- *The Professional Artist-in-Residence program:* Fall and winter residencies for experienced glass artists to work on creative projects
- *The John H. Hauberg Fellowship Program:* For outstanding artists in any medium to work collaboratively to conduct new research
- *The Visiting Artist program:* Short-term visits by visual and performing artists, designers, technical experts, critics, and curators

For more information: Pilchuck Glass School, 430 Yale Ave. North, Seattle, WA 98109; (206) 621-8422; *www.pilchuck.com.*

Organizations for Glass Artists

Glass Art Society (GAS)

Founded in 1971, the Glass Art Society is an international organization whose purpose is to encourage excellence, advance education, promote the development of the glass arts, support the worldwide community of artists working in glass, and stimulate communication to create a greater public awareness and appreciation of glass. Currently, with membership of over three thousand glass enthusiasts from more than forty-five countries, membership is open to anyone interested in glass art, including artists, students, educators, collectors, gallery and museum personnel, writers, and critics.

The Glass Art Society offers members:

- An annual conference.
- *Glass Art Society Journal:* This journal documents the lectures, presentations, and proceedings of the conference and has become the

record showing the progress and evolution of artists who have created the contemporary glass movement.

- *Resource Guide*: A reference book that showcases schools, galleries, and glass products.
- *Membership and Education Roster*: The roster provides members' names and contact information, as well as listings of educational opportunities.
- Links to their Web site and access to database information.
- *GASNews*: Published bi-monthly, this newsletter provides an ongoing exchange of ideas and information for regular communication between glass artists around the world. In addition to listings of classes, events, and other opportunities, the newsletter profiles members and student members, and highlights countries and events outside the United States.
- Web site: Lists resources including appraisers, suppliers, and artists who do commission work.

For more information: The Glass Art Society, 1305 Fourth Ave., Suite 711, Seattle, WA 98101; (206) 382-1305; *www.glassart.org*

The Art Alliance for Contemporary Glass

This organization is designed to further the development and appreciation of art made from glassworks, and to inform collectors, critics, and curators by supporting museum exhibitions, university glass departments, specialized teaching programs, regional collectors groups, visits to private collections, and public seminars.

For more information: The Art Alliance for Contemporary Glass, Box 7022, Evanston, IL 60201; (847) 869-2018; *www.contempglass.org.*

UrbanGlass

Founded in 1977 as an international center for the creation and appreciation of new art made from glass (including design, crafts, and architecture), UrbanGlass was the first artist-access glass center in the world, and is now the largest. UrbanGlass is also the publisher of *Glass Quarterly*, a magazine that provides a critical voice for glass art within the contemporary art world.

For more information: UrbanGlass, 647 Fulton St., Brooklyn, NY 11217; (718) 625-3685; *www.urbanglass.com.*

Stained Glass Association of America

Founded in 1903, the Stained Glass Association of America seeks to promote the development and advancement of the stained and decorative art glass crafts.

There are three levels of membership:

- *Accredited:* Accredited membership is available in three classes: Studio, Artist, and Supplier. A minimum of four years as a licensed business, references, and a portfolio are required for review twice a year.
- *Active:* Active membership is open to anyone involved in the craft for a minimum of two years. References are not required, and active members may join at any time during the year.
- *Affiliate:* Affiliate memberships are open to anyone interested in enriching their involvement in stained glass. Student Affiliates are available to anyone engaged in a course of study offered by a secondary school, college, or university.

Membership benefits include: a subscription to *Stained Glass Quarterly*; an annual membership directory; and the *Kaleidoscope* newsletter with industry news, member news, trade show listings, conferences, and meeting opportunities. Discounts are given to members for the Annual Summer Conference, the *SGAA Reference and Technical Manual*, and the SGAA Lead Safety Video. Services include use of the Audiovisual Library, Awards of Excellence, juried competitions, restoration standards and guidelines, and networking.

For more information: Stained Glass Association of America, 10009 East 62nd St., Raytown, MO 64133; (800) 888-7422; *www.stainedglass.org.*

Stained Glass Artists

This is a Web site that represents a collective of professional glass artists located throughout North America, who work with commission clients in their communities as well as the Web community. Members work in hot glass, leaded and stained glass panels, and gift items.

For more information: *www.stainedglassartists.com.*

These organizations will help keep you informed, inspired, and on track as your career develops. If you can, pick out at least one organization to join. Every month when you receive your newsletter or magazine, you can read about what is happening in your field around the country, as well as find out about opportunities to promote your work that you may not know about otherwise. If memberships are out of your reach right now, ask a family member or friend to give one to you as a gift.

The next chapter is devoted to profiles of craftspeople working in glass. Read them and enjoy. If you have any questions for any of the people profiled and they have a Web site, feel free to learn more about them and even contact them with your questions and comments.

CHAPTER 11

Glass Artists' Profiles

Blown Glass Artists

Harvey Littleton, Glassblower

Known as the "father of studio glass," Harvey Littleton is a well-known figure in the studio glass movement. Born in 1922, the son of Jesse Littleton, Director of Research at Corning Glassworks in Corning, New York, and the first Ph.D. physicist in the glass industry, he grew up in the world of glassmaking, in terms of its exploration as well as its artistic development. With a BA in Design from the University of Michigan and an MFA in Sculpture from Cranbrook Academy of Art, Harvey was haunted by the idea of how to make glass workable as a medium for the individual artists outside of industrial production.

Harvey's career began in ceramics, a medium that was better suited to studio production than the large-scale industrial environment required for glassmaking at that time. By the 1950s, he was a nationally recognized ceramicist, a faculty member at the University of Wisconsin, and a trustee of the American Craft Council. While on sabbatical studying pottery in Europe, he visited several small glass operations in Italy that convinced him that a compact glass studio for artists was possible. His obsession with glass led him to build his first glass studio on his farm, organize a pivotal hot glass workshop on the grounds of the Toledo Museum of Art, and travel back to Europe to seek out schools that taught glass as an art form. Littleton's ideas began to take life as his ceramics students explored the new medium, and hot glass took root in the art program at the University of Madison under his direction. In 1962, after developing the technique that revolutionized the medium by taking glass out of the factory and into the studio with Dominick Labino, Director of Research for Johns-Manville Glass Fibers Division, he left the world of ceramics. He established the Hot Glass program at the University of Wisconsin, producing the first generation of studio glass artists. The medium of glass would never be the same.

Harvey Littleton reinvented himself on a regular basis. Beginning with a career as a potter in the 1950s, a teacher from the 1950s to 1970s, and founder of the studio glass movement in the 1960s, he left teaching in 1976 to devote his energies to creating a body of work in glass. The latest episode has been as a printmaker and collector of glass. He has assembled a notable collection of approximately one thousand pieces of historical and modern glass, and hasn't made glass since 1991. "I stopped at age seventy," says Harvey. "My furnace had been on twenty-four hours a day for about eight years, a tear-down for repairs was due, and my health was bad." However, since his back surgery was completed, Harvey admits that it has been a little tempting to pick up the blowpipe.

When asked if the development of studio glassmaking has met his expectations, Harvey replies, "Yes, beyond my wildest dreams, although it still has a ways to go. For example, there is only one Dale Chihuly and there is room for lots more. Dale's success is everybody's, and we glory in it." Dale Chihuly reflects his success back onto Harvey Littleton, saying, "Without a doubt, Harvey Littleton was the force behind the studio glass movement, and without him, my career wouldn't exist. He pulled in talented students and visiting artists and was a big thinker. If he wanted a special piece of equipment, he would spend the money. He taught us to think big instead of small, all the while encouraging us to be unique."

Studio glass, unified by its material rather than a specific technique, enables glass artists to create without the pressure to conform to a specific style. Glass artists' current successes in making a living can be traced back to Harvey, who said, "Glass is expensive to make and should be expensive to buy." Harvey led the way with early successes by having a one-person show at the Art Institute of Chicago in 1963. The Museum of Modern Art in New York began acquiring his work for its collection in 1964. He was on his way.

Harvey Littleton's students from the program at the University of Wisconsin gave glass as a medium exposure in many ways, including: the eventual organization of the Glass Art Society through Fritz Dreisbach, the founding of Pilchuck Glass Center and the glass program at

Rhode Island School of Design through Dale Chihuly, the initiation of a glass program at San Jose State by Robert Fritz, and Marvin Lipofsky, who not only headed up the influential glass program at California College of Arts and Crafts, but was also the first recipient of an MFA degree in Studio Glass from University of Wisconsin under Harvey Littleton.

Many honors have been bestowed on Harvey Littleton, including the Gold Medal from the American Craft Council and the Lifetime Achievement Award from the Glass Art Society. Exhibitions of his work have been mounted in prestigious galleries and museums around the world, and his work is found in collections such as the Smithsonian Institution, the American Craft Museum, and the Mint Museum of Craft + Design.

"I have been asked by a lot of people what I think is going to happen in glass," says Harvey. "'Haven't people pretty much done everything?' 'Won't it sort of fade out?' And I tell them that as long as children are born, each one will have unique experiences from the moment of birth that are waiting to contribute to what they will become. Some of them will be influenced by glass as a material, and they will bring that unique experience to glass. What that glass will be, who knows? We don't care. We just know that they will have the opportunity to go on with it. The world is their oyster, you know. We've broken the trail for a lot of them.

"You have to ask your market to pay you," says Harvey. "Your gallery system has to encourage this. If you get a little more for your work, you can take that economic freedom to take chances and go beyond the ordinary. You can't be so concerned about selling something anymore than you can let your gallery tell you, 'Oh, we love your teapots, we sell them all, why do you do this other stuff?' We need teapots and that is good. But if you break a teapot you have had for fifteen years and you go back to the same artist and say, 'I want that teapot,' he can't just go back to his calendar and flip the pages back and make that teapot again. That's a denial of his value as an individual. It's a denial of his growth. It's a denial of him as a person. The proper function of a collector is to allow the maker to grow by making a contribution to his work so that when you buy another one, it will be better. Otherwise, you are just squeezing the person down to nothing."

Dante Marioni, Glass Artist
www.dantemarioni.com

Russell Johnson

Unlike many artists working today, Dante Marioni is not the product of a college or art school program. Growing up in a family and world made up of artists shaped Dante's world. His father, Paul Marioni, was a pioneer in the American studio glass movement. His uncle, Joseph, was a painter. Another uncle, Tom, was a performance artist. His father's friends were all involved in art. "My father's friends, all artists, definitely influenced me," says Dante. "I think my education has been from being around all these leaders of the American studio glass movement. It was a big advantage that most people in glass do not have, and I was very lucky." And since he started to blow glass at the age of fifteen, Dante has come to shape the glass world for future generations. Not only does he make 100 percent of his living through gallery sales, numerous solo exhibitions, and participation in countless group exhibitions, but his work also appears in a number of outstanding public collections, including the Corning Museum of Glass, the Mint Museum of Craft + Design, and the White House Crafts Collection. His work has even graced the covers of *American Craft* and *Smithsonian* magazines. Not bad for someone who isn't even forty yet!

When he was in high school, his family moved to Seattle. Dante began taking lessons at The Glass Eye, a production glass studio, and spent summers at the Pilchuck School, where his father taught. Summertime meant Pilchuck to Dante, and with this experience, he was able to absorb a lot about glass and working as an artist, in addition to making several meaningful connections with glass artists whom he credits as influences. "I remember going to Pilchuck with my father in the summer of 1979, when I first started to blow glass," says Dante. "We went into a studio and there were some objects that Lino had made, all these perfect little cups, bowls, and pitchers. I had never seen anything like it. That's always been something that has intrigued me as a glassblower. I was more interested in perfecting something than in inventing it." Lino Tagliapietra would become a major influence in Dante's life, as would Benjamin Moore, Dick Marquis, Fritz Dreisbach, and Dale Chihuly, all master glassblowers he met in Seattle.

Dante later worked at The Glass Eye after school, where he met Benjamin Moore. "I charged the furnace, swept up broken glass, and worked there evenings and weekends," says Dante. "When I graduated from high school, I decided to work there full-time, rather than go to college immediately like my dad wanted me to. Benjamin Moore was the first person I saw who could blow symmetrically articulate forms. Seeing him work confirmed my commitment to blow glass."

Dante's only formal education comes from the Pilchuck School and a two-month workshop he took at Penland with Fritz Dreisbach. Encouraged by Fritz, Dante created his first individual body of work, a set of tall tumblers he still keeps on a shelf in his studio. After a year in Venice working with Lino, Dante returned to Seattle to have a sellout show at William Traver Gallery, received a Louis Comfort Tiffany fellowship, and was included in the Young Americans exhibit at the American Craft Museum. At the age of twenty-three, his time as a child prodigy was over and his career was officially launched.

"Many people don't realize that glassblowing requires a team effort," says Dante. "To do it well, you need an environment that is happy and friendly, which is achieved by working with a group of friends who get along. Humor helps, too. I have been so fortunate throughout my career that some of these people happened to be my closest friends. I have known a few of them since we were kids, even before we wanted to be glassblowers. I never for a moment considered doing anything else. Working with them has turned out to be the single most rewarding aspect of this profession, and this work wouldn't have happened without them." Dante also credits his wife, Alison, with being instrumental in his career. "Alison manages my career and is very involved in every aspect except for the actual making of work," says Dante. "She is my biggest support system."

"I still consider myself a student," says Dante. "Glassblowing is quite demanding. You are constantly figuring things out as you go along. You're never too good and you're never good enough. When I am working at the bench, making a form, nothing else matters to me at that moment. When I make a shape that goes well, I feel it through my hands, and that's very satisfying. That's why I make the things I make. It doesn't always feel good; there are bad days too. But on a good day, when it's going really well, it's a great thing, and a really powerful motivator for me."

Dante suggests that people starting out make every attempt to watch and learn from people they admire. "The essence of the word 'craft' to me has always been skill," says Dante. "If you want it badly enough, observing will serve you better than any hands-on teaching or wordy explanations will ever do. Obviously you need to practice your craft, but there is absolutely no substitute for a positive role model. But the bottom line is being passionate and completely devoted to the material of your choosing."

Richard Marquis, Glass Artist

With only two requirements in mind—propane delivery and UPS service—Dick Marquis wanted a new, less crowded place to live, where he could blow glass every day. He found what he was looking for in Puget Sound. After a lifetime of doing things he didn't like and dealing with people he wasn't interested in, he packed up his belongings and moved there, to a partially finished house on ten wooded acres, to run a production business with two partners. Shortly thereafter, in 1987, he went solo. Since that time, he has earned his living making pretty much what he wants.

In addition to receiving two Fulbright fellowships to go to Italy and New Zealand, a National Endowment for the Arts grant, and an Australian Crafts Council grant, Dick has also had numerous solo and group exhibitions and has a list of public collections that will knock your socks off. He was awarded the distinction of becoming a Fellow of the American Craft Council, and given a retrospective show at the Seattle Art Museum celebrating his career from 1967 to 1997. Dick Marquis is at the top of his game, and he has designed his life to play it his way.

What his résumé doesn't tell you is that Dick is a dedicated, dyed-in-the-wool collector of things that other people aren't interested in yet. For him, the value of these objects—whether they are bowling balls, saltshakers, old black cars, cone-shaped oilcans, or kids' chemistry sets from the '40s and '50s—lies primarily in their function as a kind of scenery around his workshop and house, a visual accompaniment to his daily life and work. Away from the clutter of images with which modern life inundates us all, on this island, Dick has been able to construct his visual environment to suit himself.

Dick attended the University of California, Berkeley, after a high

school teacher encouraged his interest in art. When he arrived there in
the mid-1960s, the funk movement was roaring into high gear. He soon
discovered the brand-new Glass department, eventually receiving both
his BA and MA degrees there. He studied in Italy to develop his knowledge of Venetian blown glass, techniques he has incorporated into his
work ever since. Next he taught in Seattle and the Bay Area, followed by
stints in Australia and Tasmania, and then back to Berkeley, where he
lived while commuting part of the year to teach at the University of California, Los Angeles. At the same time, he was developing a series of production glass businesses, called Marquis Deluxe Studio, where he made
glass marbles, and HOTMIRE, or Hippies Out To Make It Rich Etc. As he
watched his neighborhood become gentrified, he began to yearn for
something different. He decided to move to Puget Sound, where he has
been ever since.

"I don't do any direct sales," says Dick. "I have a couple galleries,
and one show a year will cover our needs. I don't need much, have low
overhead, do all of my own building and shop repairs, and have never
been in debt." Dick has been able to support himself solely on the sales
of his work not only because his work is good and because he is a savvy
manager, but also because of the increasing market value of glass. "I've
been able to make my living pretty much as I want," admits Dick.
"There's more competition these days, leading to a greater degree of professionalism. The high cost of setting up and the high continuing cost of
operating a glass studio make most people have to keep on doing the
same thing just to pay the bills. In my generation, on the other hand,
people got trapped by teaching and never had the time to develop the
skills they needed to make it on their own." It's clear he enjoys the feeling of being self-sufficient and playing by his own rules.

Able to achieve a high level of craftsmanship early in his career,
Dick took that skill and used it to create a quirky, funky style combining, for example, traditional vessels with objects from his collection,
making his pieces stand out in the glass world. His work reflects a
desire to show people how he sees and experiences the work, in a
friendly juxtaposition of art and kitsch. By topping off his vibrant
glass sculpture with ceramic ducks, plastic dice, or rubber squeeze toys,
he not only pokes a finger at the studio glass movement, but he also
reminds his viewers that his art is usually seen in the context of a collector's possessions.

Clarifying a career path in production, teaching, or art will help
newcomers to the field make wise decisions. "I think people need to

decide early on if they want to do production work," says Dick. "They can either do it to work for someone else or develop a business, or they can take those skills, tools, and the nest egg they acquire and use it to become an artist. I also suggest that if they want to be an artist, that they not do the production work under their own name, because otherwise, later on, someone may say they have a piece by them when it really was a production piece, not a piece of artwork."

Dick is a firm believer in apprenticeship as a way to learn and develop. "Apprentice yourself," suggests Dick. "Do a lot and work a lot. Although there are a lot of teaching jobs available, they don't allow you to develop skills in the same way. You can obtain more skill and knowledge by doing production work. Hands-on work is a better way to learn the business than teaching. Learning how to blow glass, developing your technique, and having something to say by developing a unique vision is what's important."

Depending on the work, Dick either works with just one other person or with a crew to make his pieces. "I have different people work for me," says Dick. "They are all really good. Glassblowing is dynamic and fluid, not an isolated event. Very few people work solo. Working together also enables glassblowers to learn tricks and techniques from each other. Ninety percent of the time I work with just one other person, and with a crew the other ten percent. There are lots of skilled people in the Seattle area because Pilchuck is here providing a supportive art system, but also because the weather is perfect for the medium, neither too hot nor too cold."

Although Dick is a board member of several organizations, including the Renwick and Pilchuck, he does it out of a feeling of duty. "I'm old enough and successful enough to give back now," says Dick. "I don't go to conferences anymore unless they pay me, and I don't travel much or do workshops either." What he prefers to do is work. "In addition to glass, I still make ceramics things, even if it is only throwing and making flowerpots for the greenhouse," says Dick. "There is no pressure or expectation for this work. I also work outside in the garden and woods, work on my cars, and read a lot. I try not to put a value on what I do, whether making a shed or blowing glass or doing chores. When I retire, I plan to do the same thing."

Josh Simpson, Glass Artist
www.megaplanet.com

A semester away from completing a psychology degree from Hamilton College, Josh Simpson decided to take a year off and see if his interest in glassblowing was something he wanted to follow the rest of his life. "I built a tiny furnace and lived in a teepee," says Josh. "It was the best and worst thing I ever did. I lived in a void with no idea what was going on." During that time, he was able to develop his style as a glassblower and craftsman. After finishing his degree, Josh decided to set up a glass studio on his grandfather's property. The only problem was that the bank he approached for a business loan had never heard of anyone making a living as a glassblower and wouldn't loan him the money. After he returned with samples of his work and five thousand dollars' worth of orders from the Rhinebeck fair, the bank gave him a loan. Thirty years later, Josh Simpson's work is celebrated internationally. He not only runs a very successful glass art studio selling his platters, vessels, planets, and sculptures, but he has also had numerous one-person exhibitions, shown work in many public collections such as the Corning Museum of Glass, taught workshops internationally, received the Humanitarian Award from *NICHE* magazine and served on boards such as ACC, CERF, GAS, and Horizons. He was also awarded the Lifetime Membership Award from the Glass Art Society.

Josh did not formally study glassblowing until he had been in the field for seventeen years. "I took my first workshop at Haystack with Lino Tagliapietra," says Josh. "I had always wanted to go to graduate school for glass, mostly for the validation. I was accepted at Alfred, but for one reason or another I kept deferring. After ten years of deferring, I had developed a good studio and decided not to go." Creating work and running a business gave him a different sort of education. "When people are in school or taking a workshop, they have the luxury of time," says Josh. "They conceive an object and make it at their own pace. When you are making objects meant to be sold, you have to figure out a way to make elegant objects as simply and efficiently as you can. Customers want care and effort and time in the objects you make, but you have to work a lot faster in order to make a profit and stay alive."

"Taking workshops is a good way to get started," suggests Josh. "Especially if you can take a breather in between to figure out what was good about the workshop. If you are getting started today, you have to be good, creative, and original to compete. I've had thirty years to figure out how to make fewer mistakes."

There have been many phases to his work, from functional pieces to planets and sculptures. "Imagine walking along, looking at the horizon, looking at the mountains, and thinking you are walking in one direction," says Josh. "I thought I was making the same work, but when I look back now, I realize my perception has changed. The amazing thing about seeing older work now is that it reminds me of a mindset of that time, just like hearing a song can remind you of a moment in your life. When I pick up a piece of glass, many times I can be awash with memories, reminding me of a different time."

Josh started out making wine goblets and selling his work at crafts fairs. "I used to bring a demonstration furnace with me to fairs," says Josh. "It only took five minutes to make a goblet because I was good at it. The problem was that people didn't get the impression that it was hard to make or worth the money. From the moment I realized that, I started to take several attempts to make one and let a few crumple from too much heat to show the skill involved. I realized to a certain extent that I had to become a showman to make sales. The price didn't seem as high to customers after they saw that it took several attempts. Even today, a platter I was making ended up on the floor. Making glass doesn't always work out perfectly."

Josh has been self-supporting since the day he sewed his teepee together. "I never had another income," says Josh. Although Josh has a small crew of workers to support as well as help him create his work, he does not consider himself a production craftsperson. "Although I make a lot of work, each piece is one-of-a-kind," says Josh. "I don't use molds and I make everything by hand. I feel very strongly that if I sign a piece of work, I had to have a hand in making everything."

Josh got a Web site in 1995 and never thought it would be an important sales venue. "The reason I got a Web page and e-mail was so I could write to my wife, who is an astronaut, in orbit," says Josh. "I never thought the Web site would be a way to sell my work. I didn't even have anything for sale on my page until a few years ago. Now, however, my annual sales are equal to several good craft exhibitions and craft fairs put together. Craft fairs are slowly winding down and Web site sales are going up. It can be presented as a personal way of shopping and used as a sales tool that is no different than using the phone or a brochure. However, I am still totally surprised that people buy things over the Web site."

Josh has always been very civic-minded and involved in improving the crafts field. "I've done lots of extracurricular stuff and have recently tried to slow down," says Josh. " I helped to found CERF (Crafts Emergency Relief Fund) and was the first president. I'm still on the board. I have been very involved with Horizons, the New England Craft Program for high school students, from the beginning, and felt vested in it. I donated studio equipment. Now I meet grown-ups that first took classes there as kids. I think being involved helps the crafts field in general." When the original director of Horizons decided to make a change and sell the school, Josh became a minority partner with the new owner. He is still involved with the crafts education program there, which is currently called Snow Farm.

"Successful? Yes, I feel successful," says Josh. "All through my career, I felt as if I had just enough encouragement to continue to the next day and the next week. There are always frustrations. If you are optimistic, you can find encouragement in different events. For example, when I go to a crafts exhibition, I don't expect to sell anything. I genuinely believe this. I'm hopeful, but I don't expect to, so when someone buys one of my pieces, I'm happy."

Stained Glass Artists

Candace Jackman, Stained Glass Artist
www.jackmansglass.com

In 1977, Candace Jackman signed up for two ten-week adult education classes in stained glass because she wanted to make a panel for her front door. After she made and sold three panels, she began a career producing custom-designed stained glass windows that has spanned over twenty-five years. And today, her front door still doesn't have a stained glass window.

For the next few years, Candace kept her day job, until she took a workshop at Haystack in 1981. "I took a three-week session at Haystack with Albinus Elskus, where I learned about kiln-fired painting on glass," remembers Candace. "I went back to work for three days and gave notice on my job. I thought if I don't try it, I will never know if I can do it or not. I have run my own business full-time since then. I had to make a go of it. In the beginning, I had to use my credit card to get cash advances in the winter. It was touch-and-go in the early years, and it took a while to do well. But I was determined to make it and I like the independence of working for myself."

Early on, Candace discovered that the customers who purchased her work wanted custom designs, not ready-made pieces. "I was invited to exhibit in a show at Sugarloaf/USA," remembers Candace. "I was supposed to be put in the crafts section, but after they saw my work, I was moved to the art section. Although I sold one piece at the show, I got calls from prospective clients after the show. It didn't take long to figure out that the majority of my sales would come after the shows, not at the show itself."

Although custom work involves several contacts with clients, it is more lucrative and less tedious than production work. "Making small stuff took too much time," says Candace. "I wanted to do commissions and decided to focus on custom work for homes. It wasn't always easy, but it was more rewarding. First, I usually meet a client at a show, let him see the range of my work, and give him my Web site address if he needs to show samples of the work to someone else after the show. He gives me an order and sets up an appointment for me to go to his home, see the space where he wants the piece, and take measurements. Then I design the piece and bring it back to his home to install it. Overall, it's at least three or four contacts. The upside of all the personal contact is that it gives me and the client a story to tell about the piece, which I can then use as a selling tool for my future pieces."

In the beginning, when Candace was starting her business, she did a lot of shows to get established. "I used to do twelve to fifteen shows a year," says Candace. "This year I am only doing four. I always ask my clients where they saw us, and it turned out that they tended to see us at the bigger shows as well as the smaller ones. I decided to just do the bigger shows, cut down the number of total shows, and see what happened. I didn't want to stand around at a show when I could be working in my studio. I cut down gradually and found that I am just as busy as when I did more shows. I figured I could always add more shows if it affected sales. I'd like to reach the point where I just do one show a year, but that's kind of scary."

Customers also find Candace in other ways besides shows. "Some of our customers are referrals," says Candace. "Although we have some repeat customers, most people have only one space to put a special piece in their home. We get inquires from the Web site from places outside of Maine, but I usually say no because I'm more comfortable working close to home. I have done a few pieces out of state, mostly for people I had already met. My daughter designed the Web site to function as a gallery where I can show samples of my work. There aren't any prices on it, and I primarily use it as a follow-up tool for people I have met at shows. I also use it to share information and help other people find sources. I do that at shows too. I'm very open with sharing information because I think it is better to share. I tried doing some other advertisements a few years ago and hardly got a response. I don't think it works as well with custom work."

Learning how to price her work for the long-term survival of her business was an important step for Candace. "I took a pricing workshop in the beginning," says Candace. "Then I doubled my prices and still had enough work, if not more. The funny thing is that I needed to place a higher value on my work so that other people would value it. There are some customers who think that low prices mean your work is not as valuable. I talk to a lot of people at shows, and I always suggest they think about pricing and come up with a formula that works for them. I use a system that is based on the size of the piece and the amount of time it takes, and then I estimate the cost of my materials too. I timed myself years ago to see how long it would take me to solder and cut glass, and I still base my prices on those figures. Then there is design time, time at shows, and meeting with clients. I developed a form that I use for every project to make it easier."

Feeling comfortable with running a successful business has taken time. "I have an inferiority complex," admits Candace. "I have a hard time accepting compliments. However, when I look back at what has been accomplished in over twenty years, it amazes me. I am grateful that people want to commission my work because although it does enhance their home, what I do is not a necessity item. I feel very lucky to have made this business a success."

Bert Weiss, Glass Artist
www.customartglass.com

"In 1971, I dropped out of college and hitch-hiked my way across the country," says Bert Weiss. "On the way home, I decided I wanted to be a self-employed craftsperson. I figured all I needed to do to make stained glass was get a glass cutter, a knife, pliers, and a soldering iron." A few workshops later, Bert was able to complete a commission that paid for his study at the League of NH Craftsman and Haystack. Thirty years later, Bert Weiss Art Glass produces custom fused and slumped glass pieces that can be used as furniture, windows, or doors for public and private commissions.

"I moved to Exeter, New Hampshire, and took at class at the League of NH Craftsmen shop there," says Bert. "The teacher was a real pro and got me going. Then I took a workshop at Haystack with a master craftsman named Helmut Schardt, who taught traditional techniques. It was a three-week session and I learned a lot. I was able to go home and practice and actually pay for the workshop with my first job. I learned that because my strong point is not design, I didn't have to try to be a designer. I'm a good mechanic. So I found people to collaborate with who had complementary skills, which has worked out well." Bert teamed up with a watercolor painter and installed a very ambitious piece ten weeks later in Portland, Maine. He was on his way.

The next influence came in the form of another workshop at Haystack with Albinus Elskus, author of *The Art of Painting on Glass.* "I don't use the traditional technique that Albinus taught us," says Bert. "I adapted it. However, I still use the tools he taught us to use. My pieces are made of kiln-fired glass and are more technically driven." Two more workshops at Haystack and then one at Pilchuck rounded out Bert's formal education. "The workshop I took at Pilchuck was an amazing session in hot glass casting using sand," says Bert. "I studied with Paul Marioni. It was a graduate-level, experimental class with forty students, six teachers, and no structure. About one-third of the group worked in flat glass like I did, and we just watched the teachers work. I met a lot of West Coast people, who are so knowledgeable about glass. It was a real eye-opener."

During the early days, Bert supplemented sales of his work with cooking jobs. "I've done some cooking on the side to generate income when I needed it," says Bert. "I cooked for places like Outward Bound and the summer program at Portland School of Art. Cooking for a living is now a thing of the past." Bert primarily makes his living from doing commissions, supplemented with a couple lines of things to take to shows, such as sushi plates. "I go to shows to break even," says Bert. "Mostly the shows are a way for me to make connections to get commission work. I usually don't make any significant sales at the shows. Architects are my market and I do shows like the Boston Society of Architects show or the Philadelphia Furniture Show to connect with them. Currently I'm working in $2 million homes with clients who want to commission a craftsman to make things for their home. For example, right now I am doing two sinks and a window for a home on Cape Cod."

One of Bert's strong points has been having good equipment. "My father sold temperature control equipment to the glass and steel industry, so I was able to design a state-of-the-art control system," says Bert. "There aren't many others in my field who have such a sophisticated setup. I had built my first kiln myself and after attending Pilchuck, I built a big kiln that can fire a door-sized piece of glass. I consulted with a lot of people. This kiln is well suited to my work and sets me apart because someone else can't just go out and buy one like it."

A great source of support for Bert has come in the form of a community bulletin board on the Internet for people who work in warm glass. "I talk to people all over the world," says Bert. "It gives me both emotional and technical support from my peers. Most of my life I have worked without any real peers to talk to. We are having our first conference this year and will meet each other for the first time. Now I have a community and it has made all the difference." Bert is also a member of the League of NH Craftsmen and does their annual fair at Mount Sunapee, one year getting a $30,000 commission from the fair!

Bert utilized his Web site to supplement the marketing work he does after meeting potential clients at a show or fair. "I get referrals from the Web site," says Bert. "It provides contacts for jobs that range from small to large. However, I usually don't get direct orders until people have seen me and talked with me."

Bert suggests that people considering a crafts career focus on pricing. "Don't quit your day job until you have money in the bank," advises Bert. "If you are making money selling your work as a hobby, then you can probably do it. Starting from scratch takes a lot of investment. Most people do not understand pricing. You need to charge a lot of money to make a living from just doing your work. Look at the wholesale and retail structure and don't sell your work for wholesale prices—you will undercut the pros and go out of business."

PART FIVE

Metal

CHAPTER 12

Facts and Organizations for Metal Artists

C areers of craftspeople who work in the medium of metal include a wide range of professions. In this section, you will find profiles of traditional and sculptural blacksmiths, jewelers, artists, teachers, designers, consultants, and publishers. Many of the people in this section have worked through several stages in their crafts careers, or have combined different interests to earn a living or to live in a way that suits them best.

Insight Survey Statistics on Jewelry Artists

Today's craftspeople working in metal have a lot of options. In the Insight Survey on Jewelry Artists conducted by *The Crafts Report* in May 2003, the average gross sales for full-time jewelry artists, based on fifty-one respondents, was $114,046. While there may be variations for black-smiths or designers, here are the results for jewelers:

Percent of Gross Sales from Various Sources
- 40% shows
- 10% wholesale shows
- 7% sell directly to galleries
- 41% own gallery/studio
- 2% consign to galleries
- 1% Internet
- 1% other

Amount Spent on Materials
- 2% less than $1000
- 39% $1000 to $10,000

- 24% $10,001 to $20,000
- 22% $20,001 to $50,000
- 14% $50,000+

Number of People Working in Studio
- 34% work alone
- 42% 1 to 2 people
- 20% 3 to 5 people
- 0% 6 to 10 people
- 4% 11 or more

Time Spent Selling Crafts
- 2% less than 1 year
- 14% 1 to 5 years
- 35% 6 to 10 years
- 16% 11 to 15 years
- 33% more than 15 years

Fifty-three percent owned a Web site, 25 percent sold their work through an online gallery or crafts site, and 39 percent provided the only source of income in their household.

According to Cindy Edelstein of the Jeweler's Resource Bureau (*www.jewelersresource.com*), in an article titled "Making a Living as a Jewelry Artist" in the July 2002 issue of *The Crafts Report*, the best way to find and maintain your market as a jeweler is to do wholesale shows. "You get the chance in three to five days to meet dozens of retail store owners and fellow artists," says Cindy. "You get to do market research by strolling the aisles, obtain informal credit reports by gabbing with exhibitors, do public relations by meeting with editors, and gain industry intelligence and saturation by talking to everyone and looking at everything. To find the right markets for your work, research crafts shows, talk to peers and your existing customer base, and then just roll the dice. Repetition is the key to all advertising and promotional venues, and it often takes a few shows before buyers are willing to work with you."

Organizations for Metal Artists

The organizations listed here are designed for occupations such as blacksmiths, jewelers, designers, and teachers, as well as aspiring craftspeople and others who are interested in the field of metal.

Artist Blacksmith Association of North America (ABANA)

Founded in 1973 by a handful of smiths in Georgia, ABANA has grown to a membership over five thousand strong, with fifty chapters. Membership benefits include:

- Subscription to *The Anvil's Ring*. A quarterly magazine dedicated to the craft of blacksmithing, *The Anvil's Ring* offers special feature articles on a broad range of topics such as architectural iron, decorative design, primitive artifacts, hand-forged tools, historical references, advice to beginners, news of regional affiliate events, and exhibitions. Reports on tools, equipment and supply sources, employment opportunities, and blacksmithing instruction also make it an excellent resource.
- Subscription to *Hammer's Blow*. A quarterly publication full of tips and techniques for professionals and beginners alike, this comes in a three-hole punch format for easy cataloguing in a notebook.
- The ABANA International Conferences. Held biennially in the United States, this members-only event includes: demonstrations, panel discussions, and lectures featuring experts in the field from North America, Europe, Asia, and Australia. Dedicated to sharing knowledge of technical, aesthetic, and business aspects of the craft for everyone from beginners to established professionals, the conference draws thousands of smiths from around the world.
- Member discounts on products and services.

The ABANA Web site also offers a lot of information to the general public, including sources for equipment and an extensive list of places to study blacksmithing. Anyone who doesn't believe that each one of us can make a difference should read the description of the founding of the organization for inspiration.

For more information: ABANA, P.O. Box 816, Farmington, GA 30638; (706) 310-1030 or 769-9556; *www.abana.org.*

Society of American Silversmiths (SAS)

Founded in 1989, the Society of American Silversmiths is devoted solely to the preservation and promotion of contemporary silversmithing, including the production of hollowware, flatware, and sculpture. SAS educates the public about silversmithing techniques, silver care, restoration, and conservation as well as about the aesthetic value of this art form through its free consulting service. Members have access to:

- An outstanding benefits package, including the ability to obtain comprehensive insurance through a partnership with MemberNet USA
- Technical and marketing expertise
- An extensive library
- A referral service that commissions hollowware, flatware, and sculpture
- Generous discounts from suppliers offering precious metals, tools, equipment, business insurance, long-distance calling, casting and plating services, art and antique books, photography, and more
- An archive that has contains résumés, over 1,400 slides, 400 photographs, and a maker's mark registry for identification
- A silver restoration hotline
- Membership listings and a members' discussion group online, plus an online gallery for Artisan-level members
- Complimentary passes to the Manufacturing Jewelers and Silversmiths America Expos
- An online members' news exchange
- Discounts on artisan silver and silverworks demonstrations

Supporting memberships are open to all who are interested in the art and history of handcrafted silver, while associate memberships are available for students. Artisan-level members are juried into the Society based on their outstanding technical skill and are provided with support, networking, and greater access to the market.

For more information: SAS, P.O. Box 72839, Providence, RI 02907; (401) 461-6840; *www.silversmithing.com*.

Society of North American Goldsmiths (SNAG)

Currently with over six thousand members, SNAG was founded in 1969 to provide a meeting place for contemporary jewelers and metalsmiths, to encourage the free exchange of information inside the field, to promote the field to a wider audience, and to recognize outstanding creative achievement. Although the name uses the term "goldsmith," the organization is intended to appeal to all contemporary jewelers and metalsmiths. Membership offers:

- An annual conference
- A subscription to *Metalsmith* magazine
- A members-only newsletter

- An e-mail news service
- A Web site that includes professional guidelines, provides advice and checklists relevant to artists working in all media, and addresses such topics as exhibitions, contracts, claims for damaged work. The site also includes a bibliography of where to obtain legal and professional advice.
- Awards for students and emerging artists
- Workshops
- Major exhibitions of modern jewelry and metalwork

SNAG offers three different membership categories, each tailored to a specific level of involvement in the field, for studio jewelers, designers, metalsmiths, sculptors, educators, students, collectors, gallery owners, curators, and craft enthusiasts, as outlined below:

- Silver: Five issues of *Metalsmith* magazine, including the annual *Exhibition-in-Print*
- Gold: Five issues of *Metalsmith* magazine, five issues of *SNAG News*, a discount on the annual conference fee, SNAG's membership directory, and access to all SNAG services
- Platinum: Multiple-year memberships are available with an additional 5 to 10 percent discount on the annual full membership fee

Student membership is available at a reduced rate to anyone attending an accredited educational institution full-time.

For more information: SNAG, 710 East Ogden Ave., Suite 600, Naperville, IL 60563-8063; (630) 579-3272; *www.snagmetalsmith.org*.

The organizations listed above will help keep you informed, inspired, and on track as your career develops. If you can, pick out at least one organization to join. Every month when you receive your newsletter or magazine, you can read about what is happening in your field around the country, and find out about opportunities to promote your work that you may not have known about otherwise. If memberships are out of your reach right now, ask a family member or friend to give one to you as a gift.

The next chapter is devoted to profiles of craftspeople working in metal. Read them and enjoy. If you have any questions for any of the people profiled and they have a Web site, feel free to learn more about them and even contact them with your questions and comments.

CHAPTER 13

Metal Artists' Profiles

Designers

Deb Stoner, Artist
www.debstoner.com

Fred Soelzer

"It's hard to explain to someone what I do," says Deb Stoner. "Depending on their interest, I might say jewelry or eyeglass design or pet photography. So usually I just say I'm an artist. I have specialized in teaching eyeglass design and I'm known as an authority. If I were a designer for one company, I would never have the freedom to do what I do now: teach, photograph, and design. By doing several things at once, it keeps me plugged in, keeps me refreshed, and keeps my ideas fluid. My Web site has different pages for each interest. This is who I am."

Deb originally got her undergraduate degree in Geology. "For years I regretted that my degree wasn't in jewelry design," says Deb. "I had no idea that a major in jewelry existed when I went to college. I now believe that getting a degree was important just for the discipline and learning and that it didn't matter what I majored in. Plus, science was a great intellectual backdrop for learning how to think in a specific way that is different from the way many artists think."

After graduation, Deb worked in a jewelry store for five years. "I got really good at technical stuff," says Deb. "I cast every day, did zillions of ring sizings and chain repairs. I got the chops there, learned about speed and production (and my aversion to both!). I highly recommend that students or people just starting out have a similar learning experience."

Deb decided to go to graduate school at San Diego State University.

"It was good to go to graduate school already knowing how to make stuff so I could focus on design and art," says Deb, "rather than technical things." Following graduate school, she became an Artist-in-Residence at the Oregon College of Art and Craft. "It was a great follow-up to graduate school," says Deb. "I had a year to explore and work with the support of the school. I worked out ideas I had in graduate school with the intention of making money with them. Then I got a teaching job there and taught for the next four years."

At this point, Deb decided she needed a new pair of glasses and decided to make them herself. "I starting exploring eyeglasses when I needed a pair," says Deb. "I went shopping and decided I could make my own. Ha, what folly! I then got hooked on what was to become one of the most fascinating design problems I have ever encountered." Without knowing it at the time, this simple decision would alter the direction of her career.

Haystack heard of her work with eyeglass design and asked her to teach a workshop. "I got really focused to teach the first workshop at Haystack," says Deb. "I researched historical eyewear. Then I organized a show called 'Op Art: Eyewear by Jewelers' that traveled, and I gave a talk about my work at the SNAG conference." At this point, Deb quit her teaching job at OCAC and went to Europe for ten months, teaching in the University of Georgia's Studies Abroad program in Italy. "After teaching in Italy, I lived in Portugal with no car, no phone, and plenty of time to explore and work," says Deb. "I worked with extreme technical limits, using only a hammer, saw, file, and simple torch. I felt very free from my own expectations of what I should do."

When she returned home, she arrived with new ideas about how she wanted to live her life. "I started my freelance eyewear design business and got Donna Karan as a client, among others," says Deb. "While I made prototypes and created new designs for fashion industry, I continued to create my own designs to sell to companies." The next two years were spent working as an eyeglass designer for Anne Klein Company, until she lost her job when the company was sold and the Design department was dissolved. A short stint teaching at the university level taught her that she enjoyed teaching, but in a workshop setting rather than a degree program. "I took a teaching job to see if university teaching was a career path and learned that it wasn't, at all," says Deb. "Then I taught at Penland for the fall concentration and realized that as a teacher, I'm much better suited to short-term, intense, focused experiences. I have taught a bazillion workshops now and I love the process."

Another direction was added to her repertoire when she started a new business as a pet photographer. "I specialize in hand-colored black-and-white dog portraits," says Deb. "It is so fun and satisfying on a personal level. I continue to make one-of-a-kind eyewear, and I'm working on a prototype to make limited-production eyeglasses in titanium and gold. I also play the accordion in a couple bands, and I like to cook and enter cooking contests. In this scattershot way, I keep cobbling together an interesting life, which coincidentally includes my career. I don't measure success by how much money I make, but more by how interesting a life I have. I'm living off my savings now, while both businesses are in the startup phase. I feel it's a good way to spend it if I can get to do what I want. I like the luxury of being self-employed and being my own boss."

Deb suggests that people interested in a crafts career should just do it, not wait until they think they are ready. "It's a process," says Deb. "Just let loose of what's keeping you tied to a job. You need to be free to be who you are. Don't start a business undercapitalized, but by the same token, you don't have to pour your life savings into it either. It's always helped me to do a few things at the same time. It's also wise to hire out when you can. For example, I could do my own accounting, but I'm not interested in doing it. Your mind has to be free to be creative."

Jill Kenik, President, Acropolis Studios, Inc.
www.acropolisstudios.com

David Kenik

"I always thought I would be a craftsperson, go back to get my MFA degree, and live out my fantasy of having my own production line," says Jill Kenik. "After working for Swank, Inc. as the Men's Accessories Designer for seven years, I realized I liked working for industry. My job there was like another college education. I learned that a designer needs to be able to manufacture, not just draw pretty pictures. I never went back." Now the owner of her own product development company, Acropolis Studios, Jill specializes in jewelry and giftware, helping clients with the product design, models, and consulting to get their ideas from concept to fruition.

"When I was in high school, I had a definite interest in art," says

Jill. "I had relatives who were graphic designers and weavers. Although my high school art program wasn't great, my Aunt Jean was a jeweler and an excellent mentor for me. I decided to attend the Rochester Institute of Technology and I declared my major in Metals as a freshman." Jill earned her BFA degree in Metalcrafts and Jewelry from the School of American Craftsmen at the Rochester Institute of Technology in 1985. During her senior year, when there was a discussion about how to make a living in the field, a teacher who knew Jill's strengths suggested that she consider working in industry.

"I started as a designer at Swank right after graduation, and although I made less money there than someone working at Wendy's, I loved it," says Jill. "It was a good combination of things for me because I was strong technically and enjoyed working within tight constraints. It was an incredible learning experience. I rolled my sleeves up and learned all aspects of the business, including the speed required to build things. Every job was a huge learning opportunity, and I found that I could still come up with beautiful pieces within the constraints of production. I found I liked figuring out how to do the production the first time, then having someone else execute the production of the pieces themselves. For someone who doesn't like to do the production, industry has something to offer artists. Also, most artists don't realize that industry is willing to take phone calls for small jobs. The nature of retailing is changing, and there doesn't have to be a division between industry and artisans anymore."

Jill went on to work for several other companies in production and product development, learning more about manufacturing, before the opportunity came to work for herself came in 1994. "At age thirty-two, I not only had a lot of contacts and knowledge, but I was about to lose my job," says Jill. "It took some quick stepping, but I opened my business in a spare room using a Visa card with a credit line. I slowly built it up from there, and my husband was very supportive. Although initially my income was half of what I had made at my job, I had low overhead, with most of my costs in labor. I worked out of the house for a year, maintaining a 9-to-5 (plus a 7:00 to 10:00 P.M.) schedule. To get an emotional break, I rented a small office, and the business slowly grew. Three years later, I hired my first employee. Eight years later, I have three bench people, plus a CAD/CAM system that is worth another two employees. It's a great place to work, and we are extremely creative."

Acropolis Studios works on a wide range of projects ranging from boxes, baby rattles, frames, and rings to you name it. But they don't manufacture the products themselves; they just do what needs to be done to help a client get a piece off the ground. "We might start with a blueprint or a drawing on a napkin," says Jill. "We help the client make a prototype or model so they can do a look-see and then take it to the next step in the manufacturing process."

Jill has also learned to make the switch from being the primary designer to being a supervisor. "Sometimes I am forced to work on the bench, and it's refreshing," admits Jill. "I miss working on the bench, but I have a lot of other things that I enjoy. This is a very creative job. We make stuff every day. It's hard and it's scary, but I'm making a good living and it's a great way to go through life. I always wanted to make money and have three square meals a day plus health insurance, and this allows me to do it all."

The decision to purchase a CAD/CAM system has allowed for more job satisfaction for the staff. "I want to make the best product I can, and the computer system has helped me achieve that goal," says Jill. "I researched and discovered that I needed the system for the survival of my business. It allows master sculptors to be good at what they are good at and not have to do all the boring stuff. Two years ago, we would have made changes using pencil and paper. Now, we can make twenty changes in twenty minutes on the computer. It allows a more creative approach and is very freeing."

Jill decided to create a Web site for her business and has found it to be a good addition to the business. "The Web site paid for itself within the first two weeks of setting it up," says Jill. "It's a link to industry, and we get about fifty hits a month. It's set up as a portfolio site and is geared to the CAD/CAM system. It's basically a resource to show potential clients samples of our work."

Jill did go back to school, but this time receiving an MBA degree in 1997, not an MFA. "I'm running a business," says Jill. "In the MBA program, I did a business plan, analysis, and research. I'm a businessperson who is sensitive to good and bad design. Although I never thought I would run my own business, I am passionate about this business. It's 100 percent mine and I lose sleep over it. I'm going to keep doing what I'm doing.

"If you are going to succeed, decide what you are good at and maximize yourself," says Jill. "Take some business classes that include bookkeeping and how to put together a marketing plan. Don't invest in the studio until the numbers make sense to do so. Realize that the decision to run your business may mean that you are no longer making art for art's sake."

Jewelry Designers

Arline Fisch, Jewelry Artist, Professor of Art Emeritus

William Gullette

In a video accompanying the exhibition "Elegant Fantasy: The Jewelry of Arline Fisch" at the American Craft Museum, Arline Fisch appeared at the opening wearing an aluminum brooch the size of the Ritz. "Women want dramatic, exciting, sensuous jewelry," says Arline. "And they want to be noticed." Noticed is what one would be in any of her dramatic designs.

With a career that spans over forty years, Arline Fisch is one of the leaders of the modern art jewelry movement. She is the recipient of numerous honors and awards, including the Gold Medal for Consummate Craftsmanship awarded by the American Craft Council, an Honorary Life Membership in the Society of North American Goldsmiths, and a Lifetime Achievement Award from the National Museum of Women in the Arts. She has been named a "Living Treasure of California" by the State Assembly. In addition, she is a respected professor emeritus at San Diego State University, where she founded the jewelry program.

Arline started her career in 1952, when she received her BS degree in Art from Skidmore College in Saratoga, New York. She went on immediately to receive her MA in Art at the University of Illinois in 1954. "Although my family was always very encouraging to me, I was on my own after college," says Arline. "I was always able to support myself, whether through grants, teaching, or receiving Fulbrights."

Early on in her career, Arline received four Fulbrights. "The first one was in 1956 to go to Denmark," says Arline. "That was to learn technical things. The amount of instruction available at that time was small. Then, ten years later, I received a second one to go back to Denmark to do research. For the other two, I was requested to teach in Austria and Uruguay as part of the Council of International Education. These were two different programs, but also under the Fulbright name."

After teaching briefly at Wheaton College in Massachusetts and then at Skidmore College, Arline was hired to start the undergraduate Jewelry department at San Diego State University in 1961. SDSU quickly developed a graduate component as well. "Teaching has been an integral part of my life," says Arline. "I have always taught what I am involved with. When I was at Skidmore, I taught two days a week and still had time for my own work. When I first started at SDSU, I was expected to not only teach four to five days a week, but if I wanted tenure, I had to have an active exhibition schedule as well. I had to negotiate my schedule to be able to have the time to produce work so that my qualifications would be at a suitable level for promotion. Although I was able to receive a workable schedule, I was never able to convince the administration that a studio on campus would benefit the program. Now that I am retired, it is a loss not to have the interaction with students. Although I am still doing workshops, it is not the same kind of teaching where I was able to develop long-term relationships with my students. I am still in touch with many of my students from SDSU, even exhibiting and visiting with them."

Arline has exhibited extensively in the United States and around the world. "In the beginning, I entered every competition out there," remembers Arline. "Early in my career, there weren't that many available, and I had to get my work seen. My work has been marketed and shown almost exclusively through galleries and museums. I can't sell anything to anybody. I have no sales ability or even a lot of entrepreneurial drive. I always supported myself through my teaching income. However, I have been able to help others find their way.

"Many times when I would be introduced to parents of the students in my jewelry program, they would ask me how their son or daughter would be able to make a living after graduation," says Arline. "I always told them to keep investing in their children, even after graduation, until they are able to establish themselves. Earning a college degree is only the first part of the equation.

"At this point, I keep asking myself, do I really need to make more work?" says Arline. "I still enjoy it. I do other things, but they are not as compelling as what I do in the studio. At the moment I'm not doing less, I'm doing more. I want to be more selective and make more involved pieces. I had opportunities right from the beginning, and I took advantage of them. I also gave up other things. I started at age twenty and I had a way of falling into things.

"If you want to teach, you can find a way to teach even though it is competitive," says Arline. "Community colleges, craft centers, and workshops are viable alternatives to college teaching. The workshop level has grown so much over the years. Be willing to take risks and take advantage of circumstances. It is not always the most talented who are successful. It takes a combination of talent, commitment, and a certain type of drive to be successful. I had a student who saw the potential for a business from something she did for class. She had the ambition and passion. I saw her in her booth at a crafts fair at the Armory in New York, and it was fun to see her work in her booth. I had twenty students in that class, but she was the only one who saw the potential from what she learned in class, and her career has evolved from there."

Tim McCreight, Master Metalsmith

Robert Diamante

"When I got out of graduate school, I knew I wanted to teach, but I couldn't get a teaching job," remembers Tim McCreight. "I did other jobs for awhile, taught continuing studies, and did a little production work. Then I got a teaching job! Although it was full-time, I needed more income. I felt that I had three options: produce work to sell at fairs, do commission work, or write a book. I didn't want to do fairs because I had two young children and didn't want to travel. I hadn't had too much luck with commission work, and always seemed to underprice my work. I decided that writing a book would mesh well with teaching and make me better at it. Books had always been an important learning source for me. The first book led to another one, and I inched my way into publishing." What Tim didn't know at the time was that his publishing company, Brynmorgen Press, would go on to produce over twenty works, including several books that are now considered indispensable for every metalsmith, such as *The Complete Metalsmith* and *Practical Casting*. "*The Complete Metalsmith* is a bench reference for teachers and is written from the maker's point of view," says Tim. "Writing and publishing my own books got my name out in the field. It opened up a lot of doors for me."

Not only has Tim been successful in publishing, but he has also made his mark in teaching, exhibiting, consulting, and public service. He has been Professor of Art at Maine College of Art since 1987, President of Brynmorgen Press since 1985, and a consultant with Mitsubishi Materials Corporation since 1996. He has also served on several boards, including Haystack, the American Craft Council, and the Society of North

American Goldsmiths, where he also served as President. "I take my commitments to these organizations seriously," says Tim. "Although I can't say I love it, it is a way for me to give back and contribute to the field. I will always pitch in if someone asks me. I have enjoyed learning from these organizations and have grown as a result of my involvement."

"In the beginning, one of the first hills I had to climb was the notion that the arts are actually made by regular people," says Tim. He took a few art courses in college and had no idea what he wanted to do, although he always felt drawn to teaching. His father was a Presbyterian minister and his mother was a schoolteacher, and as a result, he grew up in a house where books were abundant and education valued. Tim took a jewelry class in college and set up a small worktable in his dorm room. Although he began selling his jewelry right away, he didn't think of it as a possible career until he visited a professional jeweler while on a vacation with a friend. "On that day, the universe shifted a little bit," says Tim. "Jewelry became more than a hobby to me; it became a possible road to take."

Tim went on to earn an MFA degree and began teaching at the Worcester Center for Crafts in Worcester, Massachusetts. "I taught there for twelve years," says Tim. "There had been a resignation, and the Director came across some of my work in the gift shop there and contacted me. I moved there a couple weeks later." At that time, the center was primarily a continuing studies program, with most of the classes held in the evening. Tim was the only teacher in the Metals department. He set up the program, purchased tools, arranged the studio, and put together the program. "I really cut my teeth there," remembers Tim. "Although being a one-person department did not offer me the opportunity to learn from another metalsmith, I was able to make a lot of mistakes more or less privately."

In the beginning, Tim made mostly earrings and rings, selling them for $2 and $5. To spend $60 on a cup seemed phenomenal to him. It was only after he had been teaching and his income became more stable that he started to make things that weren't primarily to sell. To date, his work has been in over eighty-five exhibitions around the country, including "Master Craftsmen" at the National Ornamental Metals Museum, the "National Fiftieth Anniversary Invitational" at the Brookfield Craft Center, and "Makers '96" at Colby College.

The next phase came when Tim accepted a teaching job at Portland School of Art (now Maine College of Art) in Portland, Maine. For the first couple of years after Tim accepted the new position, he did not unpack his own studio, in order to devote himself to establishing himself at the school. "What I've come to realize is that teaching, both in person and through writing, is the way I process information," says Tim. "Some people keep journals, some have long phone calls with friends. I write, teach workshops, or create projects for my courses." Not surprisingly, Tim believes that writing is part of craft, and gives his students an assignment to write a fifty-page thesis. "I'm not trying to make them into writers," says Tim. "Writing can be part of learning craft. Both technical expertise and the ability to articulate the process are important."

Recently, with other interests taking up larger amounts of his time, Tim has cut back on his teaching. "I certainly enjoy teaching, and for a long time that was how I defined myself," says Tim. "Now I'm doing less teaching, with publishing the biggest piece of the pie in terms of time and income. I'm also on a retainer doing consulting work with Mitsubishi, as well as other small jobs, and probably devote two days a week to teaching. I have enjoyed learning more about marketing as well as learning about another culture. I wish I had known a long time ago that it is possible to find help to get things done. You don't have to do it all yourself. Not knowing this earlier on slowed me down. Now, if I decide something needs to happen, I figure out different options to get it done. Early in my life, I would have said something like, 'I can't get a hundred stores to carry my work,' and it would have ended there. Now I would be open to other possibilities. There aren't just two ways to do things. We allow ourselves to narrow our options, and there usually are other ways to get things accomplished.

"Know yourself," says Tim. "Be aware of your strengths and weaknesses. Know your situation. What are your financial needs, and what length of time can you commit?"

Blacksmiths

Peter Ross, Master of the Blacksmith Shop, Colonial Williamsburg

"When I was seventeen years old, I was in about fifty bands as a drummer," remembers Peter Ross. "I was in all the school bands and two or three rock and roll bands. That was my consuming interest. Then I took a class in blacksmithing with my dad at the local museum, where we learned how to make something simple, like a hook. At the end of the

class, I participated in the museum's field day, demonstrating what I had learned to visitors. I thought it was fun, but I was much more interested in being a musician. I had hardly ever done anything like it, and it was a real departure for me." Little did Peter know that not only would he one day become one of the leading blacksmiths in the country, but that museum work was also in his future. He has been the Master of the Blacksmith Shop at Colonial Williamsburg for over twenty years, and says he can't imagine any scenario where the work would have been more interesting or he would have been happier.

After his initial experience with blacksmithing, Peter and his dad set up a forge in their garage. "If we showed a real interest, my dad would help a lot," says Peter. "After a couple months of working in that garage, I got involved with another local museum as a volunteer. I worked one day a week with the blacksmith there, and never thought it would lead to a career. In retrospect, it helped me a lot. I didn't really have an inner picture of what I wanted to make or how to do this work. What I did have there was a place to work and an assignment list of things that the museum needed. In the beginning I could hardly do any of it, but it was great training." Not only did he learn how to control the material, but he also had a goal to work towards and the tools to figure out how to do it.

Although Peter had never taken an art course, he liked to draw and had a lot of work to show by the time he applied to college. "I went to the Rhode Island School of Design and dropped out about halfway through," admits Peter. "I was put in the Sculpture department, where there was one anvil and forge, and no one teaching blacksmithing. When the head of the Sculpture department told the students he didn't want us to do any functional work, I left RISD. Then I helped a blacksmith that did historical reproductions in Connecticut for a year. By this time, I was already skilled and had learned a lot. At this point, I was ready to figure out what I wanted to do, and I went back to talk with one of my teachers from RISD, Jack Pripp, who suggested I work in Ron Pearson's shop in Deer Isle, Maine. It was vacant, and I ended up spending the next four years there until I took the job at Colonial Williamsburg."

During the time in Deer Isle, Peter worked for himself and made his living doing craft shows such as the ACC shows at Baltimore and

Rhinebeck. "I did the shows for a couple years and I didn't like it," says Peter. "I wasn't convinced that I wanted to do that for a living, and it wasn't the best market for my type of work. Although the retail market seemed interested in my work, the wholesale buyers were not. They would say, 'When you get a catalog, send me one.' I never made the commitment to do it for a living, and couldn't decide. The shows were a good way to make money, but my market was more in restoration and historical reproduction."

When Peter accepted the position at Colonial Williamsburg, the program's emphasis was changing from being geared to producing souvenirs to making historic reproductions. "It was the right time to be at the museum," says Peter. "There was a shift happening to develop knowledgeable tradesmen staff and make everything in-house. Up until then, the focus had been on providing entertainment for tourists instead of being a research program and doing preservation work. We now do a wide range of work, with more variety in six months than most shops see in twenty years. I can't imagine a scenario where the work could interest me more."

With existing professionals in the other departments to help him understand a more academic approach, Peter found himself facing high standards and lots of orders. "We had so many orders that there wasn't enough time to flounder," says Peter. "In the time I've been here, we have only run out of orders twice. The museum demands are steady and for very interesting stuff, ranging from supplying the hardware needed for historic carpentry to copying a two-wheeled cart that George Washington owned. Take making nails, for example. What did eighteenth-century nails look like? What tools and skills are needed to make them? It took years to get the right kind of nails. We were able to make nails that were similar, but not correct. It takes a long time if you have high standards, and you can only learn by doing." Other current projects include producing tools for the other craftsmen, such as: axes; hollowing knives for coopers; large andirons for a kitchen fireplace; and cooking spits.

Peter is active in demonstrating and giving workshops through ABANA to local groups. "Very few smiths are doing this type of work, and although most modern smiths are not as concerned with method and learning about history, there is an interest in carrying on the traditional methods," says Peter. "My job is to study and rediscover traditional methods. Traditional hand methods are very efficient. The notion that handwork is inefficient is incorrect. Handwork is different from modern methods and doesn't use the same steps. You can't just substitute power tools for hand tools. This is an important area of study for me. Also, most modern smiths are not connected to the modern crafts movement or to an appreciation of crafts or blacksmithing. What seems to attract a lot of people to blacksmithing is a romantic notion of being a self-reliant pioneer.

"I have been really successful in this setting," says Peter. "However, I always feel like I'm only scratching the surface. I would like to be able to watch some eighteenth-century blacksmiths to see how they really made things. I would like to keep doing what I'm doing, but perhaps in a different setting. Although I'm not as interested in a public setting, the work itself is still intriguing.

"Although I'm not advocating that everyone do historical work, expose yourself to work to see how well it's made, what forms were explored, and how the material was used," says Peter. "Unless you have studied work that has been done before, you are destined to produce naïve work."

Eric Ziner, Sculptor

"My dad used to get up in the middle of the night and go out to his shop to putter," remembers Eric Ziner. "I was in charge of making his coffee. Now that I have kids of my own, I realize why my dad did what he did. I get up at 5:00 A.M. every morning, drink three cups of coffee, and get started. I pick up a piece of metal and see if it talks to me." Eric is a sculptor who utilizes blacksmithing to create his one-of-a-kind pieces, whether they are commissioned sculptures or furniture or pieces he sells out of the gallery he shares with his wife, potter Missy Greene.

Eric's interest in making things started when he was growing up. "I'm a triplet, and we are all artistic," says Eric. "Everybody in my family turned to art. My parents were role models. My mom is a writer and teacher and my dad did sculpture and commercial art, and taught as well. My brother is into acting and my sister is a painter. When I was in high school, I used to help my dad with his work, whether it was sanding, grinding, or polishing. We made things together."

Although Eric attended a couple of different programs, he is largely self-taught. "I went to a vocational school to learn welding and improve my skills," says Eric. "After that, I drove across the country until my money ran out. I ended up in Eugene, Oregon, where I worked at odd jobs: picking rhubarb, working in the fields, working for a cabinetmaker, landscaping, and finally, welding. I decided to go back to school and enrolled at Lane College. I was able to convince the art instructor to let me make my projects at home, and I brought in work every week for critique. I started meeting other people, including a blacksmith whom I was apprenticed to for two years."

Eric's work changed from being primarily cut metal that was welded, to metal that he was able to form and bend. "Once I learned how to heat metal and saw how it bent, I never looked at metal the same again." He primarily makes animals like birds and dinosaurs, but has been getting more interested in figurative work. Although his work has changed over time, there is a common element. "I'm amazed when I look at old slides of my work and see that I was just as stylized then as my new work is now," says Eric. "Yes, some work is more sophisticated, but there is a recognizable style. I am using less stuff now and paying more attention to form. It could be yesterday. I am still excited about what I do to create a visual story and entertain viewers."

Although the West Coast had an idealistic grand scale that was appealing to Eric, his family was on the East Coast. "I started traveling East during the summer," says Eric. "I would spend the winter out West and work at the forge and then drive cross-country and paint houses during the summer." Eric continued to move between the two coasts until he began teaching blacksmithing at the Guilford Handcraft Center in Connecticut. He met Missy there, and they did a show together, then decided to move to Maine in the early 1990s. They have maintained their own seasonal gallery and done juried crafts shows of Missy's work ever since.

Missy does several large crafts shows around the country each year, and Eric is an integral part of the success of her efforts. "Missy and I are a team," says Eric. "I help her with packing, shipping, and at shows. It can take hours to set up and break down her booth, and I help her with it. We also bring our kids with us."

Commission work has been a primary source of income for Eric. "I got my first big professional job from a Yale professor who had received a Percent for Art commission," says Eric. "I helped him by building the pieces and then did the installation. It was a big job, and lots of fun. Commission work requires more thought and planning than other work. These days, my commission pieces are a combination of forged work and found objects."

Eric loves contact with customers and produces most of his work during the spring, which he then sells during the summer in their own gallery. "The work I produce to sell in our gallery is not my real work," says Eric. "Although I've had galleries approach me to carry my work, I like the personal contact with customers and want to sell it myself. I know I am missing out on a market by turning the galleries down, but I like to know where my stuff is going and make eye contact with the person who is buying it. I find it equally important to share the story of creating the piece with customers, and the sharing adds value to the piece for the people who are buying it. People enjoy the recycled nature of the work as well as information about the various parts. I want to put the work into context for them. However, it's a mixed blessing when someone comes and says, 'I'll buy it.' I really like my work and want them to have it, but it's almost true that they want it more if I say they can't have it! I want to know that they are not just spending hundreds of dollars for something because it's the last day of their vacation and they want to bring something home. The charge I get from talking to customers is immeasurable."

Although most of the people who visit their gallery enjoy seeing the work as well as meeting Eric and Missy, the small percentage that say they love the work and want to invest in it by buying a piece are the ones who leave a lasting impression. "The people who want to invest in us are essentially endorsing our lifestyle and commitment to the work," says Eric. "It's as much a mind game as it is making a sale. I want customers to be happy, but if someone saw my work and said it was cute, I wouldn't want to hear that. I work hard and I want my work to be taken seriously, even when the piece may be humorous."

In addition to benefiting from contact with customers, Eric also benefits from contact with his peers. "My ABANA membership is the only venue where I can see my peers and keep track of them," says Eric. "Peers are important for me. The group provides a chance to meet with other blacksmiths and keep up with my contacts on the West Coast. My critics and supporters are both my customers and other blacksmiths.

"Nothing is perfect," says Eric. "You have to extend yourself beyond what is practical by getting up each morning and getting to it. Assess your endeavors, because time is limited. We are at the prime of our lives right now and have recently moved to a new house, where we have built our dream studios. Although the last couple years for me have been consumed with the move and construction projects, I am ready to get back in the studio. I love it! What better reason is there to do it than that? If you enjoy your work and your life, then you work to live. I don't do it for the money. I'm going to keep doing this for as long as I can."

Mixed Media

J. Fred Woell, Studio Artist

Fred Woell is a jack of all trades and proud of it. Well known nationally and internationally for his metalwork and sculpture, he is a gifted teacher, avid photographer, poet, and mainte-nance man extraordinaire. In 2001, Fred officially retired from paid employment. "I keep saying I'm retired so I don't have to be under pressure to perform on a job," says Fred. "This opens up my days to do different things. It brings closure to a chapter in my life. I can look back and appreciate what I've accomplished."

Fred received a BFA from the University of Illinois in 1958 and an MFA in Metalwork from Cranbrook Academy of Art in 1969. He has taught at various colleges and universities off and on from 1969 until 1993, including the University of Wisconsin, Madison; the Program in Artisanry at Boston University; the Swain School of Design; and SUNY New Paltz. He was the Assistant Director of Haystack twice and was Head of Maintenance until he retired. "Teaching has been high on my list, including both college teaching and doing workshops around the country," says Fred. "The neat thing about doing workshops is the per-missive atmosphere, where students can learn without being under the gun to bring their work to a high artistic standing. I can give them a lot of information in a short time and congratulate them on both small and large successes without worrying about grading them." Many of Fred's college students and his students from workshops have gone on to make their mark in the field of metals. "Although I don't remember many of the people from the workshops," says Fred, "Many of them have come back to thank me in the long run. Teaching and learning is a discovery on both ends of the stick, for student and teacher, with an opportunity to fail and to have surprises. Taking risks is hard for the student but can also be hard for a teacher. The best teachers are able to do it."

Fred's teaching philosophy is student-centered rather than focused on an institutional agenda. "When the creative process is seen as nurturing, healing, and related to self-discovery and esteem, it allows students to see themselves and their work as something they can succeed at without having to rise to some social standing where success is based on making money," says Fred. "Art is about the unknown, not about the things you already know. A good teacher has learned how to talk with students and have critiques without the student feeling diminished in the process."

A turning point came for Fred in 1987, when a friend who was hospitalized with a nervous breakdown wrote him a letter. "That letter made me decide to leave a teaching situation that wasn't working for me anymore," remembers Fred. "People who are thinking about making a change not only need a plan of action; they also need to assess their skills and think about their marketability. They don't need to sit around and think about it for ten years. I suggest that when people take the risk, things will happen to support it. Do something you want to do. Take the chance. It's important that you do it. If you stick with your belief, in the long run it will pay off if you are persistent." Fred recommends a book called *Feel Free* by David Viscot for those who stay at a day job and wish to leave but never do.

Fred has self-published a book called *Handouts from the 20th Century: A Collection of Teaching Aids Created and Gathered by J. Fred Woell During His 20 Years of Teaching*. The book includes a variety of information such as: jump-starts for creativity, how to make a résumé, pricing and keeping track of your work, and how to approach a gallery, as well as technical information on soldering, rolling mills, forging, cold connections, casting, tools, and much more. "My workbook sells well to my students," says Fred. "It has been a nice surprise for me. I decided to self-publish it after I looked over all my handouts from my teaching over the years."

Fred also recommends that aspiring metalsmiths join an organization like SNAG. "The organization has grown and expanded to include offerings for upcoming artists," says Fred. "They sponsor awards and scholarships as well as sponsor artists to bring metals to the schools. It's a good value."

Fred is currently working in several media to express his ideas. "I'm always fascinated with something," says Fred. "Right now I'm trying to get comfortable with video. My curiosity centers around the concept of serendipity, when something triggers something else in your mind and becomes part of your own work. For me, making is not linear.

I'm all over the place. Whether I'm doing photography, videos, sculpture, or poetry, all these different interests keep me going. Poetry is a way for me to try to be creative with words. It creates a shift of opportunity and is different from making. Planning a house was also helpful to my other work. A project I used to assign to my students was for them to design something that someone else would make. This made them think through the details and learn how to communicate their ideas to others in a different way."

PART SIX

Wood

CHAPTER 14

Facts, Educational Opportunities, and Organizations for Wood Artists

L ike so many media in the crafts world, wood art takes many different forms. Profiled in this section are craftspeople working in wood who design and make fine furniture, college professors, an industrial designer, a boat builder, woodturners, and a spoonmaker who doesn't just carve his spoons—he finds them waiting for him to discover them in a tree. Many of the people profiled here have worked through several stages in their crafts careers, or have combined different interests to make a living or to live in a way that suits them best.

Insight Survey Statistics on Wood Artists

Today's craftspeople working in wood have a lot of opportunities to make a living. In the August 2003 issue of *The Crafts Report*, the Insight Survey on Wood Artists was based on twenty-two respondents who earned an average of $51,636 in gross sales. Here are the details:

Percent of Gross Sales from Various Sources
- 38% retail shows
- 22% wholesale shows
- 29% sell directly to galleries
- 5% own gallery/studio
- 2% consign to galleries
- 1% Internet
- 2% other

Amount Spent on Materials
- 0% less than $1000
- 67% $1000 to $10,000
- 19% $10,001 to $20,000
- 14% $20,001 to $50,000
- 0% $50,000+

Number of People Working in Studio
- 59% work alone
- 32% 1 to 2 people
- 5% 3 to 5 people
- 5% 6 to 10 people
- 0% 11 or more

Time Spent Selling Crafts
- 5% less than one year
- 9% 1 to 5 years
- 14% 6 to 10 years
- 32% 11 to 15 years
- 41% more than 15 years

Forty-one percent owned their own Web site, 50 percent sold their work through an online gallery or crafts site, and 32 percent said their business was the only source of income in their household.

Martha and Jerry Swanson, wood artists living in Montana, have been making wooden salad bowls since the 1980s as their sole source of income. "We credit some of our success to a local potter who gave us some great advice years ago. He looked at our bowls and the variety of sizes we were offering and said that we needed to get clear on what we do," says Martha. "I think that many starting out in crafts are faced with the temptation of taking a diluted approach and decide to make a whole line of products in the hopes of making money immediately. We have found that we were better off biting the bullet and focusing on making one product. It's the same product year after year, but we have the reputation of good and reliable quality with style." The Swansons currently make three main bowls in a few different sizes, in addition to a vessel series and some accessories, from a combination of domestic and exotic hardwoods.

Educational Opportunities for Wood Artists

Profiled here are just a few of the many places where you can learn the craft of woodworking. In addition, there are many schools for studying wood, whether as a workshop or for a degree, all around the country. See chapter 4, "Educational Opportunities, Residency Programs, and Apprenticeships for Craftspeople," for more information.

Center for Furniture Craftsmanship

The Center for Furniture Craftsmanship is a year-round woodworking school that encourages individual excellence and self-expression through workshops that focus on furniture making as well as design and related skills like carving, marquetry, and finishing. The Center was founded in 1992 by Peter Korn, a furniture maker since 1974, who has not only written several books (*Working With Wood: The Basics of Craftsmanship* and *The Woodworker's Guide to Hand Tools*), but also spent six years as the Program Director at the Anderson Ranch Arts Center.

The twelve-week intensive program is designed for people who are considering making furniture as a profession, interested in taking a sabbatical from their present career, or simply want to enhance their skills. Class sizes are small, and experience ranges from novice to advanced.

Assistantships are available to provide emerging woodworkers with an unsurpassed opportunity to learn from outstanding master craftsmen and acquire teaching experience. Responsibilities range from machine room supervision to working with students, shop maintenance, and errands. Lodging and a small stipend are provided for a period of eight to ten weeks.

Currently, the Center is in a quiet phase of a fundraising campaign to expand its programs and facilities. Although the Center will keep the small, intensive atmosphere it is known for, the campaign will provide additional shop space to offer more classes, as well as a gallery and library to offer more programming to the public and create a major artists' community for furniture makers.

For more information: The Center for Furniture Craftsmanship, 25 Mill St., Rockport, ME 04856; (207) 594-5611; *www.woodschool.org*.

Wooden Boat School

In 1980, this school grew out of a magazine aptly called *Wooden Boat*, which had been started by Jon Wilson in 1974. "The school offers something for just about everyone who shares an interest in the unique worlds of boat building, woodworking, and seamanship," says director Rich Hilsinger. Located on sixty-four acres on the coast of Maine, additional courses are also offered at off-site locations in Maryland, Virginia, Michigan, and California.

Courses run from early June through September, and usually last one or two weeks. The main requirement for participation is the desire to learn; as a result, students range from novice to professional. Classes are small, and learning extends into evening socializing and boating. Scholarships are available for one-third of the tuition costs, and are awarded to people who could not otherwise afford to participate in our courses. Preference is given to those working in the marine trades and to students contemplating a career in the marine industry. In exchange, scholarship students are expected to do periodic tasks in the shop, in the kitchen, and on the waterfront.

In addition to running the magazine, a mail-order business, a three-day WoodenBoat show, and the school, Jon Wilson is responsible for starting *HOPE* magazine, which features people who make a difference on local, national, and international levels.

For more information: Wooden Boat School, P.O. Box 78, Brooklin, ME 04616; (207) 359-4651; *www.woodenboat.com*.

Woodturning Center

A Philadelphia-based arts institution, gallery, and resource center, the Woodturning Center is dedicated to the art and craft of lathe-turned objects. Through its programs, the Center not only encourages existing and future artists, but strives to cultivate a public appreciation of the field of woodturning as well. Founded in 1986 in response to the success of an unprecedented series of ten symposia on lathe art held in Philadelphia between 1976 and 1981 and organized by Albert and Alan LeCoff (now the Executive Director) and woodworker Palmer Sharpless, the Woodturning Center has become an internationally recognized source of information and assistance to artists, hobbyists, galleries, museums, collectors, and educators. In 2000, the center expanded tenfold, moving from an office in Albert's home to adjoining storefronts on

Vine Street in Philadelphia's Old City District. The move provided space for operational needs and also allows the Center to engage the public with a gallery, library, store, and storage area displaying a collection of more than five hundred objects.

The Center offers:

- Exhibitions and a collection
- Conferences
- Membership
- Annual international residency exchange program
- Publication of a quarterly journal newsletter, *Turning Points*
- Print and visual archives
- Library
- Community service outreach and training programs

"I don't spit out work," says Hugh McKay, a woodturner from Oregon who was one of five Resident Fellows at the Center. In eight weeks, he transformed a 125-pound block of wood into a sculpture called "Quad pot w/reveal," which explored the paradoxes of geometric shapes. "I knew it would not be very saleable, so I used the stipend I received for the residency to financially justify taking the time to see it through." Like many turners, McKay has benefited from the exponential growth of his field since the 1970s, during which it evolved from turners working in isolation to a network of artists, curators, and collectors all over the world. The Wood Turning Center has played a critical role in this development, along with organizations like the American Association of Woodturners and the Collectors of Wood Art.

A recent exhibit called "Wood Turning in North America Since 1930" included more than 130 works and was accompanied by two symposia and an extensive catalog providing the first critical history of lathe art.

The Woodturning Center conferences are held every four years and are responsible for countless artistic and personal alliances worldwide. For example, Stuart King, a turner from Great Britain, met Pierre Mille, a French archeologist, at the 1997 conference, where Mille gave a talk on turned flasks by Ion Constantin, a Romanian. King was so intrigued that he traveled to Romania to meet the artist. "Now in his seventies, Ion may be the last woodturner to make drinking flasks, a tradition that goes back to the sixth century," says King. "His every stroke is accurate and meaningful, with no energy wasted. He turns simple technology into an art form."

For more information: Woodturning Center, 501 Vine Street, Phila-delphia, PA 19106; (215) 923-8000; *www.woodturningcenter.org.*

Organizations for Wood Artists

American Association of Woodturners (AAW)

An international organization dedicated to the advancement of wood-turning, the AAW's mission is to provide education, information, and organization to those interested in turning wood. Founded in 1986, membership is now close to ten thousand worldwide, with hundreds of local chapters. The AAW provides:

- *American Woodturner.* A quarterly magazine that includes: feature articles on a wide variety of topics; technical articles; profiles of craftspeople; a turner's tip column; a gallery of photos; book, video, tool, and product reviews; a national bulletin board; and a calendar of regional events.
- Annual Symposium. Held in a different part of the country each year, this is the largest gathering of woodturners in the world, and includes: panel discussions, demonstrations, slide shows, design workshops, an Instant Gallery where members can show off their latest work, a trade show, a local tour for spouses, and an auction.
- *AAW Resource Guide.* Published annually, this guide includes names and addresses of all members, supply sources, contact information for local chapters and workshops, and a list of books and videos.
- Demonstrator Connection: A free service that coordinates informa-tion for local woodturning groups and individuals.
- Educational Opportunity Grants: These grants, which allow mem-bers to attend woodturning workshops or further proposed research and development projects, are also available to local chapters to help finance visiting demonstrators or other educational events.

The beginnings of the organization can be traced back to a confer-ence held at the Arrowmont School in Gatlinburg, Tennessee, where a juried show opened with a three-day symposium. "With all the meeting and greeting of old friends and new," wrote David Ellsworth in the pre-mier issue of *American Woodturner,* "it soon became clear that what had brought us to Tennessee was more than just a lust for tools and tech-niques. It was a thirst for the process of learning. Several hundred turned objects were on view in both formal and informal displays, as if the energies of the past decade were brought before us in a moment. If there was a single thought on everyone's mind, it must have been, *Where do we go from here?"*

A survey was submitted calling for the formation of an association, and after a brainstorming session, an invitation to serve the organization went out to the attendees. A vote was taken, an ad hoc board was formed, and work began on framing a charter. By the next year, the AAW was formally named and incorporated as a nonprofit organization. Members make everything from decorative and functional bowls, boxes, and vessels to furniture and architectural spindles, toys, tools, musical instruments, and sculptures. Professional woodturners, amateurs, gallery owners, collectors, and wood and tool suppliers form the majority of the group.

For more information: American Association of Woodturners (AAW), 3499 Lexington Ave. North, Suite 103, Shoreview, MN 55126; (651) 484-9094; *www.woodturner.org.*

Furniture Society

Founded in 1996, the Furniture Society seeks to advance the art of furniture making by inspiring creativity, promoting excellence, and fostering an understanding of this art and its place in society. The Furniture Society is not a woodworking organization, because fine contemporary studio furniture can be made out of virtually any material or combination of materials. Created in a studio or small shop, studio furniture is often made by the designer or by someone in close collaboration with other craftspeople to create truly original designs.

Membership benefits include:

- A newsletter
- A copy of and listing in the *Resource Directory* and Web site directory
- Conference discounts
- Book discounts
- E-mail updates

If you are interested in learning more about the studio furniture movement and its makers, consider ordering two books available through the Furniture Society: *Furniture Studios Two: Tradition in Contemporary Furniture* and *Furniture: The Heart of Functional Arts* (published by the Furniture Society).

For more information: Furniture Society, Box 18, Union, VA 22940; (434) 973-1488; *www.furnituresociety.org.*

National Woodcarvers Association (NWCA)

The National Woodcarvers Association is made up of amateur and professional woodcarvers, with around 50,000 members worldwide. Ever since its humble beginnings in 1953, the National Woodcarvers Association's aims have been to:

- Promote woodcarving fellowship among its members
- Encourage exhibitions and area get-togethers
- List tool and wood suppliers
- Find markets for those who sell their work

It publishes a bimonthly magazine called *Chip Chats* exclusively for members, which doesn't include any paid advertisements.

For more information: National Woodcarvers Association, 7424 Miami Ave., Cincinnati, OH 45243; (513) 561-0627; *www.chipchats.org.*

The organizations listed above will help keep you informed, inspired, and on track as your career develops. If you can, pick out at least one organization to join. Every month when you receive your newsletter or magazine, you can read about what is happening in your field around the country, as well as gain information about opportunities to promote your work that you may not have known about otherwise. If memberships are out of your reach right now, ask a family member or friend to give one to you as a gift.

The next chapter is devoted to profiles of craftspeople working in wood. Read them and enjoy. If you have any questions for any of the people profiled and they have a Web site, feel free to learn more about them and even contact them with your questions and comments.

CHAPTER 15

Wood Artists' Profiles

Boat Building

Paul Rollins, Boat Builder

"I wasn't academically inclined," says Paul Rollins, "and had only done some canoe camping as a kid. But visible from my high school's windows were the sails of a boat at a nearby shop, and I found myself daydreaming about that. After attending the University of New Hampshire for a couple years, I worked construction before I got really fascinated with boatbuilding. I decided to build a boat and found a mentor named Bud McIntosh in Dover, New Hampshire, who gave me guidance." Paul has been building, repairing, restoring, and designing wooden boats for the past thirty years.

In the beginning, Paul worked in construction to supplement his work with boats. "I built a sailboat and peapod boats with the money I saved working construction," remembers Paul. "Then I began to get work passed on to me from Bud, such as oars, flagpoles, masts, and then finally, a thirty-six-foot lobster boat hull that needed to be built. Although I am self-taught and took some technical courses such as welding, I have found that tearing old boats to pieces is a wonderful way to learn how to build."

After a couple of years, Paul was able to give up his work in construction and concentrate on his boat business full-time. "I have been one hundred percent self-supporting since very early on in my career," says Paul. "Initially I had a loan from my Dad and used some of my own savings to get started. Bud gave me enough referrals to get established, and I bought my own barn and shop, and got started. However, if I had spent more time at cocktail parties than in the shop, the business would have grown faster."

The boat market is dependent mainly on word of mouth, although Paul does advertise in magazines such as *Wooden Boat* and *Maine Coastal News*. "It pays to have been in this business about three generations," says Paul. "Your name needs to get firmly established. With twenty-five years plus in the business, I am just getting to that point now. If the business would continue a couple more generations, it would really be a going thing."

Although Paul's market lies mostly in wood hull work, with an occasional powerboat to work on, he tends to work on forty-foot cruising sailboats. "I am working on a cruising sailboat right now that was built in 1934," says Paul. "The family that owns it has a summer place in Castine, Maine, and they have friends with similar boats. They enjoy racing around and having regattas. I live in la-la land, very removed from most people. It was a battle to get established. Some years I have felt successful, but the future is always uncertain. The funny thing about this business is that it has always been ahead of the economic cycles, so you can feel what's coming ahead of time. Oddly, it has been steady during the current downturn."

Paul has always employed several helpers. Each project can take up to a year to complete. He is not in the business of maintenance and storage as some of his competitors are, because he is located away from the water.

Currently Paul is working on a very different type of project away from his shop. "I was busy and didn't need another project, but I couldn't say no to this one," says Paul. "The Shelburne Museum in Vermont is building a replica of an eighty-eight-foot-long cargo schooner from 1861 that was designed to go down the Hudson River through the canals to carry freight to New York City. These boats were narrowly built to comply with the width of the canals, with this one only measuring fourteen and a half feet wide. Canal boats—both those that sailed and those that were towed by mule teams from a footpath on shore—grew in size as the canals were widened and deepened every twenty years or so during the mid-nineteenth century. Two wrecks are sunk in Lake Champlain, and they taught those of us involved in this project to scuba dive so we could go down and look at them. A team of archeologists had also spent time studying the wrecks and documenting how they were built. Working in a museum setting seems very relaxed to me. I am working with a lot of volunteers and don't have to be conscious every minute of deadlines and prices. I teach the volunteers, talk to visitors, and camp on my own boat when I am there. I like working with the volunteers. We get at least five a day, ranging from retired guys to kids and old ladies. Some are very productive. We plan to launch the boat in the summer of 2004." Following the launch, there will be a victory cruise retracing the steps the boat would have followed routinely 150 years ago.

"I suggest that people interested in pursuing a crafts career follow what they like to do," says Paul. "If you are lucky enough to find something you enjoy despite the stretches required, then do exactly what you want to do. If you don't have that intensity, keep your day job. It is good to get started while you are young. I also suggest that people not go to boat school. I think the only way to learn is to have to think it through, to go through the whole process and make every decision. I have made up my own methods, which has been an advantage, rather than being given guidance and materials in a school setting. I was fortunate enough to be passionate enough about what I was doing despite all the ups and downs. I am still having fun and despite the arduous labor, I find the work satisfying."

Woodturners

Peter Bloch, Woodturner
www.woodshades.com

"I'm self-taught," says Peter Bloch. "I went to a tool store, bought some tools, and just got started. For five years, I did wood sculpture purely as a hobby. I didn't want to think of myself as an artist. I wasn't into talking about it. I just wanted to do it. When I finally decided to make turning my living, I made functional work at first, such as bowls, clocks, desk accessories, and jewelry boxes. The work always had a sculptural look to it, however, and the objects became less functional and more artistic over time. The field is very competitive now and it was difficult to sell them. While I was working, something accidental happened and I started to see the translucency of the wood. I experimented with perfecting the technique for five years, never thinking it would produce something I would sell, and then I discovered Aspen wood. This wood provided an effective, dramatic object, and I began making the translucent lampshades that are now ninety percent of my business. This experience taught me the importance of taking the time to experiment and play without worrying about making money." Peter learned what many CEOs know about the importance of research and development time leading to future success.

To make one of Peter's lampshades, he starts with a two-hundred-pound log of green wood and ends up with a twelve-ounce shade. Although he originally found all the trees himself and got permission from property owners to cut them down, he now purchases sets of logs from loggers that are delivered to his shop and stacked for months to age. A typical shade and base might take him two to three and a half days, with a lot of variations depending on the wood. Peter can make about seventy-five lampshades a year, with the limiting factors being mainly the amount of physical effort and time required to make each one. "I like the hard parts such as being rugged with the chainsaw, and I like the finesse required at the end," says Peter. "Although I am physically exhausted after making a lampshade, I love putting the shade on a lamp and seeing it appear."

Peter also likes running a crafts business. "I've become aware of how important it is for me to think of my job as a whole," says Peter. "Not breaking it down into parts I like and parts I don't like, such as sweeping the floor. I see the big picture of it all and I love everything it has been able to do for me. If I go away for a week or two, I feel the absence of being in the shop and I am anxious to get back. However, I also enjoy the business aspects of it, such as designing a brochure or working on my Web site or a video. Although I had to learn how to talk to customers because I am not naturally outgoing, I learned to be myself and communicate my enthusiasm, passion, and story to customers. Customers don't just buy an object; they are buying it from a craftsperson who has a story to share."

Peter does about five crafts shows a year. "All my shows are retail," says Peter. "I don't do any wholesale shows because I don't want to take orders. All of my lampshades are one-of-a-kind, and each one is so different that I am better off selling them cash-and-carry. Occasionally I will do a special order, and I also do some consignment through galleries. I send out postcards religiously before every show I do. I just did a mailing of a thousand pieces for a show that is coming up. My mailing list has about two thousand names on it, either of people who have purchased a piece from me or of people who were very interested."

Peter uses his Web site to support his sales efforts at shows. "Rarely does a customer buy immediately," says Peter. "The Web site supports that by acting as a support system for people who already know about me. I don't use it to make direct sales. About fifty percent of my customers are repeat customers. One client has bought fourteen lampshades! He has three houses and has given them as gifts as well. I give every customer who makes a purchase a ten-minute video I made, and they are grateful for it. Then they act like promoters for me, and it has led to a lot of sales.

Peter also values his association with different crafts organizations, especially the League of NH Craftsmen. "I am very involved in the League," says Peter. "The League has been terrific, especially early in my career. I do the annual crafts show at Mt. Sunapee, and having my work at the galleries around the state is another great way to sell. It is also a badge of honor being League-juried, and I am proud of my affiliation. If the League hadn't been available to me, I would have had more of a struggle."

Peter had also made his mark in several woodturning organizations, including one that he founded. "I do a fair amount of volunteer work and run the New England Woodturners Symposium every three years," says Peter. "We usually get about three hundred attendees, and it attracts many professionals. I have attended the national symposia put on by the American Association of Woodturners several times, and have been very involved with the New Hampshire Chapter of the AAW, which I founded.

"Looking ahead, I am so happy making the lampshades, I don't foresee making something else. But I'm almost fifty now, and I'm not sure about how I will handle making them when I am older. I try to set aside time for experimenting and playing too. After all, that's how I discovered the whole lampshade thing to begin with!"

David Ellsworth, Studio Woodturner
www.ellsworthstudios.com

"I started out studying architecture at Washington University in St. Louis," says David Ellsworth. "I remember one of my professors called me into his office, laid my drawings out, looked at them, and said nothing. Then he told me to go to the Fine Arts department, where I belonged. He understood that I was in the wrong program." David transferred and graduated with a

Brian McNeil

BFA and an MFA in Sculpture from the University of Colorado. His accomplishments and honors include: being named a Fellow by the American Craft Council; receiving a Lifetime Membership with the American Association of Woodturners (of which he was President for five years); and obtaining Fellowship Grants from the Pew Foundation, the National Endowment for the Arts, and the Pennsylvania Council for the Arts. He started the Wood Program at the Anderson Ranch Art Center in Colorado and has exhibited and taught extensively all over the country. He currently makes his living teaching workshops out of his own studio and selling his work through galleries.

"My first exposure to woodturning began when I was fourteen," says David. "By the time I received my degrees, I had also worked in metal, fiber, and polyester. But it was my experience working in clay that led me to consider the intimate power of the vessel form. Clay had a similar centering process to turning, and my love for the material of wood returned."

Originally David sold his pieces at crafts fairs and gallery shows. "I did full-time production work, where I turned things like salt and pepper shakers," says David. "These sets retailed at eighteen dollars then, and I have only one set left. If I could find a set today, I would pay five hundred dollars for it. The production work provided good discipline, a solid work ethic, and a foundation of ideas and ideals. The mountain crafts fairs were the best, because they were more honest and responsive to the work than selling through a gallery. The value of having a gallery is different than a crafts show. In the beginning, I just sold my work through galleries until my major galleries closed and I had to start all over again. The arts are not intended to be a safe field. You need to diversify to survive, and have a variety of sources of income."

David runs a school out of his studio, teaching and hosting as many as eighteen to twenty workshops a year. "Running the workshops is like a full-time job," says David. "It occupies an enormous amount of time. The students range from those with no experience to those at the intermediate level. My name is pretty well known in the field, so most know that I have a school and I mostly get students through word of mouth. My Web site is also an enormous help getting the word out; I didn't have it until five years ago. I designed the site so that the students have to contact me directly for information. As soon as I put up the Web site, my workshops were full for six months in advance. I didn't anticipate this, and have increased the number of students I will take from four to five. I have an extensive crafts collection in our home and it's part of the educational experience. I also advertise in *AAW Journal* and *Woodshop News*."

In addition to those workshops he offers at his own home and studio, David also teaches ten to twelve workshops every year, both domestically and internationally. "I have to learn from students and vice versa," says David. "Real learning is an exchange. We share experiences, and they can see themselves moving in a direction. There is not only one right way to learn. Sometimes it is easier to tell someone what doesn't work than what does work. If a student can gain a sense of self in a positive manner and allow creative expression to occur, then art can grow and satisfaction can be achieved as part of the creative process, of which craft is the foundation."

David has also written sixty plus articles for publication, mostly about turning. "I put my heart and soul into these articles, and then later, a new group of students will come along who have never known about an article and the process starts again," says David.

David doesn't sell his work through his Web site, but relies on galleries for sales. "I don't sell over the Internet; I inform people about my work," says David. "Selling over the Internet could be disappointing, as there is no continuity to the sales and no history. Galleries provide lots of things, including documentation. I continue to produce one-of-a-kind pieces in a series, and depending on my exhibition schedule, I produce fifteen to twenty new pieces a year. I like to live with my pieces and then get them back." David usually works in a series where he can explore ideas, challenge concepts, and expand the dimension of his work into a broad visual language. "I consider the skill of my craft to be the foundation from which my artwork has evolved. The identity of each object is a glimmer of the collective body that is my life's work," says David.

David has been very involved in professionally developing the field of woodturning. "A group of woodturners attended a conference in 1985 at Arrowmont, and we decided to set up an organization that is now called the American Association of Woodturners. We give scholarships, produce a quarterly journal, and host an annual conference. We started with two hundred thirty members and now have over ten thousand members in two hundred chapters in North America. It is a fundamental organization for anyone interested in turning." David served as AAW's President for five years and has been awarded a Lifetime Membership for his service.

In addition to teaching and making his work, David sells tools, has produced instructional videos, and has done consulting work. "I have a variety of sources of income to support my family," says David. "They tend to fluctuate with the economy." The tools are designed by David and are used to turn hollow forms. "Hundreds of my students in the woodturning field have used these tools," says David. "I make them myself, and these are the primary tools I use in my own work, so I'm confident that they are both functional and versatile."

"In the future, I want to keep doing the same thing I'm doing now," says David. "The field is constantly changing, and I am looked upon as a leader. I'm always looking for new experiences, travels, and evolution to move forward with my work, whether subtle or dramatic. I can't predict what's going to happen, and I feel lucky when something occurs. We need to be aware in order to receive it when it comes to us."

Furniture Makers

Wendy Maruyama, Furniture Maker, Educator
www.sdsu.edu/art

Wendy Maruyama has the distinction of being one of the first two women to earn an MFA in Wood in 1980. She only happened to take woodworking in a required course at a local community college. "My interest in wood really started in college," remembers Wendy. "I took a required general crafts course that included woodworking, and I was hooked. I was interested in crafts, especially metalworking, and my early interests in furniture possibilities were sculptural rather than rooted in tradition. When I finished at the community college, I transferred to San Diego State University as a Metals major, but by the time I graduated, I was a Wood major."

Although Wendy had a great mentor in Arline Fisch, head of the Jewelry program at SDSU, she took several semesters of furniture making with Larry Hunter, who suggested she consider graduate school. "The motivators in the field for me at that time were Larry, Wendell Castle, Tommy Simpson, and Jack Hopkins," says Wendy. "I didn't even know who Tage Frid was! Then I saw the work of Alphonse Mattia, Tage Frid, and Bill Keyser. Alphonse's work caught my eye, and I followed him from Virginia Commonwealth to Boston University's Program in Artisanry. BU didn't have an MFA degree yet, but I had much to learn and it was a fortunate move for me. It changed my life and my destiny, and working with Jere Osgood was an honor."

In between the two years Wendy was at BU, she attended workshops at Haystack and Penland, where she met Bill Keyser. "I was encouraged to apply to grad school at Rochester Institute of Technology and get my degree in Furniture Design and Woodworking," says Wendy. "My first teaching experience was at the Appalachian Center for Crafts, where I served as assistant to Tom Hucker, who was the master craftsperson. I really learned to teach the hard way, because the only real experience I had regarding teaching was watching my professors do demonstrations. It is truly one thing to watch and another to teach it yourself. Now my students have teaching assistant positions that give them a good background in teaching foundation courses. They are also exposed to a multidisciplinary platform of study that results in making our students much more versatile as teachers. They are finding jobs teaching a range of subjects, from design to sculpture and furniture, along with courses in drawing and 3D. I wish I had been able to have that experience as an MFA student."

Wendy has found her teaching career to be very rewarding. "I am sure I am a much better teacher than I was twenty-three years ago," says Wendy. "I want to keep teaching, and only wish I had another person to teach with. It has been exhausting running a program alone all these years. There just isn't enough time to do everything. Sometimes I vacillate between wanting to keep teaching and wanting to do only my own work. Teaching has been a challenge, but it has been rewarding to be able to create a program on a shoestring and still be able to produce winners. My students work hard to get where they are, and teaching has kept my mind young and in the forefront as well. For me, the best reward of teaching is seeing my students teach all over the country."

Although much of Wendy's energy has been devoted to teaching and building the wood department at SDSU, she has also found time to create and exhibit numerous pieces of her own. "Traveling often sparks a new series of work," says Wendy. "For example, travels to France, England, and Japan have been the nucleus to several bodies of work. Other times, looking at flowers for color ideas and going to sculpture exhibitions helps me along. In addition to teaching, I sell my work through galleries and do commission work. Recently I also ventured into public art projects, designing benches for public spaces. In the eighties, my sales were twice that of my teaching salary, and then in the nineties, they were roughly thirty percent of my regular salary. Now that I am a full professor, I find myself with less time to build, and my income from work sold is about ten percent."

Wendy was Head of the Woodworking and Furniture Design program at California College of Arts and Crafts in Oakland from 1985 to 1989, and is now Professor of Woodworking and Furniture Design at San Diego State University, where she has been since 1989.

She has also received several awards, such as: a Japan/U.S. Friendship Commission grant; a Research, Scholarship, and Creative Activities grant from SDSU for the establishment of an exchange program between her students at SDSU and Takumi Jyuka, Japan, in 2000; a Fulbright grant for a residency in England in 1994; and a four-time winner of the National Endowment for the Arts Visual Artists Fellowship for residency in Japan (1995), England (1994), France (1992), and the United States (1990).

Her exhibition list is astounding, with numerous solo exhibits at well-known crafts galleries, such as: Joanne Rapp Gallery in Arizona, Peter Joseph Gallery in New York, Snyderman Gallery in Pennsylvania, and Savannah College of Art & Design in Georgia. Her work is in many private and public collections, including: the Philadelphia Museum of Art, Pennsylvania; the American Craft Museum, New York; and the Mint Museum of Art + Design, North Carolina.

Wendy has also been an active civil servant, devoting herself to several crafts boards to contribute her expertise. "I just retired after nine years on the Haystack board," says Wendy. "I am now the Vice President of the Executive Committee of the Furniture Society. Board involvement is very important to me because it keeps me on the pulse of the field and I feel I have much to contribute to help the field and students." Wendy has also served as a juror and curator for several important exhibitions, a board member of the James Renwick Alliance in Washington, D.C., and a panelist for several conferences and task forces.

"I feel successful," says Wendy. "For woodworkers just starting out, I recommend that they never lose sight of their vision and try to be as open-minded as possible. So many furniture makers today have tunnel vision. Versatility, resilience, productivity, and an inner spirit, combined with commitment as an artist and object maker, are what it takes."

Rosanne Somerson, Furniture Designer and Maker; Professor and Department Head

"I started out as a photographer," says Rosanne Somerson. "I had a lot of technical experience as a photographer because I had graduated early from high school and spent a year in Denmark studying photography. Thinking I would be a Photography major, I took a furniture course my freshman year at Rhode Island School of Design and found I liked the three-dimensional aspect of furniture. I was also starting to dislike working with all the photography chemicals, although I seem to have traded them for sawdust and chemicals. I learned to work in the wood shop quickly, in spite of the fact that my teacher at first called me 'Ten Thumbs.' Working with wood was completely new and very challenging for me. There wasn't a formal furniture design program at RISD at that time, so I tried the Sculpture department. The Department Head was uninterested in functional work, so I ended up earning my degree at RISD in Industrial Design in order to do furniture. One of the best things I did was take a semester off my junior year and study at Peters Valley Craft Center. When I came back to RISD, I was convinced that furniture design was what I wanted to do. I graduated and opened my own shop." Years later, with many other experiences under her belt, Rosanne returned to RISD to run the graduate program in Furniture, never dreaming that the program would evolve into one of the most successful undergraduate and graduate furniture design departments in the country.

After graduation, Rosanne continued to work with her RISD professor, Tage Frid, doing the photography and writing for his first book and writing for *Fine Woodworking* magazine. In 1985, when Tage Frid retired, Rosanne was asked to teach at RISD. "At the time I was asked to teach, I had been out on my own for ten years and my professional life was going great," says Rosanne. "It was supposed to be a part-time job. I didn't have a lot of teaching experience, I didn't have an MFA degree, but I had worked hard in the studio I shared with my husband, Alphonse, and had good luck showing my work. I also had a fairly large professional profile writing and researching book projects, as well as writing for *Fine Woodworking*. The combination was hard to find else-where. Each applicant also had to present his teaching philosophy to the students and faculty. Mine was about creating a process of learning for them rather than imposing a particular point of view. I took the job and designed the curriculum. In 1994, the Interior Architecture depart-ment was having problems, and I was asked to consider merging the Furniture Design program with the Interior Architecture department into one new department. I thought they should be separate depart-ments and submitted a proposal that was passed by the faculty in 1995. As a result, I became a Department Head and the Furniture Design department became a new major. It has been highly successful and gone from a small department to now both an undergraduate and a graduate program with eighty-nine majors! We often have a waiting list for stu-dents. It was the right idea at the right time, and we got a lot of support to make it happen."

For the first nine years of teaching, the position remained part-time, and Rosanne was able to do commissions and make work for exhibits in her studio. Then the needs of the department grew to the point where Rosanne's position became full-time. "I had studio assis-tants at home, but with the increase in my hours at RISD, my work at home became more a combination of making and directing," says Rosanne. "I try to have something of myself in everything I do. During the years we produced work for Peter Joseph Gallery, we did a lot of high-pressure studio production. We had six people working for us full-time, and looking back on it, I see it was an important period to get a lot of work done. The gallery closed and we reinvented the studio. I have to admit I was relieved to have more control again, although the gallery connection was great for producing." Rosanne's income has been a com-bination of teaching, commissions, and sales of her work.

Rosanne has continued to dedicate herself to her teaching, too. "At this point, I can easily do the teaching, but I want to relate to the stu-dents and help them on their journey, so I vary the curriculum every year. It requires enormous amounts of energy to do it well. I love RISD and am committed to the school. It's a phenomenal environment, although I do look forward to having a sabbatical."

Rosanne has also served on several boards as a way to help further the field. "I love being on the Haystack board," says Rosanne. "I get more than I give. I'm so addicted to that environment and school." She is also a member of the ACC and Furniture Society advisory boards. "I feel an obligation to be involved with these organizations because I am in education," explains Rosanne. "It's fun to help shape them, and I learn something from everything I do.

"Perhaps I have accomplished a lot, but I have a long way to go," says Rosanne. "I'm close to fifty now, and reevaluating the future. Some years I have been able to fit the puzzle pieces together better than others. I am much more critical of my own work, and I want to make pieces better and clearer. Although at times my own work feels self-indulgent, there is a lot of travel left in my work. With the teaching, I give back concretely every day. There is a balance between the two that is important. I also have two incredible kids who deserve lots of energy. Success changes with kids. I am proud of them *and* the department at RISD.

"It's a huge commitment to a way of life to do this work," says Rosanne. "It takes significant inner drive to express a personal point of view. Craftspeople need to push and evolve their own ideas rather than looking to others for influences, and to constantly grow their work in unplotted territories. There are inevitable frustrations in pushing into new arenas, but we are in a sense evolving our culture at the same time. This is very important in our contemporary times, where this commitment is crucial.

"Having low overhead is very important in the beginning," says Rosanne. "I suggest people consider working in a cooperative studio to share expenses, because with all the different materials used today, a shop needs to have as much equipment as a small manufacturing plant. If the overhead can be kept low, then there won't be as much of a need to take on work that someone doesn't really want to do. It is more valuable to be able to do your own work and have a less showy shop. Your own career is the biggest design project you will ever have."

Jere Osgood, Artist-Craftsman

In 2002, Jere Osgood received the Award of Distinction from the Furniture Society, an honor given to outstanding artist-craftsmen for lifetime achievement in the studio furniture arts. Thomas Hucker, who studied with Jere in the 1970s, presented the award to his teacher. "Three of us got heavy awards at that ceremony," joked Jere. "I had to give an acceptance speech, and they actually quoted what I said

Brian Wilder

later. I will have to be more careful about what I say next time." Jere's work has been exhibited widely, and he is represented in collections such as the Museum of Fine Arts in Boston, the American Craft Museum in New York, the Renwick Gallery of the Smithsonian Institution's National Museum of American Art in Washington, and the Currier Gallery of Art in New Hampshire. He has been named a Fellow of the American Craft Council for his extraordinary contributions to the field and has taught countless students through his association with Rochester Institute of Technology, the Program in Artisanry at Boston University, and numerous workshops. Since 1985, he has worked full-time in his studio doing commissions and exhibition pieces.

Jere's career in wood officially started in 1957, when he first started maintaining his own shop. Initially Jere studied architecture at the University of Illinois until one of his projects led him to working with wood and furniture. He transferred to the School for American Craftsmen at Rochester Institute of Technology (RIT) and received his BFA in Furniture Design there in 1960. This was followed by study in Denmark through the Scandinavian Seminar. He has been selling his work and teaching woodworking ever since.

"I used to say to my students, I'm not really here, I'm working in my shop," remembers Jere. "I'm just doing this temporarily. I didn't want to be a professor, but I ended up staying at the Program in Artisanry for ten years. Every once in awhile when I was teaching, I remember thinking, *I'm losing work*, so when the Program was going to move to New Bedford, I didn't really see leaving teaching and going back to work in my shop full-time as risky. Plus, my son was still in school and I didn't want to be away overnight. If I had stayed with the school and commuted to New Bedford, I would have felt I was away from him too much. It was a good decision on my part."

Originally Jere made and sold accessories, before the option to sell work through crafts fairs and galleries existed. "I spent about ten years doing accessories, which paid for my machinery and my truck," says Jere. "I was busy producing one hundred forty-four of this and two hundred eighty-eight of that. Fairs weren't available then, and I used to take samples of my work around in the early years. I made things like bookends and paperweights, and was one of the few people making wooden clocks. I had a whole line of clocks and did a lot of turning too. There was a division of the ACC called "America House" where I started selling my work before I was even a student. Just as crafts fairs came along, I stopped doing accessories. Slowly I shifted my work towards furniture."

In 1978, Jere started an association with Pritam and Eames, a gallery devoted to selling and supporting the makers of studio art furniture. "It's been a wonderful ride working with Pritam and Eames," says Jere. "Prior to that, I sold my work in New York and Philadelphia, and did private commissions."

Jere is also well known for developing lamination techniques, about which he has published several articles in *Fine Woodworking* magazine. "Over the years I have worked on some totally new lamination processes for furniture, primarily to carry out my own design ideas," says Jere. "I have developed these techniques to the point now where I envision a whole range of new pieces that are functional but not encumbered by traditional furniture forms. I know that my methods are liable to appear fussy or confusing to people who are accustomed to using a band saw to make curves from heavy, solid stock, but they will appeal to assemblers and people who enjoy complicated joinery. I prefer to spend time on the planning and drawing instead of on carving huge amounts of waste from unformed, heavy stock."

Jere has found memberships in crafts organizations to be a positive thing. "It gets me out of the shop," says Jere, "but I don't belong to be busy." He is a founding member of the New Hampshire Furniture Masters Association, which represents small shops of both traditional and contemporary craftspeople. "They are my peer group," says Jere. "We have a monthly meeting, an annual auction, and several exhibits a year." He is also a juror for wood for the League of NH Craftsmen, and a member of the ACC, the Furniture Society, and the Guild of New Hampshire Woodworkers.

"I think it's important to encourage students to think on their own," says Jere. "I would encourage people starting out to do it because everyone should have a job they like doing twenty-four hours a day, and not get tired of it. Being a craftsperson is not an eight-to-five job. On the other hand, don't expect to make a lot of money at it. Chances of success financially are small. In general, I try to give people the facts, encourage them to do it, and tell them to keep their eyes open. They have to have business sense. Artists can be flaky, but they can get it together to sell their work."

These days, Jere is still doing commission and exhibition work while occasionally teaching a workshop, and he has no plans to retire. "I teach once in awhile, maybe one or two classes a year," says Jere. "It keeps up my interest in teaching, and it's a nice change to get out of the shop. I can work by myself and not see anyone for a week. Although I can make more money working in my shop, the teaching is sort of a vacation for me, even though I am exhausted at the end of a day of teaching. I'm not planning on retiring." In addition to woodworking, Jere likes to read, maintains a flower garden, and enjoys spending time with his two granddaughters.

Industrial Design

Julie Morringello, Designer of Furniture and Housewares

"Ever since I was a kid, I loved drawing and making things," remembers Julie. "I had a dollhouse and got kits of miniature furniture for it, but found using them frustrating. I decided to make my own, so I bought some balsa wood that could be cut by hand. A friend of my parents was an architectural model maker. He saw my work and asked me to work for him after school making trees. I made trees all through high school and believe me, they had to be just right. I had no idea what to do for college, and a painter I knew suggested I consider art school. I applied and got in everywhere. I was really excited about art school and enjoyed learning and taking classes. I was torn between sculpture, interior design, and industrial design. I eventually chose Industrial Design as my major, even though I didn't want to do either appliances or products. I had seen the furniture design studio at school and knew that was what I wanted to do, but it wasn't a major yet, so I picked Industrial Design. Sculpture wasn't geared to wood. By picking Industrial Design, I was able to learn about many different materials and how to work with them, including taking courses in the wood shop." Julie received her BFA degree in Industrial Design from the Rhode Island School of Design in 1989.

After graduation, Julie worked for a year as a carpenter. "I am glad I did it," says Julie, "but I found it so physically exhausting that I was unable to stay awake past seven at night. A couple friends of mine were starting a cooperative called Birth of Venus Studios, a five-thousand-square-foot cooperative that included individual studio spaces and shared access to fully equipped metal and wood shops. I worked there for the next eight years. I had time and a place to make my work. I feel like this was the true beginning of my work, and it started to evolve." A few of these friends got together and formed the Stone Boat Association of Studio Furniture Makers of Southeastern Massachusetts, through which they organized and sponsored local exhibitions, lectures, and a studio tour for high school students.

Julie supplemented sales of her work with a job teaching wood to adults with mental disabilities, before deciding to go back to school for her MFA degree. "I had a job that I loved, but eventually I hit the top of the pay scale and had nowhere to go," says Julie. "I was getting older and I had done work in furniture, but I wanted to focus and get critiques. I took a workshop at Haystack, and that experience made me want to go back to graduate school. It was an 'aha!' moment and when I got home, I applied."

Julie earned her MFA degree with honors in Furniture Design from RISD in 1997. "My graduate class in wood was small," remembers Julie. "I was really interested in making furniture that was inspired by an object like a chair but had references to a bed, for example, with aspects of comfort as a focus. Then I began to make things that were more geared towards production and less towards one-of-a-kind items, although my focus was not design for production. I was able to fuse varying interests with this work. I graduated and continued to work in the cooperative studio."

Julie had done all kinds of part-time work to make ends meet, including making shelves and things for kitchens, as well as teaching outside of the studio. She saw a part-time job with benefits advertised, which involved designing frames and sounded just right for her. "I designed frames for Fetco Home Décor as a Senior Designer for a couple years before I decided to move to Deer Isle, Maine," says Julie. "I asked the company if I could work at home and ship the work. I did a presentation and they accepted it. This enabled me to move to a remote location with a job, to share a house and studio with my new husband, Gene Koch. I usually do drawings for the frame company, mostly on the computer, with an occasional mock-up or sample. After toying with the idea of doing my own work one hundred percent of the time all these years, I find I have tremendous freedom in what I do, and I like it. When you design something for someone else, it is a different type of making."

Julie has also taught at several of the country's leading art and crafts schools, including: Haystack Mountain School of Crafts, Arrowmont School of Crafts, the Worcester Center for Crafts, and the Rhode Island School of Design. She has received several awards, including: the

Charlotte Perriand Award for "demonstrating a virtuosity in bringing ideas for furniture alive and off the blank page," and an honorable mention for her work in the Chair Show at the Asheville Center for Crafts in North Carolina. Scholarship awards include Haystack Mountain School of Crafts and the Bernice Bienstock Furniture Library Scholarship, for "excellence in design that addresses furniture and its relation to industry." With an exhibition record that spans more than a decade, Julie has shown her work at leading venues around the country, such as the Houston Center for Contemporary Craft in Texas, the Fuller Craft Museum in Massachusetts, Pritam and Eames Gallery in New York, the RISD Museum in Rhode Island, and Joanne Rapp Gallery in Arizona. Not bad for somebody who started out making miniature trees!

"These days, I am trying to decide if I should come up with my own line or go back to doing just my own work," says Julie. "It can be isolating to work from home. Although I prefer working alone, it is not the same thing as not seeing other people. I have a stack of things I want to make, and want to build a separate studio for myself so I have more space. I will keep doing what I am doing for now, and move on to something related when the time is right."

Having a support system of friends has also been invaluable to Julie. "Working in the cooperative studio and now being married to another craftsperson has made pursuing this career a lot easier," she says. A founding member of Birth of Venus Studios, Julie is also a member of several organizations, including a national group called the Furniture Society, and a state wide organization called the Maine Crafts Association, and is Vice President of a local group called Seamark Workshops, which offers arts and cultural enrichment to Deer Isle and the surrounding communities.

Julie suggests that people thinking about a career in studio furniture should stay focused on what they want and build their life around it to be successful. "Designing and making furniture affects every life decision," says Julie. "My work has to be foremost in my thinking at all times. For example, I am foregoing getting a new car right now because doing my work is more important to me. My top priorities are my health, my family, and my work."

Utensils

Dan Dustin, Hand Spoonmaker

Rudy Hauk

Dan Dustin comes from a long line of people who split wood when they needed things, including axe handles, sleigh runners, and shingles. In the simple object of the spoon, Dan has found a living, a philosophy, and an art. After graduating with a degree in Sociology, Dan decided to make his living as a woodworker and put an ad in the *Christian Science Monitor* that said: "Useful Things, Hand Made of Wood: What May I Make for You?" He was surprised to find out that people wanted wooden spoons. He started out carving spoons with a band saw and was not pleased with the results. One day, he was splitting firewood and the wood separated in such a way that a spoon was produced. "I cleaned up around the split and there was a spoon more beautiful than anything I'd made before. After that, I split wood like crazy looking for spoons," says Dan. "Now I've got x-ray vision. The tree doesn't know it's growing a spoon, but I do." Experience with thousands of trees has taught him how to see into the tree and predict where a spoon is forming.

Dan's ability to extricate these naturally made spoons has earned him not only his livelihood for over thirty years, but also recognition, such as the Brookstone Wood Award and the League of NH Craftsmen's Sunapee Education Award; publicity on radio and TV programs such as "New Hampshire Crossroads" and "Evening Chronicle"; and features in *Yankee Magazine* and *Fine Woodworking*. He has been represented by several galleries over the years: the Craftsmen's Gallery in Scarsdale, New York; Elements in New York; Winston Limited in the Bronx; Options Gallery in Nashua, New Hampshire; and the League of NH Craftsmen in Concord, New Hampshire.

"Although I had no clue at the time when I discovered the first spoon, I'm perfectly matched to what I do," says Dan. "I think I was the first person in history to ask for real money for functional spoons. I simply refused to make a nickel another way, and I made the world buy what I wanted to make. In the beginning, I had low overhead; I lived in a log cabin with no bills and a bucket in the well. I work full-time at spoonmaking, and for over twenty years, I have made one hundred percent of my living from selling spoons. As a matter of fact, I'm working on one right now while you are interviewing me!"

In the beginning, Dan lost his shop to a fire. "I lost a beautiful shop, all my flat surfaces, my vice, workbenches. I found myself reduced to working with a stump and an ax," says Dan. "I figured I would restore my studio, but after I started working with the spoons, I realized that I no longer needed the same type of shop. Before the fire, in order to improve my work, I had dumped all my power tools, but I was still trying to do machine work by hand. I was much more successful when I stopped trying to copy machine work and began to make the spoons by hand.

"I do most of my selling at fairs," says Dan. "I know everyone who buys my work and I like it that way. The only exception these days is if someone buys my work through the League Shop in Conway. I only sell my work at one price, so a lot of shops refuse to buy my work. I don't have any galleries at present, and generally do two fairs a year. I have a following at both a fair in New York and the League's annual fair at Mt. Sunapee. I have been going to both for over thirty years, and do a post-card mailing before each show. A breakthrough in my work came from one of my New York customers who picked up two spoons, fit them together, leaned her face into the booth, and said, 'Stupid, make one into a fork.' That's how my salad sets were born. Many of my customers are other artists as well as professional people. These people often say, 'Dan, we envy you because you can do what you do for the love of it. You live for us.' There is a thirst for quality, and to them I seem to represent someone who doesn't have to think in terms of money or markets."

Dan is also an accomplished musician who plays the flute, as well as a music teacher. "I have taught flute for forty years, usually having only a couple students at a time," says Dan.

"If you want good advice, advise others," says Dan. "Although I hesitate to give advice to others, my advice to someone interested in making a living selling his craft is to do what he loves, find a way to live cheaply, start selling, even if you have to operate at a loss in the beginning, in order to find out if you are good enough," says Dan, "and then raise your prices. Then, if it is looking good, switch your career." Dan also suggests that aspiring craftspeople have a classical education.

"I see each spoon as a performance. Like the revered potter, Hamada, who asked each pot, 'What do you want of me?,' I ask each spoon what it wants of me," says Dan. "The fact that they are beautiful comes from the function. I am now putting away spoons for my retirement. I make more money than I need, and sometimes feel like the cat that ate the canary."

PART SEVEN

Transitions and Support Systems

CHAPTER 16

Making the Transition

After reading the profiles, how do you now translate the stories and advice offered into making it on your own? How do you keep yourself inspired and on the right track? What if you are a young craftsperson (or the parent of one) and want to find out ways you can get started on a career path in crafts? This section is designed to help you set goals and write a simple business plan. It offers ways to keep yourself inspired and provides guidance for the next generation of craftspeople. It's as easy as 1, 2, 3.

Bridging the Gap

If you are thinking about starting a business, you are in the first phase of the transition. What can you do to help bridge the gap between where you are now and where you want to be in the future to ensure your success? Do you have to do it on your own, or do you have people who will support you while you are growing your business?

In their book *Making It On Your Own*, Sarah and Paul Edwards offer the following suggestions for finding a cash cushion while you are growing your business:

- Start your business on the side while you still have a job. When it gets going, leave your job.
- Take a part-time job that will cover your basic expenses while you get your business underway.
- Do temporary work to get your business underway.
- If you're living with a partner, cut expenses and live off one salary while you start your business.
- Use your savings or other sources of income—like retirement

funds, a sabbatical, divorce settlements, or an inheritance—as a cushion.

- Take out a second mortgage on your home or arrange to get a consumer line of credit, such as the kind some banks are offering to very small businesses, which enables you to borrow if and only if you need to. These loans are secured with the equity in your home or other assets.

As several of the craftspeople profiled suggested, you can start your new crafts career on the side and see how it goes. If you are able to set up your studio and generate sales of your work, for example, while you are still earning a paycheck, then you may be ready to do some long-range planning to begin the transition process from part-time selling to making a full-time income from selling your crafts. Or maybe you would prefer to get a job working for another craftsperson to learn how she operates a crafts business, and when you feel you have learned enough, strike out on your own. Or an opportunity may present itself that you feel is worth taking the risk of going out on your own, as happened to quilt artist Elizabeth Busch, who said that if it didn't work out, she could always get another job. Whatever your dreams are for your work, it's time to turn those dreams into a plan of action.

In order to formulate a plan, it's a good idea to start out by doing some soul searching and picking some specific goals that you want to achieve. Continue to revisit this process to keep yourself on track as your business grows and your career evolves. It's an ongoing process.

Soul Searching

Before you set some tangible goals for yourself, let yourself dream a little. "Your career is going to be the biggest design project you will ever have," says Rosanne Somerson, furniture designer and maker. What do you want to do with your life? How can you design your life to accomplish your dreams?

Some of the questions in the Self-Assessment Quiz may have gotten you thinking about the basic issues of making your living as a craftsperson, which include:

- Finances (whether you need to have a regular paycheck to feel secure or if you can handle earning money sporadically)

- What kinds of support systems may be valuable for you (such as joining an organization or finding a space in a group studio)
- How to market your work (Would retail shows or wholesale shows better serve your needs? What about the other career options available?)

Take some time to evaluate different career options in crafts. Whatever your goals, stop and think about what the different roads are that you could take to achieve your aims. Is the type of work you want to make appropriate for your goal? Are you willing to make compromises in order to achieve your goals, or do you feel strongly about keeping your work free from the requirements of the marketplace? For most craftspeople, selling their work brings different demands to their work than making their craft just for pure enjoyment. Although there are a couple of craftspeople profiled in this book who are able to generate enough income from selling their work through solely doing gallery shows or commissions, the majority of people make some work to sell and some work for their own enjoyment, and may also have an additional source of income to complete the picture.

If you can decide what you are aiming for and what feels right to you, as you start to make the changes necessary to organize your life around your craft, everything else will be easier to plan and should allow you to focus on developing your work.

Goal Setting and Business Planning

Although most people measure the success of a career or business by the bottom line (how much money did I make?), there are other measures of success that are just as important. For example, the satisfaction of working for yourself rather than an employer, getting your first big wholesale order, getting accepted into a juried show, or taking advantage of a residency are all measures of success that you should feel proud of as you accomplish them.

Although success is something that can only be determined by you, a simple way to measure your success is to set goals for your career that are both obtainable and measurable. For example, setting a goal of getting into three juried crafts shows in one year would be a measurable and obtainable goal.

What are some goals that you would like to set for yourself? Take a few minutes to write down at least three. Now that you have some goals to get started, start developing a plan of action to accomplish them. Remember, setting goals is not about limiting yourself, but about giving you a framework to make them happen. Putting together a simple business plan can be very helpful.

Business Planning

What is all the fuss about planning a business? After all, you may have already started working in crafts and haven't needed to do any business planning yet. But if you don't have a plan, how are you going to know if your career is doing well? Business planning can include projecting what you want to accomplish with your career, creating a time line for achieving those objectives, and devising methods to measure your success. It can also help you clarify your goals so that you can make informed decisions, be prepared if you decide to submit an application for a bank loan, or even know whether you should disband your crafts career and do something else.

If you are thinking right now that there is no way you will be able write a business plan, then keep reading and use the simple outline included in this chapter to help you get started. Would you go on a trip to a new place without a map? Would you start a new career or business without taking the time to write a business plan? To help keep you from feeling lost, plan to set aside a couple hours each week to work on each section of your business plan, and before you know, you will be looking at a finished product.

A business plan should not be done once and filed away, but reviewed and updated on a regular basis to help you keep measuring your success and to help you figure out what to do next to advance your goals. A business plan should be seen as a tool to help you manage your business more efficiently so that you can spend more time in your studio.

Whether you are in the first year of your career or the tenth, you will always be learning new things and moving your career forward. No matter what stage you're at, there will always be a next one. Even if you knew everything you needed to know to advance your career, the whims of the market are not within your control, and everyone needs to learn to be flexible.

How to Write a Business Plan

Although what you are about to do is typically called "business planning," you can also call this process "writing a career plan." If you are more interested in pursuing a crafts career than in specifically running a crafts business, follow the same steps outlined below with your career goals in mind.

A business or career plan should include:

- The purpose of your business
- What the value of your product is to your customers
- Why you are qualified to run the business
- How you will market your work
- What makes your product different from your competitors' products
- Financial projections for several years

Here are the steps you should take to write your business plan:

1. *Start the plan with a simple summary of your business idea.* Write a summary as though you are trying to attract the attention of a potential lender or investor financing. You want to make it really easy to understand. A couple of paragraphs are all you need. Include why you started your career and describe your overall ideas.
2. *What is your business?* Describe your business and each product or service separately, using terms easily understood by non-craftspeople. Tell what you make and how it is used, and whether it is a new product or one already established in the market. You may want to include a few photographs of your work and your studio if you are applying for financing.
3. *Why are you qualified to run this business?* Explain how you learned your craft and discuss any business background you may have, as well as workshops you have taken. Attach a résumé, a listing of shows and awards, and any articles that may have been written about you and your work.
4. *Who are your customers?* Identify and give descriptions of the general types of people who will buy your work.
5. *What is the value of your product or service to the customer?* Think about the features and benefits that a customer will experience after

they buy a piece of your work. Will it bring beauty to their life? Will they be thought of as someone who purchases unusual gifts or has a unique house? Will it add to their collection? Does your piece serve a function?

6. *Where are you located, and how does this affect or enhance sales of your work?* Do you travel to market your work at fairs and live in a remote area to keep expenses down? Are you located in a retail district with a lot of tourist traffic? Or do you have a showroom open to the public?

7. *How do you market your work?* What are your marketing goals, what resources can help you, and what steps do you need to take to accomplish your marketing goals? Here is a sample marketing plan to help you get started.

   a. *What specific goal do I have to market my work?* My goal is to locate three crafts fairs where I can sell my furniture in the Northeast, where I can make sales of approximately $15,000 each or $45,000 total.

   b. *What resources will I use to help me?* I will buy a guide listing crafts fairs, look in magazines such as *The Crafts Report* for ideas, call my local crafts organization for referrals, go online, and ask other craftspeople for suggestions.

   c. *How will I contact people or places for information?* I will look at Web sites, make introductory phone calls to show promoters, attend fairs, and do follow-up calls with exhibitors. I will research fairs by requesting applications, speaking with a show producer on the telephone, attending several crafts fairs, and calling up exhibitors with questions after the show.

   d. *How much time and money can I spend?* I can spend three hours every week for the next two months working on my marketing goals and spend $500 for books and magazines, phone calls, and travel to visit shows in my region.

   e. *What are the steps I need to take?*

      STEP 1 Buy crafts fair guidebook and magazines with fair listings; check Web sites

      STEP 2 Call my local crafts organization and other craftspeople for ideas

      STEP 3 Call or download applications and deadline information

      STEP 4 Review applications, contact with questions, and ask for suggestions

STEP 5 Visit shows and speak to exhibitors afterward

STEP 6 Submit applications to my top three show prospects

STEP 7 Do the crafts fairs I am accepted into and evaluate the results

STEP 8 Continue this process until my sales meet my marketing goals

8. *Who are your competitors?* Give some examples of other craftspeople who make similar work, how they market their items, and what their prices are, to give the reader a comparison to the competitors in your field. Not only will this help you clarify what competition you may be up against in selling your work, but this will also enable a non-craftsperson who may be reading your business plan to understand your plan in the context of your field.

9. *Why are you different from your competitors?* Give a couple examples of other craftspeople who run a similar business. Is there enough demand to handle both businesses?

10. *What financial information should you include?* If you are writing a business plan to get a loan from a bank, try to think of the plan from the lender's perspective. The lender will be attracted by your business, but will also be aware of the risks involved in lending you money. The lender will want to know:
   - How much money you want to borrow.
   - What you want the money for.
   - When you will be able to repay the money.
   - If your business has a setback, what is available to secure the loan? The lender's concerns have nothing to do with how good your work is or whether or not they like you as a person, but rather, can you make your loan payments?

To prepare the financial projections for the business plan, you will have to make certain assumptions based on your projected income and expenses. Check out the Insight Survey in the section on your crafts medium for some ballpark figures if you are just getting started. If you have already sold some work, you should have an idea of your basic expenses and be able to project them for your own experience. Or ask another craftsperson or crafts administrator if she can share information with you to help you prepare projections.

For the business plan, forecast your financial situation for the next three to five years. The lender or investor wants to know that enough money is being requested to fund the business, and be able to understand the long-term intentions of your business. Remember, it takes many craftspeople several years to get a crafts business off the ground financially, so don't worry if your numbers show someone who isn't able to take a salary right away, for example, or requires additional capital to get started.

Review the sample outline of a business plan and take some time now to see how much you can fill out. What you already know about your business will be just as informative as the sections you have not figured out yet.

Remember, this is not rocket science. If you write down several specific goals for your business, draft your business plan, and use it as a way to measure your success and help you make important decisions, then you will be well on your way. Consider taking a small business management course that includes writing a business plan if you need help and structure to get it done. It will be well worth it.

CHAPTER 17

Keeping Yourself Inspired

What do you do for inspiration? Do you always have plenty of ideas and energy, or do you get discouraged once in awhile and wonder where you are going with your crafts career? Figuring out ways to keep inspired and developing a support system are very important aspects of attaining success as a craftsperson. Finding a mentor, reading crafts publications, belonging to a crafts organization, networking with your peers, or simply going to fairs, galleries, and museums to see other people's work can all help to keep you on the right track.

Finding a Mentor

In *Making It On Your Own*, Sarah and Paul Edwards say that if you were an Olympic athlete, enthusiastic audiences would cheer you on to great feats. Your coaches would encourage, prod, and guide you to success. If you were part of a top sales team for one of the nation's leading corporations, you would attend regular seminars and training programs with experts to charge you up and build your skills and confidence. But if you are one of today's growing number of self-employed craftspeople, who cheers you on? Who picks you up? Who gives you the boost you need? Although chances are you have to do most of that yourself, there are other people and places to help.

A mentor or trusted advisor can help by teaching you how to run your business, introducing you to important people, and providing support and encouragement. Many people become mentors after they are established in their careers because they want to give back to the community, pass on techniques, and teach someone else the business skills they worked so hard to master.

What should you look for in a mentor? Someone who is successful in her professional life, who is willing to donate her time to help you, and who has a lot of contacts that she can share with you to help you get connected in your field or area. Establish a regular time to get together, maybe once or twice a month to start, and write up a few things that you would like to accomplish together. Review your list periodically with her to see how far you have come, as well as to make changes in your plans. Mentoring and being mentored require time, expertise, and an open mind to be successful. Just like a good teacher, the mentor may find that she learns as much as the student.

In addition to finding someone to have an ongoing mentoring relationship with, consider short-term arrangements, such as assisting craftspeople at a crafts show to learn how to make sales and interact with customers. Here are a couple of suggestions:

- The Rosen Group, sponsors of the Buyers Market of American Craft, offer mentoring opportunities at their shows, where new exhibitors can be matched up with a seasoned craftsperson exhibiting at the show. Call The Rosen Group at (410) 889-2933.
- The Mentor Program through the American Crafts Council also assists artists who are entering the wholesale market for the first time, by providing them with financial support and one-on-one guidance from an experienced exhibitor. Because the success of a mentoring relationship rests on effective collaboration, the program requires that a new artist and his/her mentor apply to the program as a team. If accepted, each is given a free booth space in a specific ACC wholesale market. In addition, the new artist receives a stipend, disbursed in installments and contingent on the achievement of certain criteria which are periodically evaluated. For more information, please contact the ACC Show Office at (800) 724-0859.
- Call your local crafts organizations or show promoters for referrals if you are interested in being matched up with a current exhibitor as a short-term mentor.
- Call your local Chamber of Commerce to look for a general business mentor in your area who can assist you with the non-crafts side of your business, such as finances and marketing.
- Contact the Small Business Association (SBA) at (800) 8-ASK-SBA or *www.sba.org* for more information on mentoring programs.

- Contact the Service Corps of Retired Executives Association (SCORE) at (800) 634-0245 or *www.score.org*. SCORE is dedicated to helping small businesses through no-fee mentoring—either as a confidential one-to-one mentorship or as team business management counseling.

If you are ready to start your business but would like someone to talk to for support and guidance as the business develops, finding a mentor or mentoring program may be a solution. Depending on where you live, you probably won't have to look far to find a mentor. Even a chance to assist and learn from another craftsperson or business mentor on a short-term basis can be valuable. With someone guiding you for a longer period of time, the possibilities are endless. Remember, a mentor does not necessarily have to be a craftsperson.

Potter Bill Strickland, profiled in *HOPE* magazine in an article titled "This is My Clay," not only benefited from having a mentor himself, but has also created two mentoring programs in Pittsburgh, Pennsylvania, that have helped increase the percentage of at-risk teenagers who have gone on to college as well as helped adults in his vocational program find jobs. "I'd watched my neighborhood go from a healthy community to a ghetto," says Bill Strickland. "I needed to find a way out. But there weren't many examples of successful people in my community." Bill discovered a mentor in a ceramics teacher at his high school, who encouraged him to take control of his life and do something more than he had done before. Bill believed in him and went on to found the Manchester Craftsmen's Guild, an after-school program, to teach neighborhood children the same pottery skills that had motivated him. Three years later, he took over the Bidwell Training Center, a neighborhood vocational training program, and tested his ideas on how to rebuild his community with children and adults.

Are you interested in starting a mentoring program for youth in your area? In a recent issue of *American Craft*, the National Endowment for the Arts announced it had launched a program called "Challenge America: Positive Alternatives for Youth," awarding several hundred grants totaling close to $2 million for projects featuring artists-in-residence in schools and civic or community organizations. "Research has shown that engaging young people in art encourages positive behaviors such as cooperation and trust," says former NEA chairman Bill Ivey. For more information, contact the NEA at *www.nea.gov*.

Publications

Subscriptions to magazines, periodicals, and newsletters will help keep you informed and give you tips and ideas to sell your work, as well as encouragement to help you have a more successful career. "Join organizations to keep you connected, even if it just means getting a subscription," says quilt artist Elizabeth Busch. However, even though magazine subscriptions are a legitimate business expense, the costs can add up, especially if you get more than one. Consider subscribing with a friend, asking your public library to subscribe, or visiting the library at your local crafts organization as an alternative to subscribing to magazines on your own. Or suggest a subscription to a magazine you want as a gift idea to your friends and family.

Although there are many magazines to choose from, subscribe to at least one magazine created solely for your medium as well as a general business magazine for craftspeople, such as *The Crafts Report* or *American Craft*, to keep up on industry news. If you aren't familiar with magazines designed for craftspeople, look in the medium-specific sections of this book to see what magazines the organizations publish, in addition to the ones profiled here. Here are ten sample magazines to consider.

- *American Craft*, 72 Spring St, New York, NY 10017; (800) 724-0859; *www.craftcouncil.org*. Founded in 1943, this magazine is published bimonthly by the American Craft Council and features interviews and profiles of craftspeople and books, articles on crafts history, and profiles of emerging craftspeople in the "Portfolio" section. Informative listings of opportunities such as exhibits, events, and workshops are located in the back of each issue.
- *American Style*, 3000 Chestnut Ave., Baltimore, MD 21211; (410) 889-3093; *www.americanstyle.com*. Published by The Rosen Group, this magazine is primarily geared towards crafts collectors.
- *Ceramics Monthly*, P.O. Box 6102, Westerville, OH 43081; (614) 523-1660; *www.ceramicsmonthly.org*. Published monthly, this magazine is geared towards the ceramics field, including profiles, how-to articles, opportunities, and lists of suppliers.
- *The Crafts Report*, P.O. Box 1992, Wilmington, DE 19899; (800) 777-7098; *www.craftsreport.com*. This business journal for the crafts industry is published monthly to inspire the professional craftsperson and crafts retailer, with articles on business management, industry

news, and current trends and issues, as well as a forum for exchanging ideas, encouragement, and recognition. The "Crafts Showcase" is an advertising section is specifically for craftspeople.

- *Fiberarts*, 67 Broadway, Asheville, NC 28801; (828) 253-0467; *www.fiberartsmagazine.com*. For craftspeople working in the fiber arts—spinning, weaving, surface design, and wearables—each issue includes profiles, how-to articles, opportunities, and lists of suppliers.
- *Fine Woodworking*, The Taunton Press, P.O. Box 5506, Newtown, CT 06470; (203) 426-8171; *www.finewoodworking.com*. Published monthly for woodworkers, this magazine includes profiles, how-to articles, opportunities, and suppliers.
- *Hand Papermaking*, P.O. Box 77027, Washington, D.C. 20013; (301) 220-2393; *www.handpapermaking.org*. Published for craftspeople working with handmade paper, each issue includes profiles, how-to articles, opportunities, and lists of suppliers.
- *Metalsmith*, 710 East Ogden Ave. #600, Naperville, IL 60563; (630) 579-3272; *www.snagmetalsmith.org*. Published by the Society of North American Goldsmiths (SNAG), each issue includes profiles, how-to articles, opportunities, and lists of suppliers.
- *NICHE*, 3000 Chestnut Ave. #300, Baltimore, MD 21211; (410) 889-3093; *www.nichemagazine.com*. Also published by The Rosen Group, this publication is for crafts retailers and galleries, with profiles and advertising opportunities for craftspeople.
- *Sunshine Artists*, 3210 Dade Ave., Orlando, FL 32804; (407) 228-9772; *www.sunshineartist.com*. A monthly publication that calls itself "America's premier show and festival publication," with show reviews, extensive listings, and business articles.

These magazines are only a sampling of what is available. Magazines are a good way to keep up with what's going on in your specific field and the crafts world in general. Check out the resource section in *The Crafts Report*, or ask other craftspeople for more ideas.

Networking and Organizations

Joining a crafts or business organization can be an excellent way not only to network with other craftspeople and businesspeople, but also to connect to opportunities you might have missed out on if you decided not to join a group. So, what is networking, and which organizations should you consider joining?

Networking

Chances are, if you are thinking of being a full-time craftsperson, you are intrigued with the idea of just working in your studio and being left alone by the outside world. While there are craftspeople who love contact with the public and selling their work, the majority of people attracted to the field would prefer to work in their studio. Many people also feel as if they're not supposed to talk about themselves and their work because that would be bragging, or having a big ego, or seem pushy. But how will anyone know about your work if you don't talk about it? If you don't tell them, who will? The good news is that with a little practice, even shy craftspeople can learn to interact with customers, buyers, and gallery owners in a way that fits their comfort level and personal style. "Although I had to learn how to talk to customers because I am not naturally outgoing, I learned to be myself and communicate my enthusiasm, passion, and story to customers," says woodturner Peter Bloch.

Networking is simply going to places that attract the kind of people who are your customers to have a chance to meet them, talk about your business, find a way to show them your work, and keep in touch with them. How do you know which organizations your customers belong to? For example, if you are interested in breaking into the interior design market with your furniture, you may want to join the local chapter of the American Society of Interior Designers (ASID). If your products are garden sculptures, you might want to join the local garden club. You get the idea.

Networking also gives you the opportunity to meet other people in business to share valuable tips and information, take workshops, and gain access to much-needed business services, such as group health insurance. The Chamber of Commerce and your local crafts organization can both be valuable sources for basic business tips and networking. If you are thinking about hiring employees for the first time, the Chamber of Commerce may be just the place to either take a workshop or ask for a referral of another local businessperson who has recently improved the same area in her business. Interested in trying a new market for your work, such as wholesale shows? A crafts association would probably be a good place to start for advice and referrals.

Just joining an organization or attending a couple of events isn't enough. You have to get out there, mingle, and figure out ways to let people know about your business, or it doesn't count. Here are some ideas to help get you started:

- *Attend events and talk with people.* Ask people questions to start a conversation, such as, Have you been to these meetings before? How long have you been a member? What is your business? Many of the other people there will feel just as awkward as you do at first, and will be happy to have a conversation with someone. Outline a few questions ahead of time so that you are prepared when you meet someone new.
- *Join a committee and help organize some of the events.* Although this requires a time commitment on your part, you will get to know several people very well by working on a committee, and more importantly, they will get to know you. Perhaps you could host one of the meetings at your studio, or donate one of your pieces to be used as a door prize, to increase your visibility in the organization further.
- *Exchange business cards.* The object of the game is not to give away as many of your business cards as you can, but to get cards from the people you think should know more about your business so you can follow up with them and keep them informed about your business. People expect to exchange business cards at meetings, so feel free to suggest it if you think someone may be a potential customer or can refer you to someone else.
- *Keep in touch with the people you meet.* Although this may sound obvious, put them on your mailing list and invite them to see your studio or visit your booth at a fair. While they may not have a need to purchase one of your pieces now, something may come up later on, and they will remember you. People like to work with people they know. "Devise a system to keep track of all of your sales and code it carefully to use it for targeted mailings to keep customers informed," says potter Mark Bell. The same applies to people you meet who seem interested but may not have purchased a piece yet.

There is no right or wrong way to network. You are probably already doing it but didn't realize that by attending a workshop, talking to people at a meeting, or asking for (or providing) referrals, you were actually promoting your business.

Crafts Organizations

Joining a crafts organization may be one of the best business decisions you can make, and is an easy way to network with your peers. A crafts organization will usually give you information and announcements of upcoming events; access to having your work sold in a shop, fair, or show; slide registries; a link to your Web site; group health and studio insurance; workshops; magazine subscriptions; and the chance to meet other craftspeople in your area. Contact your local crafts organization for membership information and benefits.

Many crafts organizations also publish a guide to crafts galleries, shops, and individual showrooms, which are usually distributed for free in information booths, shops, and galleries, in cooperation with the Department of Tourism in your state.

In addition, there are numerous organizations dedicated to specific media. If you don't see one of interest here, check out sources on the Internet, such as the listings provided at *The Crafts Report*'s site, *www.craftsreport.com*.

Here are a few crafts organizations to consider, in alphabetical order:

- The American Crafts Council (ACC), 72 Spring St., New York, NY 10013; (212) 274-0630; *www.craftcouncil.org*. Membership includes a subscription to *American Craft* magazine, access to group health insurance, a library, free admission to their museum, and information about the ACC juried crafts fairs.
- Arizona Designer Craftsmen, 218 West Knox Drive, Tucson, AZ 85705; (520) 791-4063; *www.intrec.com/adc*.
- Arkansas Craft Guild, P.O. Box 800. Mountain View, AR 72560; (870) 269-3897; *www.arkansascraftguild.org*.
- Craft Alliance of Missouri, 6640 Delmar Blvd., St. Louis, MO 63130; (314) 725-1177; *www.craftalliance.org*.
- Florida Craftsmen, 501 Central Ave., St. Petersburg, FL 33701; (727) 821-7391; *www.floridacraftsmen.net*.
- Kentucky Art & Craft Foundation, 609 W Main St., Louisville, KY 40202; (502) 589-0102; *www.kentuckycrafts.org*.
- League of NH Craftsmen, 205 North Main St., Concord, NH 03301; (603) 224-337; *www.nhcrafts.org*.
- Maine Crafts Association, P.O. Box 8817, Portland, ME 04104; (207) 780-1807; *www.mainecrafts.org*.

- Michigan Guild Artists & Artisans, 118 N 4th Ave., Ann Arbor, MI 48104; (734) 662-3282; *www.michiganguild.org.*
- Ohio Designer Craftsmen, 1665 West 5th Ave., Columbus, OH 43212; (614) 486-4402; *www.saso-oh.org/odc.*
- Pennsylvania Guild of Craftsmen, P.O. Box 820, Richboro, PA 18954; (215) 579-5997; *www.pennsylvaniacrafts.com.*
- Southern Highland Craft Guild, P.O. Box 9545, Asheville, NC 28815; (828) 298-7928; *www.southernhighlandguild.org.*
- VT State Craft Center: Frog Hollow, 1 Mill St, Middlebury, VT 05753; (802) 388-3177; *www.froghollow.org.*

Again, don't overlook the opportunities that may be available to you through local business associations like your local Chamber of Commerce, as well as other small business management organizations like the SBA or SCORE. Although the membership will be made up of a wide variety of types of businesses and professions, there are valuable contacts to be made here and services to use.

For example, many Chamber of Commerce offices have information booths where you can put your brochures so that visitors can find your showroom. They also offer workshops on various business topics, and sometimes provide access to group health insurance. Chambers host a variety of functions to help promote different businesses in the area, such as early bird breakfast meetings, annual dinner meetings, and after-hours business receptions held at different business locations. Call your local Chamber of Commerce for details.

The most important thing is to find an organization you like, where you can increase your skills, meet other people, and get the word out about your business. Remember, networking is just talking about your business.

Places to Go

Where can you go to get ideas, be inspired, meet other craftspeople, and continue your education? Crafts fairs, shops, galleries, and museums can all provide ways to keep you on track as your work and business grow.

Fairs

Why attend a crafts fair? After all, aren't you busy trying to get your career off the ground? Attending a crafts fair can be an important tool in doing market research for your work. Not only can you see what kind of work is displayed (and what is selling), but you can also get ideas for how to design your own booth, discover the kind of customer a fair attracts, and informally talk to exhibitors (if they aren't busy making a sale!) to get valuable tips and feedback. However, in this section, I am suggesting that you attend crafts fairs primarily to see new work, get pumped up by talking with your peers, and have some fun!

With the wealth of crafts fairs held all over the country these days, finding a crafts fair shouldn't be too hard. However, if you aren't sure where to start, several publications are designed to help potential visitors, exhibitors, and buyers find just the fair they are searching for. Here are a couple places to start your search.

- *The Crafts Report* lists fairs and shows in every issue, usually reviewing a specific region of the country. Their Web site, *www.craftsreport.com*, also features a section called "Craft Show Finder," with which you can search by show name, time of year, state, category, type of craft sold, and show promoter, to help you find the show you need.
- *Sunshine Artist* contains thousands of listings and hundreds of reports about arts and crafts shows, festivals, and events all over the United States. Listings are categorized by state and date for easy planning. Reports cover real experiences and come from regional correspondents, official reviewers, and artists. These reports and listings give you all the information you need to plan entries, inventory, displays, marketing, and travel. Check out their Web site, *www.sunshineartist.com*.
- The American Craft Council provides craftspeople with the opportunity to display and sell their work through a program of public shows and wholesale markets presented annually in various cities. This organization is the crème de la crème of the crafts fair world, and gives aspiring craftspeople something to work towards after seeing the work of exhibitors. Check out their Web site, *www.craftcouncil.org*.

You can also find information about fairs in other magazines, through crafts organizations, and by talking with other craftspeople. Or you can find out about them the way the general buying public does: by purchasing some pieces and getting on a mailing list, seeing an advertisement, or hearing about it on the radio. Bring a friend and enjoy!

Shops and Galleries

How would visiting a shop or gallery help you further your career? By visiting shops and shows, not only can you see what type of work is being exhibited, but you can also see what is selling, observe how the staff interacts with customers, and do some networking, especially if you attend an event such as a trunk show or an opening reception. You can also be inspired by seeing the type of crafts work that sells in shops for gifts, as well as the more cutting-edge work usually shown in galleries for collectors. Get together with a friend, frequent shops and galleries on a regular basis, and enjoy! This is supposed to be fun, right?

If you don't know where there are any crafts shops or galleries, where can you find this out? There are gallery guides published in all major cities, as well as guides available through information booths or crafts organizations. Look at the gallery and gift shop listings on *The Crafts Report*'s Web site, *www.craftsreport.com*, as well as monthly reviews of galleries in other magazines for ideas.

Museums

How could attending a crafts museum exhibit help your career as a craftsperson? Not only will seeing crafts exhibits be inspirational, but there are usually lectures, workshops, and other events available as part of a package designed by the museum to educate the public. Also, museums may be a potential market for some craftspeople to sell their work through museum shops, related events such as demonstration days, networking during opening receptions, and member events.

There are also career opportunities for craftspeople in the museum field, either as an employee or for special projects. For example, several of the craftspeople profiled work with museums, such as blacksmith Peter Ross at Colonial Williamsburg in Virginia, or boat builder Paul Rollins's project at the Shelburne Museum in Vermont.

In addition to museums devoted solely to exhibiting crafts, such as the Museum of Art and Design (formerly known as the American Craft Museum) in New York, the Mint Museum of Art + Design in North Carolina, and the Fuller Craft Museum in Massachusetts, there are also medium-specific museums, such as the Quilt Museum in Massachusetts or the Corning Museum of Glass in New York.

For a listing of museums and art centers around the country, check out the ACC Web site, *www.craftcouncil.org*, under "Resources," or go to the American Association of Museums' Web site, *www.aam-us.org*. The AAM also posts job openings in a database that you can search online by location or by specialty that may be of interest to you.

Whether you attend a fair, visit a shop or gallery, or see an exhibit at a museum, you are not only giving yourself a chance to be inspired and helping yourself stay on track with your career plans, but you are also doing market research. As a self-employed craftsperson, it is easy to become isolated when producing work in the studio is your main focus. Make time to get out and see other work, talk to other craftspeople and business owners, and keep a journal to have time to regenerate and participate in a lifelong learning process.

CHAPTER 18

Special Programs for Young Craftspeople

This section is dedicated to supporting a new generation of crafts-people (and their parents) by providing information about programs available for high school students who are wondering what the next step may be as they begin to climb the rungs of the career ladder. For recent college graduates, I recommend that you review the "Career Options" section, as well as the section on residencies and apprenticeships, as possible next steps for you.

"If I had only known then what I know now, how different my life would have been!" It's a common saying, but a true one. Even though more opportunities exist than ever, it is still not easy for young people to find all the resources available to them to decide the best way to pursue a career in crafts.

This chapter offers programs that may be able to help you get started, as well as advice. If you don't see an opportunity listed here in your area, consider calling a program that interests you to see if they are aware of their counterparts in your part of the country, or just contact the nearest crafts or art school.

According to Maryon Atwood, Director of the Worcester Center for Crafts in Massachusetts, craftspeople of today tend to be older than their counterparts of the 1960s and 1970s. "I see the trends of each person having multiple careers reflected in our professional crafts program," says Maryon. "Most of our students have attended college, even earned degrees, and have a lot of experience. These students are very serious, motivated, and aware of the preciousness of time, and are interested in what I call a 'heart's desire career.' Many craftspeople are just starting their businesses at midlife, changing careers to realize their dream of making a living from their avocation, and bringing vast amounts of professional experience to running their crafts business.

Others are self-directed high school or college students who would like to pursue a career in crafts but are not sure how."

As we learned in the CODA survey at the beginning of this book, the crafts field today is made up of people whose average age is forty-nine. In response to the concern about recruiting enough young people to replace today's craftspeople, many schools and organizations have put together programs and opportunities to help ensure that properly trained and nurtured craftspeople will continue to enter the field.

Programs for High School Students

There are programs available for high school students considering a degree in art and crafts at many schools around the country. Programs include continuing education classes on Saturdays, intensive weekend workshops, and extended programs during school vacations or summer. Extended programs are designed to immerse high school students in a creative environment to help them decide if art or crafts is something they want to pursue. After all, if you think you like making things out of clay or wood but have only had the opportunity to work with them for one class period a week in school, how do you know if you will still enjoy it if you do it for several hours every day? It's a good idea to figure this out *before* you apply to college or art school, and the following programs have been designed to help you do just that.

Maine College of Art in Portland, Maine (MECA)

MECA offers Saturday classes for high school students during the school year, as well as a summer program called Early College that provides an exciting and challenging opportunity for approximately fifty motivated high school students to explore their creativity and earn college credit in a four-week intensive visual arts program.

Early College allows students to expand their skills, strengthen their portfolios, experience themselves as serious art students, interact with peers who share their interests, and proceed at a rigorous pace with a workload similar to the first semester at an art college.

The curriculum includes instruction in Drawing and 2-D and 3-D Design, as well as elective offerings in Painting, Photography, Jewelry and Metals, and Film/Video. Students have classes from 9:00 A.M. until 5:00 P.M. Monday through Friday, and are required to put in at least ten hours per week of additional studio work during the evenings and on weekend afternoons or evenings. The basic program is supplemented by critiques, visiting artists, and field trips. Classes are taught by college instructors from MECA, as well as by working artists. Teaching assistants are advanced students or alumni who work with the faculty in classrooms and monitor the evening/weekend studio time.

For more information: Maine College of Art (MECA), 97 Spring St., Portland, ME 04101; (207) 775-3051; *www.meca.edu*.

To find other art schools that offer programs similar to the Early College one at MECA, contact the art school nearest you, the College Art Association at *www.caa.org*, or the National Association of Schools of Art and Design at *www.nasad.org*.

Haystack Mountain School of Crafts in Deer Isle, Maine

Haystack offers several programs for young craftspeople, including a program for students in the local school districts called Studio-Based Learning, and a weekend workshop called Student Craft Institute for high school students throughout Maine.

Studio-Based Learning combines hands-on learning in crafts in three-day workshops with follow-up activities during the year, such as a mentoring program with local craftspeople and a collaborative residency where a craftsperson visits the schools as well. Teachers also take part by observing new teaching methods in the workshops that they can bring back to their classrooms. "The Studio-Based Learning and mentor programs have generated a lot of enthusiasm from kids and teachers about bringing more Haystack programs into the school," says Dennis Saindon, Industrial Arts Teacher at the Deer Isle-Stonington High School. "We see this year's residency with Doug Wilson, a blacksmith, as part of building a program here that gets kids involved in the kind of hands-on learning that makes sense to them. It's about gaining skills and confidence so that they have options when it's time to make decisions about careers or even avocations. In programs like the residency, they have an opportunity to learn things they can use in the real world. It's keeping traditions alive, and it gives them a creative outlet that they don't get anywhere else. I believe it keeps them whole."

Student Craft Institute for Maine high school students is modeled after a Haystack session: Students can take an intensive workshop in clay, metal, fiber, or wood, and reside on the campus for a weekend.

For more information: Haystack Mountain School of Crafts, P.O. Box 518, Deer Isle, ME 04627; (207) 348-2306; *www.haystack-mtn.org*.

Snow Farm

Snow Farm, located in Williamsburg, Massachusetts, offers intensive crafts courses in the summer for high school students. Offering workshops in clay, metal, glass, drawing, and photography, mornings are devoted to one studio, and most of the afternoon to a second studio. "Open" studio time is scheduled during late afternoons and evenings to give students an opportunity to work on pieces begun earlier in the day, as well as a chance to work and explore on their own. Considerable independence is given to all students in managing time, with the foundation of the program resting on each person's strong sense of commitment to herself and her work.

For more information: Snow Farm, 5 Clary Road, Williamsburg, MA 01096; (413) 268-3101; *www.snowfarm.org.*

League of NH Craftsmen

At their annual crafts fair, the League of NH Craftsmen sponsors a special booth called "The Next Generation" for children of state-juried League members and sponsored guests to learn to make and sell their own crafts. Coupled with children's activities in crafts that change daily, this event is a great way for other children to see how their peers are doing as small businesspeople.

For more information: League of NH Craftsmen, 205 North Main St., Concord, NH 03301; (603) 224-3375; *www.nhcrafts.org.*

Worcester Center for Crafts

The Worcester Center for Crafts offers teens and young artists:

- Classes
- Two-week Summer Fun Camps
- A program during the school year called Craft Reach/Public School Partnership, where grade-school students come to the Center for studio-based lessons linked to their social studies curriculum
- The Artist-in-the-Classrooms enrichment program in the schools,
- T.E.A.C.H. (Teaching Education, Arts, and Crafts for Healthy Kids) for middle school students, who learn to mentor younger students through bringing their training to after-school programs
- T.A.P. (Teen Apprenticeship Program), a two-year course of study in metal, textiles, clay, and wood

For more information: Worcester Center for Crafts, 25 Sagamore Road, Worcester, MA 01605; (508) 753-8183; *www.worcestercraftcenter.org.*

In addition to the programs already mentioned, three innovative programs for high school students were profiled in *The Crafts Report*, in an article called "Job Training Programs in Art: An Alternative for the 'Starving Artist'" (August 2002):

- The first program, called Studio 150, offers high school students the opportunity to work for eight weeks over the summer as apprentices to professional artists, to learn valuable job and artistic skills, create art, and earn a paycheck. Held outdoors in Kansas City, Missouri, in the city's historic Eighteenth and Vine jazz district, the program exposes artistic young people and the general public to art.

  For more information: Studio 150, The Arts Council of Metropolitan Kansas City, 1925 Central #150, Kansas City, MO 64108; (816) 221-1777; *www.artslink.org.*
- The second program profiled is Gallery 37, which offers year-round programs for young people throughout Chicago in visual, literary, media, culinary, and performing arts, with support from public and private sources. In addition to the social benefit of students from different backgrounds mingling, the students come away with a greater sense of self-esteem and the encouragement they need to flourish.

  For more information: Gallery 37, 66 East Randolph Street, Chicago, IL 60601; (312) 744-8925; *www.gallery37.org.*
- Finally, the RiverWalk Art Project takes place for four weeks in the summer, and gives artists the opportunity to work with students in the seventh through twelfth grades who want to explore a career in art and drama. The program is held under tents in the Citizen Plaza in Anderson, Indiana, an outdoor pedestrian center. The public is invited to an end-of-program picnic that includes live music, student performances, and an auction of student work to help raise money for the program.

  For more information: RiverWalk Art Project, 120 E 8th Street, Anderson, IN 46016; (765) 648-6112.

As you can see, there are all sorts of programs already in place to help young craftspeople get their start, whether they want something short-term, such as a weekend, or long-term, like a summer program. Keep in mind that the help young craftspeople need does not have to require a building or a lot of people. We can make a difference in the future of today's young craftspeople by first of all showing interest in what they are doing, and secondly by connecting them to a support system that will nurture their creativity and spirit as they develop artistically.

Just as adults need organizations and places to network, so do young craftspeople. Many organizations offer student memberships at a reduced price to help educate this valuable segment of our population, while others offer fellowships and scholarships to help young crafts-people continue on with the learning process, whether in school or by attending conferences. Consider giving a student you know a member-ship as a gift to show your support. Help her make arrangements to attend events, or even go with her to help facilitate conversations and help her get the most out of the experience.

Young craftspeople should also consider pursuing a residency or apprenticeship to have the time to develop their work as well as learn the business of being a craftsperson. See chapter 4, "Educational Opportunities, Residency Programs, and Apprenticeships for Craftspeople," for more information.

And finally, work out a way to help young craftspeople realize their dreams. I'm not suggesting that parents should pay for everything, but help out in ways that are acceptable, such as offering business loans to your children, attending their exhibitions, reading up on their field of interest, and most of all, telling them they can do it! "Many times when I would be introduced to parents of the students in my jewelry program, they would ask me how their son or daughter would be able to make a living after graduation," says Professor of Art Emeritus Arline Fisch. "I always told them to keep investing in their children, even after graduation, until they are able to establish themselves."

Conclusion

This book has taken you from the history and current trends in the crafts field to how to help nurture the next generation of craftspeople. I hope that the information provided will allow you either to bridge the gap between your present lifestyle and the one you are dreaming of, or to help you feel good about what you are presently doing with your work. If you have passion for your work and can define what you want to do with it, the possibilities are endless.

One thing is clear: Whether we call it "crafts" or we call it "art," creative people are using traditional skills and techniques to make cutting-edge work, as well as carry on traditions that are centuries old. The expansion of the crafts field into other media such as interior design and architecture is rapidly changing the definition of crafts as we know it today. It is my hope that the decision-makers in the field decide to keep using the word "craft" in the names of schools and museums, even if they choose to add words like "art" and "design" to the mix. The history behind the word "craft" is a long and honorable one, and we should not turn our backs on it.

Success is all in how you feel about yourself and your work. Anything we can each do to support one another in the quest to make a difference and push our work one step further needs to be supported and celebrated. Reach out and tell someone how you feel about their work by offering constructive criticism, attend open houses and exhibitions, invite others to your studio to see your current work, and take care of yourself by establishing a support network. A series of baby steps can add up to quite a distance in a short time, even if the movement seems slow in the present moment. Take the time to note your achievements and feel good about promoting them to others. It's okay to toot your own horn!

With all the career options available, surely one of them will match your present goals and responsibilities. Even if you have to start out at the bottom of the career ladder by sweeping another crafts-person's floor as an apprentice, you have defined a direction for your work that will eventually lead you to where you want to go. Establishing your career will take time, but someday soon you will be able to look back, see a pattern emerge, and realize that you have gotten somewhere and that you like what you have done. You can do it!

Be sure to take advantage of at least one of the educational opportunities in crafts, whether you take a weekend workshop or make the commitment to do a residency. You never know what will come out of such a program. I would have never written *Selling Your Crafts* or this book if I had not participated in a panel on marketing through the New England Foundation for the Arts, where I met writer Daniel Grant, who decided right then and there that I should write a business book for craftspeople, and kept after me for a couple years before I agreed to do it. Writing a book was the last thing I was thinking of doing, and now, of course, I am happy that I did it. You may find that you meet a mentor or a trusted friend, or even get offered a position that furthers your career too, through simply attending an event and networking.

Join an organization and reap the benefits by reading all about it, networking with your peers, and attending conferences. If there isn't an organization available that serves your craft, then join with a few other like-minded people and start one. After all, that's how most of the other organizations available today got off the ground. If you read any of the histories of the organizations profiled, you will find that they all began with a small group of people and a concept. Sounds simple, doesn't it?

Researching the profiles of the craftspeople in this book was thrilling. I wish I could share with all of you the joy and inspiration I felt after finishing each interview. My own profile appears in "About the Author," so you can learn more about my own journey.

And finally, I hope that the "Transitions and Support Systems" section provides enough information to help you become a full-time craftsperson, if that is what you desire, or helps someone you know to do it. The crafts field is full of opportunities to keep you inspired, as well as to nurture emerging craftspeople to assure the continuation of the field. And who knows what tomorrow will bring? I hope it brings a new generation of craftspeople—whether they call themselves "artists," or "craftspeople," or just say they "make stuff"—that is as committed, talented, and generous as the ones that have gone before them.

If you are interested in obtaining more nuts-and-bolts information about running a crafts business, please consider buying my other book, *Selling Your Crafts*, available in bookstores everywhere, through Allworth Press, or on my own Web site, *www.artbiz.info*. It complements this book, and is one of the best reference books out there for people interested in selling their work.

Stay well, keep in touch, and if there are times when you feel that nobody else believes in your dream to have a career in crafts, remember, I think you can do it. All you have to do is get started—today.

About the Author

I remember signing up for a mini-course in crafts when I was in the ninth grade and calling my mother at work to tell her I had gotten into it. I was so excited that I couldn't wait to learn how to work in clay, weave, and batik. I also took painting and photography that year. It was the beginning of when I began to define myself as an artist. The next year, I transferred to another school that did not offer as much in the way of art or crafts classes, so to keep myself inspired, I took an  evening class in weaving at another school and did several independent studies in art and crafts at my school during my free periods. I worked in a needlepoint store after school, stocking shelves, selling, and doing custom designs. The store had called my art teacher for a recommendation, and I had gotten the job.

I was also a good student in other subjects, and an honors student, so when it came time to apply for college, I was only sure of what I didn't want to do. I decided to try out art school and was accepted into the Lake Placid School of Art, a two-year diploma program, in Lake Placid, New York. Although I learned a lot and became very interested in non-traditional photography and collage, I missed academics and felt somewhat isolated from my peers. I served on the Board of Directors as a Student Representative, and also edited the school newsletter (a forerunner of things to come).

I graduated and transferred to Hampshire College in Amherst, Massachusetts, where students designed their own program of study and worked with faculty as mentors. It was the first time in my life that I felt I was in the right place at the right time, and I thrived there, completing the degree in two years. I developed skills as I completed my divisional exams that have served me well in my professional life, such as how to take an idea from concept to fruition and how to work with committees. However, existing in the real world after graduation was a shock for me, and it took me several years before my expectations of myself once again matched the reality of what I was able to accomplish.

After a series of false starts, I took at job in the office of the Program in Artisanry at Boston University, which offered degrees in Clay, Fiber, Metal, and Wood, marking the official beginning of my work as an arts administrator. Two years after I began, the school left BU and merged with a small, independent art school in New Bedford, Massachusetts, called the Swain School of Design. I was the only staff person to move with the school, and I worked at Swain for another two years as the registrar. Although Swain had a very dedicated staff and faculty, the school later had to merge with the UMass system because of financial difficulties due to the lack of enrollment. My experience showed me not only that I had excellent skills as an administrator, but also that I could make a difference in other people's lives by doing my job well. It has been a hard thing to replicate, and I still look back fondly on that time and group of people.

I took a series of other jobs at art schools, but it wasn't until I accepted a position as the Assistant Director at the Haystack Mountain School of Crafts in Deer Isle, Maine, that I again knew I was in the right place at the right time. The three seasons I worked there were filled with organizational improvements as well as lots of inspiration and learning for me as a creative person. The faculty slide shows during the summer season were like obtaining a minor in Contemporary Crafts History, and I met several of the people profiled in this book during my time there. Although I enjoyed working at the school, its remote location (for a single person) left much to be desired, and I moved away after I met my future husband to begin a new life in a different part of Maine.

Leaving Haystack and moving to central Maine was a culture shock, but the isolation compelled me to start my business, ArtBiz, offering business seminars, career counseling, and books to interested artists and craftspeople. I taught workshops all over New England, and have helped more than a thousand people this way. It was also during this time that I met Daniel Grant, a writer of numerous business books for fine artists, who urged me to write a book geared towards craftspeople. I did this several years later, titling the book *Selling Your Crafts*. Unlike many people who write a book, because of Daniel, I had a publisher and contract before I wrote it. It was a great way to expand the information I presented in my workshops to be readily available to a larger group of people.

I gave birth to my son, Miles, at age forty-one, and my life has never been the same since. I stayed at home with Miles until he was three. During this time, I revised *Selling Your Crafts* (it had sold over ten thousand copies) and proposed doing a new book profiling crafts careers, expanding one of the sections in the first book. The result is what you have in your hands. Writing this book has given me back a sense of my professional life, and has been both a painful labor and a joy to birth. I look forward to seeing where it leads me next.

For the future, I hope for more time to do my own creative work and to continue sharing my gifts with others, whether it is through creating opportunities for others to develop their craft, or through making a happy home. I am thankful for all of the help and guidance I have received over the years from so many people, and I am grateful when opportunities present themselves for me to return the favor. Onward and upward!

Contributors

Clay

Mark Bell
Lisa Tully Dibble
Lynn Duryea
Christine Federighi
Randy Fein
Abby Huntoon
Iver Lofving
George Mason
Mary Nyburg
Gerry Williams

Fiber

Amanda Barrow
Elizabeth Busch
Pat Castka
Katharine Cobey
Rev. Wendy Ellsworth
Dorothy Gill Barnes
Peter Hagerty
Jan Owen
Mary Ozbolt-Storer
Patricia Palson
Theresa Secord
Ellen Spring
Pamela Weeks Worthen
Gail Wilson

Glass

Candace Jackman
Harvey Littleton
Dante Marioni
Richard Marquis
Josh Simpson
Bert Weiss

Metal

Arline Fisch
Jill Kenik
Tim McCreight
Peter Ross
Deb Stoner
J. Fred Woell
Eric Ziner

Wood

Peter Bloch
Dan Dustin
David Ellsworth
Wendy Maruyama
Julie Morringello
Jere Osgood
Paul Rollins
Rosanne Somerson

Bibliography

Alliance of Artists Communities. *Artists Communities*. New York, Allworth Press, 1996.

American Craft. "*Crafting a Legacy: Contemporary American Crafts in the Philadelphia Museum of Art*," Books, Feb/March 2003.

American Craft. "Pritam & Eames," Exhibition Review, Oct/Nov 2001.

American Craft. "Turning Since 1930," Exhibition Review, April/May 2002.

American Craft. "Arline Fisch: Museum of Contemporary Arts and Design, NY," Exhibition Review, Dec 2002/Jan 2003.

American Craft. "Craftworld: Profile on Watershed," Feb/March 2001.

American Craft. "Gold Medal: Arline Fisch," American Craft Council Awards, Oct/Nov 2001.

American Craft Museum: *www.americancraftmuseum.org*, Press Release Section.

AmeriGlas Stained Glass. *www.ameriglas.com*, History Section.

Bessire, Mark. "Distinguishing Marks: Tim McCreight, Master Metalsmith," Exhibition Catalog, National Ornamental Metals Museum, Memphis, Tennessee and Mays Gallery, Portland, Maine, 2001/2002.

Bowdoin College Museum of Art. "Connections with Antiquity: Works by George Mason," Exhibition Catalog, Brunswick, Maine.

Bryd, Joan Falconer. "Interview of Harvey K. Littleton," Smithsonian Archives of American Art Documentation Project for Craft in America, March 15, 2001.

California College of Arts. "CCAC Changes Name to California College of the Arts," June 19, 2003, *www.ccarts.edu*, Press Release Section.

Center for Maine Contemporary Art. "Haystack: Pivotal Transformations," Exhibition Catalog, Rockport, ME, August 2001.

The Crafts Report. "Job Training Programs in Art: An Alternative for the 'Starving Artist,'" August 2002.

The Crafts Report. "Making a Living as a Jewelry Artist," July 2002.

The Crafts Report. "Insight Survey on Ceramics," April 2003.

The Crafts Report. "Insight Survey on Jewelry Artists," May 2003.

The Crafts Report. "Insight Survey on Glass Artists," June 2003.

The Crafts Report. "Insight Survey on Wood Artists," August 2003.

The Crafts Report. "Profile on Martha and Jerry Swanson, Woodworkers," August

2003.

Drutt, Helen. *Jewelry of Our Time: Art, Ornament and Obsession*. Rizzoli, 1995.

Duncan, Katharine. "Generations: Harvey Littleton, John Littleton, Kate Vogel," Exhibition Catalog, Southern Highland Craft Guild Folk Art Center, 1995.

Edwards, Sarah and Paul. *Making It On Your Own*. New York, Jeremy P. Tarchers, Inc., 1991.

Ellsworth, Rev. Wendy. "About Wendy Ellsworth," *www.ellsworthstudios .com*.

Finnerty, Bernadette. "CRAFT: National Retailers Association Takes Shape," *The Crafts Report*, December 2002.

Finnerty, Bernadette. "Making A Living As A Fiber Artist," *The Crafts Report*, October 2002.

Finnerty, Bernadette. "Research Values Crafts and Hobby Industry at $25.7 Billion," *The Crafts Report*, June 2002.

Finnerty, Bernadette. "The $14 Billion Crafts Industry: The CODA Survey Results Prove that Crafts Are BIG Business," *The Crafts Report*, May 2001.

Finnerty, Bernadette. "CODA to Test Economic Impact Study This Summer," *The Crafts Report*, August 1998.

Grant, Daniel. "Apprenticeships Get Your Foot in the Door," *The Crafts Report*, June 2003.

Haystack Mountain School of Crafts. "Studio Based Learning," *The Gateway*, Winter 2002.

Halpern, Nancy. "Pioneers: Teaching the World to Quilt," *QNM*, July/August 2002.

Hebert, Ernest. "People and Places," *For the Protection of NH Forest*, 2001.

Holloway, Monique. "Debate Heats Up On Craft and Art," *The Crafts Report*, March 2003.

HOPE. "This is My Clay," Fall 2001.

Jones, Robert O. *The Biographical Index of Historic American Stained Glass Makers*. Stained Glass Association of America.

Kangas, Matthew. "Dante Marioni: Apprentice to Tradition," *American Craft*, March 1994.

Klein, Dan. *Artists in Glass: Late 20th-Century Masters in Glass*. New York: Phaidon Press, 2001.

Lambdin Meyer, Diana. "The Department of Craft Development: No Such Department Exists Yet. But as Craft Moves Up on Many States' Lists of Viable Tourism Promotion Tools, Craft Artists Are Getting Major Support from State Initiatives," *The Crafts Report*, May 2001.

Laughlin, Kara. "Art on A Shoestring Budget: What State Economic Crises Mean for Craft Programs," *The Crafts Report*, May 2003.

League of NH Craftsmen. "Gerry Williams, New Hampshire's Artist Laureate," Exhibition Catalog, Gallery 205, Concord, NH, June 17–August 20, 1999.

League of NH Craftsmen. "Gail Wilson, Dolls for Disney," Member Profile, *League of NH Craftsmen Newsletter*, 2001.

Little, Carl. "Tim McCreight: Multithreat Master," *Ornament*, 2001.

Lunney, Michael. "From mandalas to sculptures . . . Haycock woman has passion for beading," *Quakertown Free Press*, Quakertown, PA, August 11, 1992.

Marler, Ruth. *The Art of the Quilt*. Philadelphia, PA: Courage Books, 2001.

Mint Museum of Craft and Design. *Harvey Littleton Reflections 1946–1994*.

Moss, Kathleen. "Circles of Light: Beaded Peyote Stitch Vessels," *Bead & Button* #15.

New Hampshire Magazine. "Warmth and Tradition, Interwoven," March 2001.

NICHE. "Designer Profile," Winter 1991/92.

Oakland Museum of California. "Elegant Fantasy: The Jewelry of Arline Fisch: Jan 20–April 22, 2001," Exhibition Review, *www.museumca.org*.

Ohio Craft Museum. "From The Woods: Dorothy Gill Barnes," Exhibition Catalog, November 21,1999–January 23, 2000.

Oldknow, Tina. *Dante Marioni Blown Glass: Apprentice to Tradition*. New York: Hudson Hills Press, 2000.

Petzak, Mary. "CODA 2003 Conference Coming in April," *The Crafts Report*, March 2003

Porges, Maria, "Richard Marquis: Material Culture," *American Craft*, December 1995.

Preview. "A Potter Combines Love of Craft with Commercial Savvy and Keeps Smiling: Lynn Duryea," August 1995.

San Diego Historical Society. "Elegant Fantasy: The Jewelry of Arline Fisch: Feb. 11–July 30, 2000," Exhibition Review, *www.sandiegohistory.org*.

Shannon, Faith. *Paper Pleasures*. New York: Grove Weidenfeld, 1987.

Skelly, Heather. "Museum is First in New England to Focus on Craft," *The Crafts Report*, October 2002.

Smith, Hyrum W. *What Matters Most: The Power of Living Your Values*. New York: Simon & Schuster, 2000.

Smith, Rolf. *The 7 Levels of Change: Different Thinking for Different Results*. Irving, Texas: Tapestry Press, 2002.

Williams, Gerry. *Apprenticeship in Craft*. Goffstown, NH: Daniel Webster Books, 1981.

Updike, Robin. "A Seamless Life: Marylou Ozbolt-Storer," *Ornament Magazine*, Autumn 2001.

Warmus, William. "A Fire in the Studio: Harvey Littleton," *Glass Magazine*, Autumn 1998.

Index

Books from Allworth Press

Allworth Press is an imprint of Allworth Communications, Inc. Selected titles are listed below.

Selling Your Crafts, Revised Edition
by *Susan Joy Sager* (paperback, 6 × 9, $19.95, 288 pages)

Creating a Successful Crafts Business
by *Rogene A. Robbins and Robert Robbins* (paperback, 6 × 9, 256 pages, $19.95)

Crafts and Craft Shows: How to Make Money
by *Philip Kadubec* (paperback, 6 × 9, 208 pages, $16.95)

Business and Legal Forms for Crafts
by *Tad Crawford* (paperback, 8½ × 11, 176 pages, $19.95)

The Law (in Plain English)® for Crafts
by *Leonard DuBoff* (paperback, 6 × 9, 224 pages, $18.95)

The Fine Artist's Guide to Marketing and Self-Promotion, Revised Edition
by *Julius Vitali* (paperback, 6 × 9, 256 pages, $19.95)

How to Grow as an Artist
by *Daniel Grant* (paperback, 6 × 9, 240 pages, $16.95)

Legal Guide for the Visual Artist, Fourth Edition
by *Tad Crawford* (paperback, 8½ × 11, 272 pages, $19.95)

The Fine Artist's Career Guide
by *Daniel Grant* (paperback, 6 × 9, 304 pages, $18.95)

The Business of Being an Artist, Third Edition
by *Daniel Grant* (paperback, 6 × 9, 352 pages, $19.95)